New England Lighthouses

Famous Shipwrecks, Rescues & Other Tales

Allan Wood

Schiffer Publishing Ltd.

4880 Lower Valley Road • Atglen, PA 19310

Dedication in Memory

This book is dedicated in memory of my Uncle Dick for his humorous approach to life, my Aunt Grace for teaching me to always put family first, and my buddy, Lisa, for teaching me to never give up on my dreams. This book is also, of course, dedicated to those special individuals, past and present, who risked their lives to help those in peril, because they felt it was the right thing to do. Thank you.

Schiffer Books are available at special discounts for bulk purchases for sales promotions or premiums. Special editions, including personalized covers, corporate imprints, and excerpts can be created in large quantities for special needs. For more information contact the publisher:

Schiffer Publishing Ltd.
4880 Lower Valley Road
Atglen, PA 19310
Phone: (610) 593-1777
Fax: (610) 593-2002
E-mail: Info@schifferbooks.com

For the largest selection of fine reference books on this and related subjects, please visit our website at
www.schifferbooks.com
We are always looking for people to write books on new and related subjects. If you have an idea for a book, please contact us at
proposals@schifferbooks.com

This book may be purchased from the publisher.
Include $5.00 for shipping.
Please try your bookstore first.
You may write for a free catalog.

In Europe, Schiffer books are distributed by
Bushwood Books
6 Marksbury Ave.
Kew Gardens
Surrey TW9 4JF England
Phone: 44 (0) 20 8392 8585
Fax: 44 (0) 20 8392 9876
E-mail: info@bushwoodbooks.co.uk
Website: www.bushwoodbooks.co.uk

Designed by Stephanie Daugherty
Type set in Gill Sans MT Condensed/ NewBskvll BT

ISBN: 978-0-7643-4078-9
Printed in China

Acknowledgments

There were many people who contributed their images and support for this book, including artists, historical societies, museums, individuals, members of the Coast Guard, whose images and expertise helped to compliment the stories, and, of course, the folks at Schiffer Publishing. I'd like to thank the following people and organizations for their contributions and support:

The folks at Schiffer Publishing for their support and belief in the success of this book.

Jeremy D'Entremont, New England's premiere historian, for his images from his collection, and his unselfish valued assistance with some of the research.

Paul and Helen Baptiste, for allowing me into their home and letting me write about their stories, and to use some of their images, their son John for coordinating everything and to my brother-in-law, Brad Goodreau, for being my connection to this great family.

Mary Anne Bader, Coordinator of Art for the Coast Guard, for providing contacts for Coast Guard artists' paintings used in this book, and Scott Price, Deputy Historian, of the Coast Guard for use of vintage images.

Jill Park, daughter of artist Sherman Groenke, for allowing me to use his painting "Launching a Surfboat."

Gwen Mazoujian, daughter of artist Charles J. Mazoujian, for allowing me to use his painting "Nantucket Lightship Sunk by RMS *Olympic*."

Susan Ahysen, daughter of artist Henry Ahysen, for allowing me to use his painting "Andrea Doria."

Artist Lou Diamond for his painting "The USLSS to the Rescue, 1880."

Brian Tague for use of images and contacts for Flying Santa(s) story.

Eric Takakjian of Quest Marine Services for vintage images used for stories involving the City of Columbus, Metis, and Portland wrecks.

Artist William Trotter for use of his painting "Tending the Buoys."

Artist John Witt for use of his painting "Ida Lewis."

Newport Historical Society for use of the Ida Lewis portrait.

Chatham (MA) Historical Society for images of the Monomoy crew.

The Mariner's Museum in Virginia for image of City of Columbus.

The Museum at Martha's Vineyard for image used for City of Columbus story.

The Museum at Portland Head Light for vintage images of the Stout family of keepers, and Annie C. Maguire wreck.

Paul St. Germain of the Thacher Island Association Museum for image of Maria Bray.

Joan Hammond, of the New Castle Historical Society, for images of Jerry's Point Lifesaving Station in New Hampshire.

Sheri Poftak of Friends of Wood Island Light, for the use of images for the keeper's daughter rescue story.

I also want to thank my parents for always allowing me to follow the path less traveled, and to help those I meet along the way. My sincere love and appreciation for my wife, Chris, for her continuous support for this project, and my two boys, Bryan and Steven, for their constant silly humor to always keep me grounded.

Contents

Preface

New England is known to have one of the most rugged coastlines in the world. This book was developed to provide the reader a series of stories that encompass the brave men and women of New England who risked their lives at or near New England's lighthouses. These individuals were not only part of the lighthouse, lifesaving, and revenue cutter government services of the nineteenth and early twentieth centuries, but also encompass a town's own citizens, local mariners, or a ship's captain and crew, who would also risk their lives alongside their government counterparts in helping those in distress. From these historic stories, the reader will discover the importance of the three branches of lifesaving services (Lighthouse, Life Saving, and Revenue Cutter Services), and their methods, in rescuing those in peril. Also, to develop a sincere appreciation for these people, and an understanding of their character in what drives them to want to help those in need, and from some of these events, what safety regulations were put in place for travel today. There are some stories where, sometimes, respected individuals can't explain what they perceive or hear around some of New England's lighthouses documented as paranormal activities, leading into controversial folklore.

This book contains not only stories about lighthouse keepers and their rescues, but also selected rescue stories by their wives, children, and even dogs. The reader will find heroic stories of crews of "surfmen" from lifesaving rescue stations that were established between lighthouses, including a famous rescue by the Wampanoag Tribe of Native Americans in Massachusetts. There is a remembrance of one of the most dangerous of all marine professions, that of being a crewmember aboard a lightship. There is a section for the reader to learn about some of New England's worst coastal disasters, many near our lighthouses that pioneered travel safety procedures used today. These special stories and others, involved coordinated efforts between those employed within the three branches of rescue service, along with local fishermen, lobstermen, or captains of steamships who would risk their lives to help those in peril. This coordination of rescue operations, especially among the branches of rescue service, evolved into our current Coast Guard.

Through much research, there have been many conflicting accounts, and finding accurate documentation was quite challenging in determining what had actually occurred in a given event. While some of the stories will always remain controversial, and some may spark heated debate as to the truth of the content, the resources utilized, such as by reputed authors and their books, newspaper articles from the period, and documented eyewitness accounts provide hopefully an honest truthful account of what really happened. To provide a visual connection with these stories, the author has used his own current photographs, along with vintage images by the Coast Guard, collections from individuals and organizations, museums, historical societies, and paintings by some famous artists who all wanted to contribute to the success of this book.

There were also accounts that were documented up to, and sometimes including paranormal sightings. The lighthouse hauntings section, though it may be entertaining, still involves a journalistic approach to the events leading up to some of these paranormal activities, through research into the folklore of the story. Many of these sightings described were by respected townsfolk, mariners, or lighthouse keepers themselves.

The reader will also find special heartwarming stories, including the story of the "Flylng Santa(s)" who rescued the keepers along the New England coast emotionally during the holiday seasons, the miracle baby rescues, and a collection of amusing personal stories by one of New England's surviving lighthouse keepers, Paul Baptiste. Paul's stories encompass many of the stories mentioned in this book as he was stationed as a lighthouse keeper, and at various lifesaving stations in New England during and after World War II. His honest and cheerful character embodies how we should always view those who serve in our Coast Guard and in all military branches today: the love of country and the unselfish duty of helping out their neighbor.

Historic Introduction

New England has arguably the most dangerous populated coastline in the world. The first lighthouse, Boston Harbor Lighthouse, in Massachusetts, was built in 1716. By the time the Constitution had created the Lighthouse Establishment Act, which became the law of the land in 1789 under Federal control, twelve lighthouses were already built in the United States. It was at this time that lighthouse control passed from the states to the federal government's Treasury Department as the US Lighthouse Service.

As more lighthouses were established along the New England coast, they were strategically placed to provide guidance and warn mariners of dangerous reefs, ledges, and shoals. Keepers' and their assistants' main duties were to maintain the lights at all costs. Their daily tasks involved tending the wicks, fueling the tanks, polishing the brass, cleaning the soot off the lenses and prisms, and maintaining the rest of the tower and surrounding buildings. They would also become involved in many rescues that occurred at or very near the lighthouse. Their rescue equipment consisted of a rowboat or some type of lifeboat, depending on the number of assistants the keeper had, and various lines and preservers for hauling survivors into the boat. There always had to be someone to keep the light burning, especially during a storm, in order to guide mariners to safety.

Shortly after the Revolution, President Washington established the beginning of the Revenue Marine Service of ships in Newburyport, Massachusetts, where

**Launching A Surfboat.
Painting by artist Sherman Groenke.** *Courtesy of Jill Park and US Coast Guard.*

the first revenue cutter was built. Today, Newburyport is recognized as the birthplace of the Coast Guard. The Revenue Marine Service used its revenue cutters in times of war and for law enforcement in protecting our shores. It wasn't until the 1830s that these fast vessels would be used for rescue purposes, mainly out in open waters off shore where lighthouse keepers were unable to help in reaching those wrecks.

During the Civil War, the Revenue Marine Service received its official designation as the Revenue Cutter Service. After the Civil War, smaller cutters were also built to patrol more closely to the coastline and were responsible for saving many lives from wrecks within harbors, or later as part of rescue coordination efforts with personnel from lighthouses and lifesaving stations.

As shipping, tourism, fishing, and whaling traffic dramatically increased after the Civil War, there came the need for lifesaving stations to be built along the shores within a few miles of lighthouses. They could provide a broader area range in rescuing stranded survivors from the many shipwrecks that occurred throughout New England. This idea of having shore-based stations began with trained volunteer services set up by the Massachusetts Humane Society and spread to each state's Humane Society. The early stations were originally sheds built for equipment. Congress established the US Life Saving Service in 1871, consisting of a

keeper, or captain, and a trained crew of six to eight men, with the necessary buildings to house these crews and their equipment. These lifesaving stations, also referred to as surf stations were built five to ten miles apart from a nearby lighthouse

These lifesaving station keepers were fishermen, or were previously involved in some other maritime occupation and had a vast knowledge of the local area and terrain. They used local mariners and fishermen as mostly volunteers, who were experienced boaters, to assist in most instances from autumn until late spring when the New England weather was the most dangerous. These men were called "surfmen" as they got their name from launching their heavy lifeboats into the thunderous

Remaquid Point Lighthouse, Bristol, Maine.

surf. They were also proudly referred to as "soldiers of the surf" or "storm warriors." These surfmen completed many successful rescues because of the nearly daily training drills they performed in using the equipment and rescue procedures, and would go out on daily shore patrols covering over five miles from either side of the station to keep an eye out for stranded wrecks.

Where the lighthouse keepers and their assistants were only allowed to attempt rescues near the proximity of the lighthouse, lifesaving stations covered a much more vast area and could assist a larger number of distressed survivors on a wreck a distance from the shore. They were more mobile and were specifically trained in their ability to rescue survivors.

Surfmen had two means of rescuing people either on board stranded vessels or near the shores. They used an extremely heavy lifeboat pulled on a cart either by horse, or by the men themselves, to a site near the wreck where it could be safely launched into the surf along the shore. This lifeboat weighed nearly half a ton and was useful in all kinds of weather. If a ship wrecked too close to shore to use the lifeboats safely, the surfmen would use a nearly 200-pound small cannon like gun, called a lyle gun, which when fired, would send a line out to the wreck up to 800 yards. The stranded sailors would secure the line to the wreck, and then the other end would be securely fastened by the surfmen to a sturdy high post, boat, or rock along the shore.

A surfman's daily routines consisted of drills in using the lifesaving equipment on the beach or rocks, and shooting the lyle gun at a practice pole as if it were a ship's mast. In a perilous rescue attempt, if a lyle gun could not be used, the surfmen would have to resolve to wading waist deep into the dangerous surf and use a heaving stick to try to get a line aboard the ship. One of their other pieces of equipment was a

Breeches buoy photographed at the Maine Lighthouse Museum.

Lyle cannon photographed at the Maine Lighthouse Museum.

breeches buoy, which looked like a life preserver with canvas pants attached to catch the survivor so he or she could be towed ashore.

The unofficial motto of the surfmen was that "you had to go out, but you did not have to come back." Many surfmen risked their lives to save shipwrecked victims, and some received Lifesaving Medals from the Government for performing their duties under extreme conditions, or from the Humane Society itself. They were the most trained and experienced boaters to launch in all kinds of weather and perform their duties, at great risk to their own lives.

Where lighthouses were built on specific locations as navigational guides, to aid mariners in distress or assist mariners in inclement weather, lightships were needed in the late 1800s as mobile floating lighthouses at dangerous locations, or within busy shipping channels where it was not possible to build a lighthouse. The crews of these relatively small vessels would endure extremely cramped and lonely

Lightship *Nantucket* Collision Sunk By RMS *Olympic*. **Painting by Charles J. Mazoujian.** *Courtesy of Gwen Mazoujian and USCG.*

conditions away from the mainland, along with extreme weather conditions in fog, violent storms, hurricane-force winds, swelling seas, and natural formations like ice floes that could rip the hull of a ship. If a storm approached and vessels were trying to seek safety in nearby harbors (or even in clear weather), lightships would remain at anchor at their designated stations during the storm and provide the flashing light or sound their fog horn to help each vessel navigate to safety.

In the 1930s, radio was used where the lightship was anchored at a designated coordinate. The ship would flash their light beacon at night and bounce the radio signal across the waves. The trans-Atlantic vessel, whether entering or leaving their destination, say a harbor, would steer towards the signals of the radio beacon or flashing light directly in the path of the guiding lightship. There was a lookout posted on the incoming vessel whose purpose was to locate the lightship from the signals received and adjust the ship's course to avoid collision with the stationary lightship. The lightship, anchored in its position was quite vulnerable in that it could easily be involved

in a direct collision with a misguided vessel. Those crewmembers that were stationed aboard lightships knew they were in the most hazardous and vulnerable position, as many lightships met with tragedy in colliding with ships.

After the Civil War, there were three branches of marine rescue service that were established to aid those in distress. They were the Lighthouse Service, the Life Saving Service, and the Revenue Cutter Service. Both personnel of lighthouses and lifesaving stations were funded by and reported to the US Lighthouse Service. Many events involving maritime rescues occurred near our lighthouses, and it is how most of us remember. What is important is to understand is that the three branches were all involved in saving lives along the coast, by the late 1800s they began coordinated rescue efforts together in helping to increase chances of saving more lives. As they continued to aid stranded survivors individually and at times alongside one another, Congress finally combined the services into what we now know as the Coast Guard in 1915.

During the eighteenth and nineteenth centuries, New England became a major commerce region for the shipping, fishing, and whaling trades. More lighthouses were built along the east coast to accommodate the needs of these industries in providing guidance to warn mariners of dangerous reefs, ledges, and shoals. However, with New England's surprising and often fierce storms, many shipwrecks still occurred.

As traffic dramatically increased, which also included tourism after the Civil War, there came the need for lifesaving stations to be built along the shores within a few miles of lighthouses, and from one another. Where the lighthouse keepers and their assistants made rescues near the lighthouse where they were stationed, lifesaving stations covered a much more vast area and could assist a larger number of distressed survivors on a wreck near the shore. They were more mobile and were specifically trained in their ability to rescue survivors.

The Revenue Cutter Service was initially involved in rescue efforts on those wrecks out in open waters,

New England Shipwrecks and Rescues

and then as part of coordinated rescue efforts with the Lighthouse and Life Saving Services. After the Civil War, the use of many successful coordinated rescue efforts between personnel of the Life Saving Service, the Lighthouse Service, and the Revenue Cutter Service, prompted the merger of these services into what we know as our current Coast Guard.

These stories provide a wide range of famous and special rescues where so many individuals risked their lives, not only those employed by the government, but also many local individuals and mariners whose personal call to duty was simply to help those in need, at times risking their lives and successfully saving those in distress, and sometimes losing their lives in the heroic process. There are also special stories of popular rescue animals, the "Flying Santa(s)" during the holiday seasons, and special personal stories of one of New England's last surviving lighthouse keepers, who was also involved in all three branches of rescue service.

Nubble (Cape Neddick)
Lighthouse, York, Maine.

The Rescue of the Frozen Lovers

At Owls Head Lighthouse in Maine

Owls Head Lighthouse marks the entrance to Rockland Harbor and has always been the site of many shipwrecks. Its tower, though only 20 feet tall, is situated over a high rocky cliff making it over 100 feet above water. These rocky formations empty into the ocean, surrounding the area.

One of the most famous bizarre rescues in Maine's maritime history occurred at Owls Head Light, in Maine, during the winter storm of December 22, 1850. Five vessels went aground in this storm between Rockland Harbor and Spruce Head, which is located about eight miles away. The weather was bitterly cold at temperatures below zero, and the gusting winds cast an icy coating from the waves on any vessels anchored in the harbor. All vessels were inside the harbor as the storm approached, intensifying as the night wore on.

At Jameson's Point Wharf, near Rockland, a small coasting schooner from Massachusetts was anchored, ready for a morning start for Boston the next morning. The captain had gone ashore, and had not returned that night, leaving Seaman Roger Elliott, the mate, Richard B. Ingraham, and passenger Lydia Dyer, who was also Ingraham's fiancé, aboard the vessel.

Late in the evening around midnight, the storm came full force into the region as the gusts intensified and the seas began to thrash about. The cables holding the schooner snapped and the heavy winds caused the boat to drift across the harbor towards the rocky shoreline of Owls Head. Ingraham and Elliot tried to control the vessel but the winds were too much for their efforts as the schooner became stuck on an icy ledge just south of Owls Head Lighthouse. It was wedged so tightly that the schooner did not sink as it filled with water, leaving the deck exposed just above the waves that would constantly break over it.

With no help in sight, or any signals of distress to send, the three frightened survivors covered themselves from head to foot with large woolen blankets creating a form of cocoon to try to fend off the icy spray and somehow stay dry. Ingraham placed Lydia Dyer first on the blanket, as he placed himself next to her, then Elliot placed himself at the other end next to Ingraham. They huddled together on the deck and waited, hoping help would arrive as they could barely see the light emanating from the lighthouse.

The tide was coming in and rising, as the frigid waves continued to break over the deck, forming an icy coating on anything they touched. The hours passed and the evening wore on with no help in sight. All three could feel themselves weakening as they were starting to succumb to exposure, while the gusting winds and freezing surf continued to pound the vessel. Their woolen blankets were becoming an icy tomb inches thick as Ingraham and Dyer were slipping into unconsciousness from the additional weight.

The intensity of the surf was also becoming too much for the schooner as it started to slowly break apart

Storm Over Owls Head Lighthouse, Maine.

Keeper's building in Owls Head, Maine.

from the waves constantly washing over her. Fearing that the couple may have already perished, or were very close to death, Seaman Elliot knew that if he could not find help soon, they would all certainly freeze to death. He assured the couple that he would find help and be back for them, but they did not hear him.

It was just before daybreak and the tide was starting to retreat. Elliot tried to hack his way out of his side of the ice-covered blanket using his sheath knife. He continued to chop away until he finally managed to free himself from its frozen grasp. He jumped off the wreck into the frigid waters, as the waves continued to thrash him around. Slowly and carefully, he would grab hold onto a slippery rock and wait for the waves to recede, and then scramble onto another group of rocks as the waves came over him. He would then hold on, as the seas would start to draw back, and start off again. His hands and feet bloodied from being slammed onto the rocks.

Finally, he managed to get close enough to climb over the ice-covered rocks using his hands and knees to the shoreline. He knew he had to keep moving in the bitter chill or he would freeze to death. He climbed up through snowdrifts up the hilly terrain towards the direction of the lighthouse. Nearly overcome with exhaustion and exposure from the freezing cold, he reached the road to Owls Head Lighthouse. Luckily, Keeper Henry Achorn just happened to be riding by in his sleigh, worried about possible wrecks from the storm. He quickly brought the exhausted Elliott to the Keeper's house. Overcome with hypothermia and barely able to speak, Elliott was still able to tell the Keeper about Richard Ingraham and Lydia Dyer still on the schooner. Keeper Achorn quickly rounded up a group of neighbors and they headed to the shoreline, following Elliot's footprints in the snow. They finally sighted the wreck, wedged on the rocks a short distance away from shore.

The waves and winds were starting to subside a little, allowing the keeper and his crew to eventually reach the wreck. There they found both Ingraham and Dyer clinging together inside the blankets under the thick coating of ice. It looked from all appearances that the couple had perished, but Keeper Achorn believed he could feel a faint pulse in each, and was determined to bring them back to the keeper's house and revive them. The men carefully hacked off whatever ice they could from the blanket then brought the ice covered Ingraham and Dyer onto the lifeboat. They carefully placed them in the sleigh and quickly brought the couple inside to the warm kitchen of the keeper's house.

While keeping the pair in cold water just above freezing to slowly bring their temperatures up, they removed their clothing and any ice on their bodies. They then covered them in warm blankets and slowly raised the temperature of the water. Keeper Achorn was convinced they still had to be alive, still feeling what he believed to be a very faint pulse on both victims.

The men took turns massaging and exercising Ingraham and Dyer's cold, limp, arms and legs. After almost two hours of exercising and massaging limbs, they were astonished to find Lydia Dyer showing signs of life. They kept vigorously on their tasks. Another hour passed and Ingraham miraculously opened his eyes and said, "What is all this? Where are we?"

The following day, Dyer and Ingraham had survived the ordeal and were able to eat a little. It took several weeks before they could get up and walk around. It was many months before they were fully recovered. They married that following June and had four children. Seaman Roger Elliott was never able to recover from exposure trying to save the pair and never went back out to sea. His struggle to stay alive and inform Keeper Achorn resulted in the miraculous rescue of Lydia Dyer and Richard Ingraham, the frozen lovers of Owl's Head.

The captain of the ill-fated schooner was never found and many believe he may have learned that, either this was his last trip and was to be fired, or he had heard about the wreck while he was ashore and left town to avoid blame.

Owls Head Lighthouse after snowstorm in Owls Head, Maine.

Abbie Burgess Becomes Maine's Teenage Heroine

At Matinicus Rock Lighthouse in Maine

Matinicus Rock lies about twenty-four miles from the city of Rockland out in Penobscot Bay, in Maine. It is one of the most remote locations for a lighthouse on the eastern coastline. The lighthouse consisted of two towers and keeper's building sitting on a windswept rock and was home to the most famous teenage heroine in Maine's lighthouse history, Abbie Burgess, who lived with her family in the wooden keeper's house.

The Burgess family, originally living in Rockport, Maine, first arrived at Matinicus Rock Lighthouse in the spring of 1853, when her father, Samuel Burgess, was made the keeper of the lighthouse. Her family also included her mother, who was an invalid and in poor health, three other sisters, Esther, Lydia and Mahala, and her brother, Benjy.

Benjy enjoyed the allure of fishing more than staying at the lighthouse and was frequently off on fishing trips. The extra duties fell on Abbie who willingly learned how to tend and operate the lights of the two towers. She became skilled enough to act as her father's assistant keeper.

Abbie soon discovered an old logbook kept by previous light keepers and was fascinated by the stories it told about storms and dangers from the sea. She would spend countless hours reading and studying their writings.

Abbie Burgess Grant, portrait.
Courtesy of US Coast Guard.

Abbie's first test of her keen senses and her awareness of her surroundings involves her mother. Upon studying the log book and learning about weather patterns on the island, she convinced her family to help change the location of her mother's room to where she believed was the strongest constructed location of the new keepers' quarters. A month later, after moving her mother, in December 1855, a great storm hit the rock and swept against the old dwelling containing her mother's original room causing some damage to the structure, while only spray hit the windows of her mother's new location.

The following month, in January of 1856, involved one her most famous acts of heroism. The lighthouse cutter scheduled for dropping off provisions and medical supplies in September, was unable to make the trip. Keeper Burgess, fearing his family would be trapped over the winter without sufficient food and medical supplies, decided he had to go to Rockland on the mainland located about twenty-four miles away. With her younger brother sent aboard a fishing vessel months earlier, Keeper Burgess gave Abbie a hug and told her of the dire need to get the necessary provisions, he then looked into her eyes and said, "I can depend on you, Abbie." Burgess hugged the rest of the family, walked out to the boat dock, jumped into his dory, and began the long sail to Rockland. The winds started to pick up as he left the isolated rock that morning.

By late afternoon that same day, on January 16, a huge storm began to approach Maine's Penobscot Bay. By early evening, it had increased in intensity with gale-force winds causing huge waves to crash over the rocks and lighthouse structures on Matinicus Rock. The storm's ferocity continued for three days. During this time, fearing the keeper's house may be taking in water and would be weakened by the storm, Abbie moved her mother and sisters to the north lighthouse tower, believing it was the strongest structure and location. The high seas were pounding on the island, causing the tides to rise constantly.

On the fourth day, on the morning of January 19, Matinicus Rock was practically underwater. Abbie waded knee deep in the freezing water to rescue her pet chickens from their coop. She was very close to them as they provided comfort in helping her to deal with the constant isolation from the mainland, and was determined to care for them as well. With the chickens safely by the tower, Abbie looked over at the old keeper's house where her mother originally had settled in when they first arrived. At that moment, a

Matinicus Rock Lighthouse, Maine.

giant wave came up and crashed over the dwelling. This time, the old home was totally destroyed, and not a stone from the foundation was left in place.

The rough freezing seas and constant pounding storms for the next four weeks made it impossible for anyone to land on the island. It became one of New England's worst storms of the century. During this time, 17-year old Abbie kept the lights burning on both towers to guide any mariners and ships in the area, while caring for her mother and sisters. There were days when hurricane-force winds would batter the buildings with sleet and snow, as Abbie made the long climb up the stairs of both towers to maintain the lights. She would fill the lanterns, trim the wicks, and clean the many glass lenses of the lights in each tower. She stood on watch for any distressed vessels, and to make sure the lights continued to burn during the day and especially at night, taking short naps each day to keep her strength together.

Abbie wrote the following regarding the experience:

> The new dwelling was flooded and the windows had to be secured to prevent the violence of the spray from breaking them in. As the tide came, the sea rose higher and higher, till the only endurable places were the light-towers. If they stood we were saved, otherwise our fate was only too certain. But for some reason, I know not why, I had no misgivings, and went on with my work as usual. For four weeks, owing to rough weather, no landing could be affected on the Rock. During this time we were without the assistance of any male member of our family. Though at times greatly exhausted with my labors, not once did the lights fail. Under God I was able to perform all my accustomed duties as well as my father's.

Matinicus Lighthouse with both towers and buildings.
Image courtesy US Coast Guard.

About four weeks after he had left for the mainland, Keeper Burgess finally made it back to Matinicus Rock, and was elated to find his family alive and well. Abbie had saved her family and kept the lights in both towers burning to warn any ships of the dangers on the rocks.

The following year, in 1857, she was again tested and proved her heroism. She was left with her brother on the rock during another storm, again, when their father needed to go to the mainland to secure provisions. During a lull in the gale, her brother went off looking for food in a small skiff. Neither her brother, nor her father came back for the next twenty-one days, during which time the family had little food and was reduced to rations of eating one cup of corn meal mush and an egg each day to survive. Abbie and the girls had feared that both their father and brother had perished in the storm.

Current Matinicus Rock Lighthouse with second tower removed.

Whitehead Lighthouse, Maine.

Finally, after three weeks, both father and son returned with plenty of food, but they found Abbie exhausted from worry about them, fearing that both had drowned. During this time while they were gone, again, Abbie tended to her sisters and mother's well being, and all the lighthouse duties of both towers to guide any approaching ships. Her tenacity and determination won her great praise from the locals on the mainland who referred to her as the teenage heroine of Matinicus Rock Light at this time.

Abbie helped her father with many of his duties so he was able to supplement the family income by lobstering, which some believe may have cost him his position as keeper, as additional income to government pay was frowned upon in those days. Abbie's father decided to retire from his position in 1861, and persuaded a friend of the family, Captain John Grant, to take the position as the next keeper. While Abbie stayed on to help train Grant, a romance quickly developed between Abbie and the new keeper's son, Isaac Grant, who was the assistant keeper to the lighthouse.

A year later, they were married and Abbie was also officially appointed assistant keeper. The couple had four children, Francis, Melvina, Mary Louise, and Harris. All were born on Matinicus Rock before Isaac Grant's appointment to Whitehead Lighthouse

in Maine, in 1875, where she remained with him as assistant keeper for another fifteen years. Abbie had stayed at Matinicus Rock Lighthouse for a total of twenty-two years.

In her last days, she wrote a moving letter revealing her love of lighthouses:

> Sometimes I think the time is not far distant when I shall climb these lighthouse stairs no more. It has almost seemed to me that the light was part of myself... I wonder if the care of the lighthouse will follow my soul after it has left this worn-out body! If ever I have a gravestone, I would like it in the form of a lighthouse or a beacon."

She died in 1892 at the age of 53 with a request to leave something about Matinicus Rock Lighthouse placed on her grave. Years later, in 1945, historian Edward Rowe Snow, also known as the "Flying Santa," honored her, and in a quiet ceremony of organized historians and townsfolk, placed a metal replica of the Matinicus Rock Lighthouse over her grave. She had spent 37 of her 53 years tending lighthouses.

The U.S. Coast Guard later honored her by naming a Keeper Class buoy tender, the *Abbie Burgess* (WLM-553).

Miracle Baby Rescues

There are two incidents near New England lighthouses involving the rescue of a small baby in each. These stories have been told over many years and are believed to be relatively accurate in truth. They demonstrate the spirit of a parent that, when all is lost in times of peril, they use their last moments to try to save their children.

Miracle Near Mount Desert Rock Lighthouse

Mount Desert Rock Lighthouse sits on a ledge and is the most isolated lighthouse in New England because of its location 26 miles away from mainland. The rocky island is only 600 yards long and 200 yards in width.

In the early 1880s, the schooner *Helen and Mary* was carrying a load of granite from Halifax, Nova Scotia, when threatening weather suddenly came upon them out by Mount Desert Rock Lighthouse, many miles from shore. The first mate, Nelson White, tried to convince Captain Parker to head towards Maine's Jonesport Harbor for safety, but the captain was eager to make his destination and receive payment for the

Current Mount Desert Rock Lighthouse with building destruction from recent storm, Maine.

cargo he was carrying. The captain's wife, who also happened to be the first mate's sister, accompanied the crew with their baby girl.

As the weather worsened, the waves strengthened and started to wash some of the deck cargo overboard. The captain realized his ignorance too late, and as he started to shout to shorten the sails, fierce gusts of wind caught the fledgling canvas and started to tip the vessel into the raging sea. As water started to fill into the schooner, the captain's wife, baby, and crewmembers were quickly put into the first of two boats. First Mate White and Captain Parker tried to drop the second boat into the rough seas, but the attempt was too

Tending the Buoys at Mt. Desert Rock.
Painting courtesy of artist William Trotter and US Coast Guard.

late. The water-filled vessel, with its heavy cargo, was starting to sink beneath the waves, sucking both men underwater. First Mate White managed to reach the surface and climbed atop a large piece of floating wreckage. He observed in horror as the first boat had capsized nearby and could not locate any survivors near it. He agonized over the fact that all passengers and crew, including his sister, baby niece, and brother in law, had perished.

A short time passed and the seas were starting to calm when he noticed a small bundle of heavy oilskin floating in the water towards him. He successfully managed to lift it out of the water and found his sister's infant daughter wrapped inside, barely wet. Ecstatic that the infant had survived such an ordeal, he tied her as close to his chest for warmth, secured himself to the deck load of wreckage, and collapsed in exhaustion. Hours went by and the weather cleared as the two survivors drifted in the seas.

By the early afternoon of the following day, White was sighted by the lighthouse buoy tender, *Iris*, and both were quickly brought aboard and given warm blankets and food. The infant had survived and was in good health from such an experience. Both recovered from the exposure and were later brought to Prospect Harbor Lighthouse for additional medical treatment. All others from the ill-fated *Helen and Mary* perished near Mount Desert Rock.

Little is documented as to what happened to the miracle baby afterwards, but many believe her grateful uncle cared for her among other family members in remembrance of his sister and brother-in-law.

Miracle Rescue Near Hendricks Head Light

The most popular story involves Keeper Jaruel Marr, who was Keeper at Hendricks Head Lighthouse near Boothbay Harbor in Maine from 1866-1895. During a fierce March blizzard in 1875, blinding snow and gale-force winds came up the Maine coastline. The captain of a small sailing vessel got caught in the rough seas as he was trying to make it ashore and could not see the lighthouse in the driving snow. The vessel ran aground on a rocky ledge about a half mile from the lighthouse point.

Keeper Jaruel Marr was watching from the station during the storm and noticed the vessel lodged on the rocks. He could see the figures of the survivors clinging to the rigging and watched helplessly as the icy waves continued to wash over them in a deathly grip. He anxiously debated as to whether he could launch his dory to help the doomed victims, but the ferocious high seas and gale-force winds bashing against the rocky shoreline would have meant certain disaster for him.

As darkness started to fall, the wind began to subside, allowing Keeper Marr and his wife to build and light a large bonfire for the victims of the wreck as a signal that help was waiting, if they miraculously could find a way to the shore. About an hour later, as he was feeding the fire, he noticed a strange large bundle floating in the waves. He ran to the boathouse for a boat hook and line, and asked his wife to assist him, as he waded into the freezing waters to retrieve the strange package.

Keeper Marr managed to resist the breaking waves and secure the bundle and himself safely on shore. Upon inspecting the bundle, he found it consisted of two small feather beds tied together, which seemed to contain something inside. When he ripped them apart he found a box with a crying baby girl. He grabbed the cold infant, and, with the line still tied around his waist, ran to the house and placed the infant near the fire to warm her. His wife quickly followed in and wrapped the baby in warm blankets to calm her down after the ordeal.

With the baby being cared for, Keeper Marr rushed back to the shore to try and signal to the victims on the wreck, but it was too late. The seas had smashed the vessel to pieces with no survivors. The wreckage was starting to collect along the shore, as the keeper looked for the box the infant was lying in and found some blankets, a locket and a message from the mother in the hopes that God would help her child. The infant survived the ordeal but all aboard the vessel had perished.

The baby girl, later named Seaborn, was believed to have been later adopted by a doctor and his wife who were summer residents living nearby, as Keeper Marr and his wife had plenty of their own children at the time. This story has been disputed and believed to have had originated from a book published around 1900 called "Uncle Terry," but ancestors of Keeper Marr believe and have written that it is actually true.

Hendricks Head Lighthouse, Maine.

Maine's Cape Elizabeth Lighthouse in winter.

The *Bohemian* Wreck
Near Cape Elizabeth Twin Lights and Portland Head Light

On February 4, 1864, the steamer *Bohemian*, was making a winter voyage leaving Liverpool, England, for Portland, Maine. The 295-foot steamer was carrying about 219 passengers consisting of 200 Irish immigrants and 19 cabin-class passengers. As was the custom in those days, immigrants would be crowded below deck at the bottom of the ship in steerage away from the other passengers. Captain Borland had his 98 crewmen aboard the vessel and was very familiar with the Portland Harbor, as he had made the journey a number of times during his eight years at the helm.

On February 22, 1864, on President's Day, the *Bohemian* proceeded up the Maine coast towards Cape Elizabeth, moving rather slowly as a hazy sky filled the night. Sometime after seven o'clock the lookout notified the captain that he spotted two lights offshore. The two lights were the range lights of the Cape Elizabeth Twin Lights a few miles south of Portland Head Light. Somehow from the atmospheric haze Borland had miscalculated the distance and believed he was seven or eight miles offshore, but in reality, the *Bohemian* was only a couple of miles away from the rocky shoreline, and was proceeding dangerously close to Alden's Rock. This was a treacherous ledge in shallow water that at the time was only marked by a silent buoy, not a bell buoy. Borland could not see Portland Head Lighthouse from his position.

By eight o'clock, the first officer had just taken the wheel when a buoy marking the perilous rock was spotted directly ahead. The captain yelled to have the engines shut off in an attempt to slow the vessel, but it was too late. The *Bohemian* struck Alden's Rock, ripping a gash in the hull. Borland tried to head the vessel toward shore, eventually reaching an inlet location about two miles from the mainland, but the disabled steamer could not proceed any further under power due to the amount of water she had taken in, and the damage inside the engine room. The steamer could only drift towards shore. The captain ordered the gunboats fired to signal the *Bohemian*'s distress, but only one could be set off as the other was already under water. A pilot boat's captain was in the vicinity a mile away and heard the one gun, but believed the ship was celebrating President's Day.

To keep the *Bohemian* from drifting back out to sea, anchors were dropped and the captain ordered the lifeboats deployed immediately. While most lifeboats were able to safely launch, a support pin in the second lifeboat gave way, spilling forty passengers into the freezing waters and drowning sixteen of them. As the lifeboat drifted ashore near Cape Elizabeth hours later, locals found only one man and child in it, both dead.

Most of the boats launched in the hysteria were not filled to capacity and contained mostly men. The frightened passengers and crew aboard the lifeboats refused to return to the sinking ship to pick up those stranded on the deck for fear of capsizing. The victims on the wreck jumped into the icy waters in hopes of being hauled into the boats, but many drowned from exposure in their struggles.

With the lifeboats dispatched, Captain Borland, four of his crew, and around seventy passengers found themselves stranded on deck. With the steamer's bridge completely covered in water, and the seas constantly sweeping over her, Captain Borland knew the *Bohemian*'s time afloat was getting shorter. The steamer was less than 1,000 feet from shore when some of the lifeboats returned to pick up survivors. Additional help was provided from residents at the Ocean House and from the Fishing House on Cape Elizabeth, who sent teams out to help the survivors and to later help in the gruesome task of picking up the corpses floating in the waters and bringing them to shore.

Some of those stranded, many of whom were women and children, who were still waiting and could not climb up the masts and rigging, were being washed overboard as the ship started to sink into the icy waters. Captain Borland managed to get about fifty passengers off the wreck to safety along with his crew. He and his remaining crew waited until all the remaining survivors were in the lifeboats before they climbed into the last lifeboat to shore. An hour and a half later, the *Bohemian* sank. In total, two crewmembers and a total of forty passengers, all Irish immigrants from the lower steerage class, perished. The nineteen cabin passengers survived.

The locals of Cape Elizabeth opened their homes in providing food, shelter, and clothing to the exhausted survivors, while the local City Hall provided temporary shelter as the survivors tried to notify their families in England and Ireland. Money was collected by the Portland Board of Trade and distributed to the survivors for clothing.

In his deposition, Captain Borland testified, "when we struck I was not certain where we were." The ship's officers, crew, and some of the passengers were asked for their recollections of the night, and were questioned as to whether the captain had been drinking. Some reported that they felt the captain was a bit intoxicated, but the chief saloon steward testified that Borland was given one glass of ale that day. There was also public outcry that the captain's crew had left so many stranded to die on the ship, while he and most of his crew survived. The jury concluded that Captain Borland was in error of judgment and was responsible for the disaster, and

Cape Elizabeth Lighthouse shines at twilight.

that his crew did not act professionally in trying to help the passengers to fill the lifeboats to capacity, thinking only of themselves. The pilot nearby who had heard the gun signaling the *Bohemian* in distress was also ruled at fault for not investigating. They also ruled that Alden's Rock should have had a bell buoy instead of a silent buoy to warn vessels passing by the treacherous rock.

Days later, some of the women from nearby Cape Elizabeth found items from the *Bohemian* wreck including bolts of wool, silks, and satins which many kept for themselves to create new clothing.

After the shipwreck of the *Bohemian* and public outcry, The Portland Board of Trade investigated the rocks and shoals nearby and had bell buoy markers placed as needed. Portland Head Lighthouse's visibility was also examined and improved by raising the tower twenty feet in 1865. A second-order Fresnel lens was also installed to generate a more powerful light.

Many years later, early accounts indicated that an Irish immigrant, John Fitzgerald, believed to be the ancestor of President John F. Kennedy, was one of the survivors, but this has been proven to be inaccurate.

Portland Head Light Shipwrecks and Generations of Service

At Portland Head Lighthouse in Maine

Portland Head Lighthouse is Maine's oldest lighthouse, built in 1791 during George Washington's presidency, and one of the oldest lighthouses in America. Its location set atop a rocky cliff on the shoreline marks the picturesque entrance to Maine's Portland Harbor in Casco Bay. There were four shipwrecks that occurred in the vicinity of the lighthouse, three a very short distance from the lighthouse, and one a few miles south of the lighthouse near Cape Elizabeth Lighthouse. Two of these, the wreck *Annie C Maguire* and the wreck *Bohemian* (previous story) are the most well known and are rather intriguing in their stories. After the tragedy of the *Bohemian*, improvements in the vicinity were made off shore and in the eventual raising of the Portland Head Lighthouse tower. Portland Head Lighthouse is also known as having four generations of the Strout family in dedicating over 100 years of combined service to the light.

Generations of Strout Family at Portland Head Lighthouse

In the 1820s, Joshua Strout's mother had worked as the teenage housekeeper at Portland Head Lighthouse for an earlier keeper, Captain Joshua Freeman. She was so inspired by the joyful keeper, that when she married years later, she named her son Joshua Freeman Strout. Joshua Strout went to sea at the age of 11, and by the time he was 18, he became a cook on a tugboat. He

Portland Head Lighthouse, Cape Elizabeth, Maine.

Portland Head Lighthouse in storm, Cape Elizabeth, Maine.

later became a captain of the brig *Scotland*, in 1854, where he sailed and transported cargo around South America. He captained other vessels and, enjoyed sailing all around the world dealing in foreign trade. It was more of a majestic adventure for these men drawn to the ocean, than being planted on shore in America in those times. With the excitement of exploration and trade to other countries, came many pleasant and often rough times. Some of the difficult periods included many bad storms, long stretches over open waters where time would seem to stand still, occasional mutinies to deal with when food supplies dwindled or had gone sour, or working with abusive captains. During the Gold Rush of California, Strout helped to transport many "Forty-Niners" to San Francisco in search of their fortunes.

Sometimes, deep-water sailors like Strout were retired to respectful positions on shore as a result of accidents, or, if they were lucky to live long enough, of old age. A severe fall from the mast of his ship, *Andres*, forced Captain Strout ashore, and in 1869, he was made keeper of the Portland Head Lighthouse, with the help of his mother. His wife, Mary, served as assistant keeper for ten years with him until 1877, when their fourth son, Joseph, at the age of 21, took over the duties as the new assistant keeper to help his father.

The Strouts loved the life at the lighthouse and Joshua would frequently meet with the famous poet Henry Wadsworth Longfellow, who lived nearby in Portland. Longfellow would visit the lighthouse a day or two each week and the two men would enjoy many pleasant conversations together, becoming close friends. Longfellow's famous poem, "The Lighthouse," was believed to have been written while sitting on the rocks by Portland Head Light as

Keeper Joshua Strout. *Image courtesy of Portland Head Light Museum.*

he was enjoying the beauty that engulfed the region. Joshua rarely took any time away from the light, as was the case of many dedicated lighthouse keepers. He is known to have gone a period of nearly seventeen years without taking any time off.

Over the years, Joshua and Mary raised eleven children at the lighthouse, but had lost three of their sons at sea. During a hurricane on September 8, 1869, Joshua barely escaped death when a fog-warning bell was sent crashing over the cliff below the lighthouse. Their most famous rescue involves the wreck of the *Annie C Maguire*, on Christmas Eve in 1886.

The Rescue of the *Annie C Maguire*

The *Annie C Maguire* was a converted bark vessel that was originally built as an extremely fast clipper ship, named the Golden State, narrowly breaking sailing distance records on some of its voyages. As a clipper ship, it had a thirty-year career involved in trade with China. Afterwards, it was converted as a three-masted bark sailing vessel for carrying heavy cargo. Its owners, however, had run into financial difficulties and owed money to their creditors. A few days prior to Christmas Eve, in 1886, a sheriff's officer had received word that the *Annie C Maguire* may be passing by, or anchoring near Portland Harbor. He stopped by the Strout's house and asked Joshua to keep an eye out for the vessel and to notify him if the vessel was sighted along the Casco Bay.

On Christmas Eve, in 1886, members of the Strout family were gathered together for the Christmas holiday at the keeper's house. Joshua's wife, Mary, had killed eight chickens a few days prior for baking her famous chicken pies. Joshua went up to the tower to remain on look out while everyone was settling in for the night, ready to enjoy Christmas dinner the next day. As the evening wore on, the winds were blowing, but not gusting, and a mixture of rain and snow was falling over the area from a heavy storm that was raging off shore.

That same night on Christmas Eve, around 11 p.m., the *Annie C Maguire* was headed for Portland Harbor on route to Quebec coming from Buenos Aires, Argentina. On board were two mates, thirteen crewmen, and Captain Thomas O'Neil's family, including himself, his wife, and teenage son, Thomas Junior. The captain had made the decision to wait out the impending storm in Portland Harbor.

The waves were starting to get rough as the *Annie C Maguire* started up along the coast. The temperature was fairly warm for that time of year with rain falling along the shore, mixing in with occasional snow squalls. All of a sudden, around 11:30 p.m., the vessel ran aground on the rocks nearly 100 feet from Portland Head Lighthouse. Apparently Captain O'Neil could not see the lighthouse in either the heavy rains or possible snow squall and misjudged his location. To keep the vessel lodged on the rocks, he quickly had the crew take down the sails and lower the anchors. He realized they had landed right next to the lighthouse and knew they would be rescued shortly.

Portland Head Lighthouse, Cape Elizabeth, Maine.

Wreck of *Annie C Maguire* at Portland Head Lighthouse.
Image courtesy Museum of Portland Head Light.

Joshua saw the wreck from the lighthouse tower and couldn't believe his eyes. He ran into the keeper's house and burst through the door yelling, "All hands turn out! There's a ship ashore in the dooryard!" The family had felt the ground shake and heard the noise from the impact of the vessel slamming into the nearby rocks. As his son, Joseph, quickly put his clothes back on, he ran out the door and was shocked to find the rather large vessel on the rocks listing to one side nearly 100 feet from the lighthouse. Keeper Strout's wife, Mary, grabbed a blanket, cut it into strips, and soaked them in kerosene. She lit them so they could be used as torches to light the area for rescuing the crew. Joshua and his son, Joseph, rigged an ordinary ladder as a gangplank between the waves and rocky ledges that separated them from the wreck. One by one, Joshua and Joseph helped each survivor over the makeshift plank to the warm safety of the keeper's house. They rescued all eighteen people safely while the ship lie wedged on the rocks.

When they reached the keeper's house, the survivors, freezing from the icy waters, had all their drenched clothing cut off and removed and were given warm blankets and clothes. Mary soon had hot coffee and food for the survivors, and helped in rubbing their hands and feet with warm kerosene and glycerin. They found that the crew had been on food rations of salt beef and macaroni for weeks, mixed in with lime juice to keep them from getting scurvy, and were quite famished. In fact, after they were provided a Christmas day dinner the next day, consisting of Mary's famous chicken pies, they loafed around for three more days consuming any food that was left. The Strout family, although only able to manage a plateful apiece of the delicious delicacies, felt it was their duty to oblige their unexpected guests. Keeper Strout did try to convince the crew that they were not at a lifesaving station, where there was plenty of food for large groups, but at a lighthouse station, were food was limited. This seemed to fall on deaf ears as the survivors continued to stay on and fill their bellies with any food they could find. Captain O'Neil and his family were very gracious to the Strout family and very appreciative of their efforts.

The following morning on Christmas day, the deputy sheriff, notified of the wreck, came to claim the ship and put Joshua Strout in charge of salvaging anything from the wreck for the creditors. When two cases of scotch whiskey were brought in the house, the selfish crewmembers drank the contents at once, got very drunk and proceeded to beat up the cook for their meager rations they were served during the latter part of the trip. Joshua Strout's son, Joseph, kept a spear-like device from the ship as a souvenir, which was probably used to fend off the local natives at a faraway port that may have been trying to board the ship.

Because the ship was so beaten up, the creditors received only $177 at auction. In trying to serve the angry creditors, the sheriff searched the ship's sea chest for special papers and cash, but came up with nothing.

Just over a week later, on New Year's Day of 1887, another storm came along and destroyed what was left of the *Annie C Maguire*. The crew had been discharged a few days earlier and sent home by the British Vice Counsel. Years later, it was discovered that the captain, with the help of his devious wife, had ransacked the chest and carried the cash, papers, and other items of value in her hatbox during the rescue.

When Joshua Strout retired as Maine's oldest lighthouse keeper in 1904 at the age of 79, his son, Joseph, already an assistant keeper, was appointed as the next generation keeper at Portland Head Lighthouse. He had a joyful reputation like his father and was affectionately called "Cap'n Joe" by the locals and mariners alike. The family also had a parrot named Billy for many years. The parrot learned to speak when inclement weather was coming it and would shout, "Joe, let's start the horn. It's foggy!"

Joshua Strout passed away a few years later at the age of 81. The Strout family combination of father and son were keepers of Portland Head Lighthouse for a total of fifty-nine years from 1869-1928. When the assistant keeper position was traditionally promoted to John Strout, Joseph's son, on his 21st birthday in 1912, he became the third generation Strout to serve in a government position at Portland Head Light.

It was on his birthday that John Strout decided to paint an inscription to commemorate the location of where years ago the *Annie C Maguire* had wrecked on the rocks close to the lighthouse. He had to chip a large portion of the rock away in order to create a flat surface on which to paint. After mixing mortar, sand and some paint together, he painted the words "In Memory of the Ship *Annie C Maguire*, Wrecked on this Point Christmas Eve, 1886." He had a wooden cross placed on top of the rock as well. The wooden cross has long since washed away along with the original painting, but the inscription has been periodically renewed and repainted over the years. It has evolved into a simpler inscription reading "*Annie C Maguire*, Shipwrecked Here, Christmas Eve 1886" which displays today for residents and tourists alike.

Along with the *Annie C Maguire*, there were two other vessels that wrecked near Portland Head Lighthouse afterwards, and were almost at the same location as the *Annie C Maguire*. One occurred during a severe winter storm on November 30, in 1887, less than a year after the wreck of the *Annie C Maguire*. The schooner *D. W. Hammond* was caught in the blizzard and crashed onto the rocks a short distance from the lighthouse. Joseph Strout and his brother Gilman ran out to the shore where they could see the wreck. They were able to get a line out to the captain and his two crewmembers on the vessel and pull them safely to shore before the vessel broke apart.

Many years later, on October 4, 1932, the seventy-two-foot schooner *Lochinvar*, carrying a cargo of over twenty tons of fish, was caught in a heavy fog near Portland Head Light. It crashed on the rocks by the lighthouse less than 100 feet from where the *Annie C Maguire* had struck some 46 years before. The cargo was destroyed but the captain and crew survived the ordeal.

John Strout served at Portland Head Light for a few years as assistant, then later served at nearby Spring Point Light, and then at the Lighthouse Depot in Chelsea, Massachusetts. The Strout family of four generations served a total of 128 years as lighthouse tenders, with over 100 years of combined service between family members, including Joshua's mother's tenure as housekeeper, at Portland Head Lighthouse. There were many family members of different lighthouses that would be involved in tending a lighthouse, including wives of keepers, or their sons, but rarely there would be four generations of family members servicing at the same lighthouse.

Other members of the Strout family served at nearby lighthouses in Maine. Len Strout was the keeper a few miles from Portland Head Light, at Portland Breakwater Light, or commonly known as Bug Light from 1866 to 1867. Arthur Strout served as an assistant keeper at Halfway Rock Lighthouse, out in Casco Bay.

Recently, there were items donated by the current Strout family from whose ancestors served in the lighthouse. Among the items donated is the original brass lamp that was in used to light the lens in the lantern room of Portland Head Light on Christmas Eve, 1886, the night of the famous wreck of the *Annie C Maguire*, crashed upon the rocks by the lighthouse.

Keeper Joseph Strout.
Image courtesy Museum of Portland Head Light and Jeremy D'Entremont Collection.

Painted commemoration on rock of location of *Annie C Maguire* wreck by John Strout at Portland Head Lighthouse, Maine.

Keeper John Strout.
Image courtesy Museum of Portland Head Light.

The Most Daring Lighthouse Rescue

At Cape Elizabeth Lighthouse in Maine

Cape Elizabeth Lighthouse, Cape Elizabeth, Maine.

Marcus Hanna was transferred as head keeper to Cape Elizabeth Lighthouse in 1873 from Pemaquid Point Lighthouse. He was to become infamous in one of the most daring rescues in lighthouse history. The rescue is not famous for the number of survivors saved, but for the incredible suffering Keeper Hanna endured in his determination to save those in distress, in risking his own life at in the attempt.

The schooner *Australia* was carrying a cargo of 150 barrels of mackerel on deck and a load of ice on the 27th of January, 1885. She was leaving Boothbay, Maine to deliver her cargo to Boston, Massachusetts the next day. On board there were three crewmen, Captain J.W. Lewis, Seaman Irving Pierce, and Seaman William Kellar.

That night, a violent nor'easter storm came over the area with bitterly cold gale-force winds and blinding snow. Keeper Hanna sounded the steam fog whistle all night despite being exhausted from having flu-like symptoms. By daybreak, the keeper trudged his way back from the tower through large snowdrifts to the keeper's dwelling in order to get some needed rest. Mrs. Hanna extinguished the lights in both towers, while Assistant Keeper Hiram Staples took the morning shift trying to keep an eye out for distressed vessels, although visibility was very poor from the ongoing blizzard.

Around midnight that same night during the storm, the *Australia* had lost her sails from the high winds while attempting to reach Portland Harbor for safety. By 8 a.m. that morning, on January 28, she ended up crashing on the rocks by Cape Elizabeth Light, near the fog signal. As the seas washed over the wreck, the crewmen had barely enough time to crawl upon the rigging. Captain Lewis lost his grip and was washed overboard, drowning in the icy waters. The two seamen, Pierce and Kellar, were trying to hang on to the rigging in the bitter cold as the temperature had tumbled to minus ten degrees below zero. As the storm continued, they were being drenched in icy water and spray.

At around 8:40 a.m., with the blizzard still unrelenting, Hanna's wife saw a glimpse of the masts of the vessel on the rocks and shouted to awaken her husband. Keeper Hanna rushed to the signal house with Staples, who hadn't seen the wreck through the

Keeper Marcus Hanna.
Courtesy of US Coast Guard.

blinding snow. Hanna and Staples hurried to the edge of the water near the schooner, where they observed the two sailors covered in ice clinging to the rigging, looking like ghoulish scarecrows. Hanna yelled that they were coming to help and for the sailors to hang on.

Keeper Hanna's wife and Staples' son went to get help from the neighbors as Hanna and Assistant Keeper Staples decided to try to find materials to rescue the men. The keeper realized he could not launch a boat in the stormy waters, so crawled through the snow to the fog signal house and grabbed an axe. He and Staples then had to crawl again over the snowdrifts to the boathouse 300 yards away and shovel the entrance to get into the building. There they grabbed a line to rescue the frozen crewmen.

Hanna tied a heavy iron weight he got from the fog signal house to the end of the line and crawled along the icy rocks with the winds still gusting at below zero temperatures. If he slipped on the rocks in the thunderous surf it could be a fatal mistake in such freezing waters. When he reached the edge of the surf, he tried a number of times to throw the line to the vessel but failed. He tried again and again unsuccessfully with the line falling short of its target each time. After many unsuccessful attempts, Keeper Hanna had to crawl back to the shoreline to briefly try to warm himself up. He could feel the stinging pain from prolonged exposure as his fingers, hands, and feet started to go numb. Assistant Staples was also suffering from the freezing cold, and briefly had to abandon the keeper. He went back to the fog signal house to try to warm up and went to check to see if any additional help had arrived.

Suddenly, a huge wave struck the wrecked schooner and smashed her further on the rocks. Hanna knew time was getting short for the men. In exhaustion from his illness, and practically frozen as hypothermia was engulfing him, he decided to risk his life and waded waist-deep into the icy ocean surf. The waves were thrashing all around him as he summoned all his strength, and again threw a line to the schooner, this time landing it near Pierce. The frozen sailor managed to barely pull his grasp away from the icy rigging and bend the line around his waist.

Hanna crawled back to the icy rocks and shouted for help with no reply. As soon as he was ready, Pierce signaled to Hanna, and jumped into the raging surf. Hanna was determined to save Pierce at any cost, and somehow managed to pull the helpless man through the waves and over the slippery rocks to safety on the shore. Hanna would later write,

> Pierce's jaws were set; he was totally blind from exposure to the cold, and the expression of his face I shall not soon forget.

Keeper Hanna realized he couldn't wait for help to arrive and quickly loosened the line from Pierce's ice-covered body. He again waded into the surf in subzero temperatures and howling winds. After several tries, the line landed within Kellar's grasp. Kellar, also frozen and badly frostbitten, was barely able to tie the rope around his waist. Keeper Hanna could feel his own strength giving out as he tried to haul Kellar over to safety. Just as Hanna was about to pass out from exhaustion and exposure, Staples and two neighbors arrived and were able to help the keeper haul Kellar to the shore.

The two sailors were then carried to the fog signal building, along with Hanna, where they were given dry clothes, food, and spirits. They were badly frostbitten and could not be moved to the keeper's dwelling until later that night due to the intensity of the storm and huge snowdrifts. The storm had removed communication within the city and most of the roads were closed for a couple of days. After spending two more days at the keeper's dwelling, Pierce and Kellar had recovered enough, along with Hanna, to be taken to the marine hospital in Portland by sled. They gradually recovered from what could easily have been a tragedy for all if not for the determination of the keeper.

Six months later, in April of 1885, Marcus Hanna received a Gold Lifesaving Medal for his selfless heroism in rescuing the two sailors. The incident was to rank as one of the greatest lifesaving feats at an American lighthouse and was one of the highest honors given for heroic service. Hannah also received the distinguished Medal of Honor in 1895 for his bravery in another rescue incident at Port Hudson.

In August 1997, the Coast Guard launched a 175-foot Coast Guard buoy tender vessel named the *Marcus Hanna*. A replica of Hanna's lifesaving medal is mounted on board. The ship's homeport is located in South Portland, Maine, near the Cape Elizabeth Lighthouse.

Ice-covered rocks by Cape Elizabeth Lighthouse, Cape Elizabeth, Maine.

Rescue of the Keeper's Daughter

At Wood Island Light in Maine

Sometimes life at a lighthouse located offshore can create problems that many of us may take for granted, especially if medical attention is needed for the keeper or members of his family. The keeper, the Coast Guard station, and the local mariners all have a deep respect for one another and always try to look out for one another, especially in stormy weather. This is a somewhat controversial story of a rescue of the keeper's little girl, which could have evolved into a tragic event from a New England storm, if not for the courage of her Coast Guard rescuers, her father, and a local lobsterman to make sure she was brought ashore safely.

Wood Island Lighthouse is located about a mile from the mainland, marking the entrance to Saco River. Laurier Burnham was the Coast Guard keeper at Wood Island Lighthouse with his wife, Lily, and two children from 1959-1963. On November 29, 1960, a near tragedy occurred when his 2-year-old daughter, Tammy, became seriously ill and it became necessary for her to get to the mainland for immediate medical attention. The seas were raging in five-foot swells, it was raining, and the area was engulfed in thick fog as a storm descended on the region early that evening. Burnham signaled the Fletcher's Neck Coast Guard Life Boat Station at Biddeford Pool that he needed assistance to bring his daughter to shore to Biddeford's hospital. They responded sending a thirty-foot Coast Guard lifeboat containing a four-man crew, which was towing a small lobsterman's type of skiff boat to bring the little girl in. When the main lifeboat came within range of Wood Island, the tiny skiff was launched and manned by two Seamen, Ed Syvinski and Raymond Bill, to transport the little girl back to the main boat.

Burnham wrapped Tammy up in blankets and warm clothing and walked her a bit of a distance to the west side of the island to the boat house and they waited for their rescuers. The two seamen were already having trouble rowing the tiny boat to shore through the wind, fog, and rough seas. They finally made it to the boat ramp on Wood Island where Keeper Burnham reluctantly handed over his daughter in such a small boat. He asked the two rescuers to contact him as soon as they made it onto the main lifeboat. The two young men agreed and set out for the Coast Guard lifeboat in the fog and high seas.

About a half hour later, Burnham received a call from the Fletcher's Neck Light Station asking what was taking so long. He replied that they had already left and feared that something may have gone wrong in the storm. Burnham announced that he was going

Wood Island Lighthouse, Biddeford Pool, Maine. *Courtesy of Friends of Wood Island Lighthouse.*

out in his peapod to search for the skiff. The station commander reminded him that he was on duty and ordered Burnham not to leave his post in the storm. Seaman Ed Syvinski and Seaman Raymond Bill were trying to maneuver the rowboat, without life jackets aboard, through the heavy waves and were about a few hundred feet from where they had left Wood Island, when all of a sudden a large wave capsized the small rowing skiff, tossing the little girl and the two seamen into the cold waters. Seaman Syvinski grabbed Tammy just as she was going under the water and held onto her tightly.

Front left to right, Keeper Laurier Burnham, Ed Syvinski, and Raymond Bill.

In the darkness and fog, neither Keeper Burnham at the Wood Island Light Station nor the two men on board the Coast Guard boat knew of what had happened to the three struggling in the chilly waters. Syvinski still held tightly on to the little girl as he tried to hold onto the capsized boat with his other arm. Fearing that they would all perish if he couldn't get help, Seaman Raymond Bill announced he would get help and took off swimming in the freezing waters towards the direction of the Coast Guard boat. Syvinski feared we would never see his comrade again. Chief Kennedy and Engineman Rouleau aboard the thirty-foot vessel miraculously spotted the exhausted Seamen Bill struggling in the chilly waters and hauled him to safety. They started to search for the pair as the fog thickened but could not find any sign of them.

As Syvinski still hung onto little Tammy and waited for help to arrive, he was determined to save the little girl even if it meant losing his own life. Nearly a half hour had passed and a large wave came over the capsized boat, separating him and Tammy from the craft. Three times as waves started to break over the two survivors, dragging them under water, Syvinski told the little girl to hold her breath as he covered her nose and mouth. Luckily, they were still in shallow waters, and each time they were dragged under, Syvinski was able to touch and push up from the bottom to the surface. The water continued to get shallower as Syvinski kept pushing off from the bottom. They finally made it to nearby Negro Ledge Island where Syvinski held her tightly to his chest, as he stood waste deep on the underwater ledge while the waves broke around and over him. He tried his best to keep the little girl as warm as possible, and kept trying to comfort her.

After an hour had passed since the skiff had left his dock, the frustrated keeper received another call from Fletcher's Neck Station, telling him that the main lifeboat found only Seaman Bill and that they were unable to locate the keeper's daughter or Syvinski. Presuming that both Syvinski and Burnham's daughter were lost at sea in the storm,

View of Wood Island from the lighthouse tower, Biddeford Pool, Maine. *Courtesy of Friends of Wood Island Lighthouse.*

they told Burnham, "We'll search for the bodies in the morning." Enraged, Keeper Burnham shouted that he was going to find his daughter. He was again told to remain at his post, as it was too dangerous to go out in the storm, and that he would be court marshaled if he went against orders. As would most any parent, he responded, "Like Hell!" slammed the phone down, and quickly ran out to launch his little peapod motorboat in the raging waters.

Burnham was quite knowledgeable of the area and he knew if they made it to any of the neighboring islands surrounding Wood Island they might be safe. He had a feeling that if they were both able to survive, that nearby Negro Island should be the first place to look. As luck would have it, at his first attempt at Negro Island, he spotted the exhausted pair. Syvinski was holding onto his daughter at his chest, as he stood waist deep in cold water on the ledge. Burnham's face lit up when he saw the two and that his daughter was still alive. He landed the peapod on Negro Ledge and got his daughter, who had slipped into unconsciousness from the ordeal and Syvinski into his boat. He brought his boat through the waves and fog towards the direction of the main Coast Guard boat. He found the searchlight and loaded both onto the boat.

With the three from the capsized boat brought safely onto the main boat, but suffering from exposure to the cold, Burnham was then ordered to return to the lighthouse. Syvinski and the little girl were put in the forward hold and given warm blankets to dry off. With the thickening fog and storm still raging the thirty-foot Coast Guard boat became disoriented in trying to return to the dock at Biddeford Pool.

Preston Alley, a local lobsterman, with over thirty years of experience in navigating the harbor, had been listening to the situation on his two-way radio and decided to risk his life and his boat in helping out to get the girl ashore as quickly as possible. He was able to find the Coast Guard boat near an area ledge called Phillip Rock, and persuaded the reluctant crew to give the girl to him so he could get Tammy quickly to her grandparents who had been waiting to bring her to the hospital. They finally agreed, and Alley made haste for the shore as the Coast Guard boat followed. Chief Kennedy radioed the hospital and told his family to bring blankets to the dock. When he and Alley arrived at Biddeford Pool, Kennedy's family members were waiting on

the dock with warm blankets, along with Tammy's grandparents. Alley carefully brought the unconscious freezing little girl to her grandparents as they laid her in their laps in their car, placed more blankets around her, and sped to Notre Dame Hospital in Biddeford, where emergency crews were waiting for the little girl.

When Tammy arrived at the hospital her body temperature had plummeted to a dangerous 82 degrees. The crew worked busily all night to try to bring her body temperature up. As the night wore on, miraculously her temperature finally started to increase. Within five days, she was released from the hospital and became known locally as the "little lighthouse child." Thanks to the brave efforts of Seamen Ed Syvinski and Raymond Bill, Chief Kennedy, Engineman Rouleau, Keeper Burnham, and Lobsterman Preston Alley, Tammy fully recuperated and had no long-lasting effects from the ordeal.

Both Seamen Ed Syvinski and Raymond Bill were suffering from exposure when they arrived at the dock, but decided not to receive medical attention at the hospital, and were not persuaded to get medical help. Syvinski, though suffering from hypothermia, was obliged to stand on the midnight watch as he was scheduled before the incident. He performed his duties that night, but became ill for three weeks afterwards. He stayed on with the Coast Guard for four years and later became an engineer. Laurier Burnham remained at the lighthouse until 1963.

Over the years, participant's families disputed accounts of what happened that night. In 1993, thirty-three years later, Tammy's sister prompted the Coast Guard to find out what truly happened that night. The Coast Guard investigated the incident and decided to present awards to Keeper Laurier Burnham and Seaman Edward Syvinski for their extraordinary courage. A Public Service Commendation was awarded to the widow of lobsterman Preston Alley, who had passed away in 1990, and whom the Coast Guard had determined had also been instrumental in the rescue. In 2010, a reunion was held at Wood Island Light between participants and their families to celebrate the 50-year anniversary of the incident. What is most important regarding this story is a little girl survived what could have been a tragic event, with the help of a group of individuals who risked their lives and safety, so she would survive and have a family of her own.

Tammy Burnham (on right) with her sister by Wood Island Lighthouse.

Daring Rescue of Survivors and Between the Rescuers

Near Portsmouth Harbor Lighthouse in New Hampshire

As lighthouses were built along the shore as navigational aids in guiding shipping traffic and local mariners, most of these buildings could only accommodate the keeper and one or two assistants. Their main objective was to keep the light burning to aid mariners in all kinds of weather. Most of the rescues by lighthouse keepers involved wrecks that occurred close to the lighthouse where the keeper and his assistants could rescue from the shore, or by a small lifeboat. In the mid-1800s, as shipping traffic increased along the coast, lifesaving stations were constructed in busy strategic locations near the lighthouses to house additional crewmembers, called surfmen, or lifeboat men. These men were highly trained in rescue efforts alone and were capable of rescuing larger numbers of individuals than lighthouse keepers and used special heavy lifeboats to drive through the surf to the wreck. These stations usually had their own captain or keeper. Both personnel of lighthouses and lifesaving stations were funded by and reported to the US Lighthouse Service. Before there would be telephones or radio, these stations were constructed usually within a few miles of their neighboring lighthouses.

The surfmen provided additional help during peak shipping, fishing, or tourist seasons. They would patrol the shoreline, keeping a close eye out for ships that may be in distress or had already wrecked on nearby ledges or sandbars, especially during stormy New England weather. Their daily routines also consisted of daily drills (except on Sundays) in using the lifesaving equipment on the beach or rocks, including shooting a cannon type of gun called a lyle gun with a survivor's line at a practice pole as if it were a ship's mast. They would also use a cart with a huge coil of rope and crank to pull in shipwrecked sailors. In a perilous rescue attempt, if a lyle gun could not be used, the surfmen would have to resolve to wade waist deep into the surf and use a heaving stick to try to get a line aboard the ship.

By the late nineteenth century, residents along the Piscataqua River that borders between the New Hampshire and southern Maine regions petitioned for a lifesaving station on New Castle Island, next

Surfmen at Jerry's Point Lifesaving Station carrying wagon with crank and coils of rope for rescuing stranded sailors, New Hampshire. *Courtesy of New Castle Historical Society.*

Portsmouth Harbor Lighthouse in snowstorm, New Castle Island, New Hampshire.

to Portsmouth, New Hampshire. The island also contained Fort Constitution (also known as Fort Point), which maintained Portsmouth Harbor Lighthouse, and was located across the river from Maine's Whaleback Lighthouse. This region was extremely busy with shipping traffic into Portsmouth, and many vessels wrecked along the rocky shoreline, out in the Isles of Shoals, or would get caught in the deep strong currents of the Piscataqua River. The government granted the request and built a Lifesaving Service Station at Jerry's Point in 1878, located on New Castle Island a few miles from Portsmouth Harbor Lighthouse. Other lifesaving stations were also built in the area and spread along the eastern coast.

By 1883, nearly five years after its construction, Jerry's Point Lifesaving station recorded forty-four instances where assistance needed to be given to stranded vessels. Keeper (Captain) Silas H. Harding and his seven surfmen had rescued sixteen survivors during this period. Harding was always impressed with his crew and would always make it well known of his admiration of their courage and big heartedness for their fellow mariners and for one another. He and his faithful crew had their experience and courage ultimately tested in not only rescuing survivors from the stranded schooner, *Oliver Dyer*, but also in bravely rescuing one another from what could have been a certain perilous fate. It became one of the bravest acts of heroism in the region's lighthouse and lifesaving history.

On November 25, 1888, the schooner *Oliver Dyer* had acquired a load of coal from Saco, Maine, and was heading to her homeport of Weehawken, New Jersey. The winds had picked up during the day and the captain decided to set her anchor just outside the entrance to Portsmouth Harbor about a half mile from Jerry's Point Lifesaving Station. The five-man crew had to stay aboard and ride out the storm, as they were unable to get in closer to shore. By sunset, gale-force winds were blowing thick snows all over the region creating huge swells and a vicious surf on the shore. Keeper Harding and his men tried their best in such poor visibility to keep an eye out along the shoreline and along the raging surf for any vessels that might be in distress. There was also the fear that those vessels anchored outside the harbor, including the *Oliver Dyer*, may end up dragging their anchors along the rocky bottom from the sweeping waves. Harding set up a heaving-stick with a rescue line attached by the patrol box to keep dry just in case they may have to use the equipment later.

The seas continued to swell from the violent winter storm. By 1:15 a.m. on November 26, huge waves began to force the *Oliver Dyer* away from her safe haven and drag her inward towards the rocky shoreline onto the rocks. The ship's anchor was no match for the surging waves and was being dragged across the bottom. The chains soon broke away as the helpless schooner moved closer to the ledges. The frustrated crew was unable to send out a visible or audible distress signal because of the howling winds and thunderous surf.

Visibility was still very poor while Surfman Robinson was on patrol. He would not see the stranded vessel until around 5:45 a.m., just before daybreak. By that time, the *Oliver Dyer* lay stranded on the ledges near Jerry's Point Lifesaving Station about a quarter mile off shore. Robinson ran back to the lifesaving station to notify Keeper Harding. Harding sounded the alarm and called all hands. He and Robinson ran down to the rocks to assess the impeding danger. They had a lifeboat nearby to push into the surf, but observed that the chains had broken away from the ship's anchor and the vessel was heading towards the rocks about 150 feet from shore.

Harding decided that the best way to rescue the stranded crew was to try to fire a line to the *Oliver Dyer*. They quickly grabbed the heavy 200-pound Lyle gun, and made preparations to fire the lifeline to the vessel. Just as they were ready to fire, a heavy sea caught the schooner on her broad side and lifted her up and over another forty feet towards the shore upon the ledges. As she lay stranded, the raging waves began to wash over the helpless craft. Harding and his men could only see the top of her masts and her lower mastheads from the shore, making the attempt of firing the line to the crew over the wave-swept deck impossible. Harding, nor any of his men, had seen that one of the crew of the *Oliver Dyer* had been swept away by one of those first rogue waves.

Keeper Harding decided that the only and best method to rescue the crew was to use the heaving-stick and line he had carefully placed in the patrol box nearby the night before. The vessel at this point had lodged itself about 100 feet from a large flat ice-covered rock which was also being breached continuously by the vicious surf. Harding made the decision to make the rescue from the rock, as it seemed the only launching point to help the survivors.

Jerry's Point Lifesaving Station, New Castle, NH, near Portsmouth Lighthouse. *Courtesy of New Castle Historical Society.*

Maine's Whaleback Lighthouse, view from New Castle Island, across the Piscataqua River.

The frightened crew of the *Oliver Dyer* could see that the wreck was breaking up and two men felt they were close enough to shore with Harding's crew nearby to make an attempt over the waves to safety. As Harding and his crew reached the rock, they saw one man had jumped from the helpless schooner and was struggling in the icy waters. The winds were blowing and the surf continued to relentlessly wash over the stranded vessel. Surfman Hall tied a line to himself, anchored by his comrades, jumped into the icy waters, and got a firm hold of the distraught crewman. The rest of the crew began dragging the survivor and Hall towards the large ice-covered rock.

Just as Hall had reached the icy ledge, and was ready to lift the man onto the rock to Harding's crew, a huge wave swept over the rock and tumbled both men and their rescuers into the water. Luckily, they were on the shoreline side of the ledge, otherwise they would have been swept seaward from the ferocious undertow and drowned. As they clung to the jagged edges of the rock, the waves receded and the men regained their footing. Harding, who had also slipped and was risking being swept seaward in the undertow, was quickly grabbed by Surfman Randall and held tightly until he could reach the rock. All the men were bleeding from being bashed around the barnacle-covered rocks, with Surfman Hall receiving the worst wounds. Harding's crew managed to climb back on the rock, while Surfman Hall and the frightened crewman quickly were hauled onto the ledge and brought to the safety of the shore.

As the first survivor was being rescued, the cook of the schooner jumped into the icy waters but was caught in the undertow, preventing him from gaining distance to the shore. Surfman Randall saw the crewmember struggling and jumped to rescue the exhausted survivor as he was being dragged seaward. The cook managed to hold onto Surfman Randall as both struggled to swim back towards the rock. They finally overcame the raging waves and made it to the safety of Keeper Harding's crew.

There were two men left aboard the stranded vessel. Keeper Harding made a throw of the heaving stick that reached the wreck for the other crewmen. They tied the lines around their bodies and under their armpits, as Harding persuaded the survivors to jump into the freezing waters. The men were then carefully dragged towards the rock to safety as waves washed over the ledge and the piercing winds continued. The seas continued to wash over the ice-covered crag as one of Harding's crew would lose their footing and be helped up again by their comrades. When all four of the crewmembers of the *Oliver Dyer* were on shore, Keeper Harding's crew could not get an accurate account if all had survived, as the exhausted crewmembers of the *Oliver Dyer* could hardly speak, suffering from exposure.

Harding decided to send Surfmen Amazeen and Randall back to the rock to see if there were any signs of additional survivors too exhausted to signal the line, or for any signs or distress signals coming from the schooner. As the two men climbed over the slush and ice onto the forbidding icy ledge, again, a huge wave came over the rock and both men lost their hold. Amazeen held onto to Randall, as Randall tried to gain footing for both men while the undertow attempted to carry them away towards the raging sea. They screamed and were able to remain near the rock as the rest of Harding's crew ran over to bring Amazeen and Randall to safety on shore.

Harding's men tried to see if there any more survivors on or near the wreck and believed they had all the survivors. When they came back towards the freezing crewmembers, one of the survivors was finally able to tell Harding that one of the men had been washed overboard and that no one else was on the wreck. The rescuing efforts of the crew made all exhausted, drenched, bloody, and freezing from exposure to the bitter winds.

The survivors of the *Oliver Dyer* were cared for at the station for two days. Crewmembers of the schooner and Keeper Harding's crew of Jerry's Point Lifesaving station survived without any long-term effects from their ordeal. Harding and his men learned later that day from the crewmembers of the missing sailor, Giuseppe Puez, who was observed by one of the sailors to have been washed overboard. The lifesaving crew searched the shoreline for two days, but the body was never found. The *Oliver Dyer* and her cargo were deemed a total loss, but the surfmen were able to retrieve some of the personal effects of the survivors.

The incident made Harding and his surfmen local heroes and their efforts caught the attention of the investigating officer Lieutenant Shoemaker, who recommended that their brave efforts be given the Gold Life Saving Medal, the highest Medal of Honor to Keeper Harding and each of his men. The Secretary of the Treasury agreed and granted the request on January 10, 1889. Keeper Harding and each man of his crew had risked their lives in not only trying to save the crew of the *Oliver Dyer* from their perilous position from that dangerous rock, but also saved one another as each were washed over into the icy and deathly grip of the thunderous surf. The recipients of the award were Keeper Silas H. Harding and Surfmen G. W. Randell, E. S. Hall, Ernest Robbinson, S. F. Wells, John Smith, and W. A. Amazeen.

Jerry's Point Lifesaving station remained in service until 1908 and was used during the war efforts. A replacement light station was built across the Piscataqua River on the opposite shore near Fort Foster on Wood Island in Kittery, Maine, near Whaleback Lighthouse. It is known today as the Wood Island Lifesaving Station, but is sometimes still referred to as Jerry's Point Lifesaving Station.

View across Piscataqua River, Wood Island Lifesaving Station, also referred to as Jerry's Point Lifesaving Station.

Acting Lighthouse Keeper Becomes Local Hero

At Isles of Shoals (White Island) Light in New Hampshire

The Isles of Shoals consist of nine islands split between the Maine and New Hampshire borders about ten miles away from the mainland. The shoals are rocky islands that spawned a small local fishing community, which soon developed into an important local fishing center for centuries. The shoals also became a safe haven for those who led less productive lives, like Blackbeard the pirate. It was also a haven for tourists, poets, and writers, as it still is today.

The Isles of Shoals' dangerous location along the coastal shipping route amid New England's frequent inclement weather caused many shipwrecks. In 1821, a lighthouse was built on one of these rocky islands, White Island, and became known as the Isles of Shoals, or White Island Lighthouse. It helped to protect the many local mariners, shipping traffic that would pass by the islands, vacationers, and those heading into Portsmouth's busy shipping port.

One of the most famous rescues in the region occurred in March of 1855, not by the present lighthouse keeper at that time, but by a local islander named John Bragg Downs, who agreed to act as temporary keeper while the new keeper was preparing to bring his family from the mainland to the lighthouse. The Downs family had been living near the desolate White Island for generations and was part of a group of families known as the original

"shoalers." John grew up on nearby Appledore Island away from the mainland and enjoyed the view of White Island Lighthouse. He would frequently visit the keepers and learned many of the duties in tending the lighthouse and surrounding buildings. He was a salty man of medium build who was also renowned as one who could always be counted on as a great resource of information, or for any assistance. He was also known to drink a cup full of rum three times a day to maintain his good health.

During the winter of 1855, the new keeper to Isles of Shoals light, Captain Richard Haley needed to head to the mainland to Massachusetts to make preparations in order to bring his family to live at Isles of Shoals Lighthouse. He decided to ask a local "shoaler" John Bragg Downs, to stay at the lighthouse and act as its temporary keeper until he returned. Downs gladly accepted the task and also brought a friend to keep him company and act as his assistant while Haley was away. He was comfortable in his new position and its responsibility and enjoyed tending to the lighthouse duties with his friend. Five days into his temporary position, he could see a major storm was brewing.

On the sixth day, the area was hit with a monstrous snowstorm, causing huge waves from the winds and high tide. These waves were sweeping across the islands as the evening progressed. Downs and his friend decided to stay at the keeper's house to ride out the storm.

Meanwhile, a Russian brig, headed for Salem, Massachusetts, with a cargo of tallow and hides got caught in the storm. The captain was unable to see the lighthouse beacon that night in the blinding snow, and believed he was many miles away from the mainland. To his horror, and too late to change course, the vessel was carried by the thrashing waves near the rocks by White Island. One huge wave lifted up the vessel and

Isles of Shoals (White Island) Lighthouse by rocky cliff on White Island, New Hampshire

Isles of Shoals
(White Island)
Lighthouse on
White Island,
New Hampshire

lodged it between some jagged rocks a short distance from the lighthouse. The captain prepared the crew to be ready in case the vessel started to break apart during the night. There was nothing the crew could do but wait until daybreak and try to ride out the storm.

Just after midnight, there was calm in the blizzard, and the captain saw the light of the beacon through the snow a short distance from their position. This was a very lucky but very dangerous situation. He knew the vessel may break apart from the pounding waves and all might perish in the freezing seas if they could not get help from the shore.

One of the sailors of the vessel, a large burly man, volunteered to be lowered over the wreck and get help. The captain knew time was precious and told the sailor to make haste. The sailor was lowered over the bow in the night, lit only by the beam of the lighthouse illuminating through the snowfall. He had to time his endeavors, so that as the huge waves would recede, he would try to lunge himself onto a barnacle-filled rock, and hold fast as they would wash over him, dragging his skin over the jagged edges. As he slowly made his way to the shore, he became increasingly cut and bruised with each rock he tried to hold to avoid the undertow, and as each frigid wave passed over him. He finally reached a ledge above the waves and started to scramble over the rocks up an incline towards the lighthouse, knowing time was precious for the safety of his comrades. Bruised, bloody, and freezing, he made haste for the keeper's house where he could see a light inside.

Acting Keeper Downs had been watching for any vessel most of the day and that night but could not see anything in the blinding snowstorm. At about the same time, during a lull in the storm around midnight, he told his friend to catch a quick nap while he prepared

something to eat. His assistant could not relax, and watched Downs prepare a small meal while he gazed at the door. The noise of the surf crashing over the rocks could easily be heard from their comfortable dwelling. His friend shouted over the noise, "Well, John, what would you think if somebody was to knock at the door just now?" Downs responded, "Think! I should think it must be the devil himself, for no human could land on White Island this night and live."

In almost as if in response, came a loud rap on the door from the outside, startling the two men. They couldn't believe that so late in the evening during a raging storm, someone or something was trying to get in from the outside. The raps continued and Downs quickly lit his lantern and opened the door. There stood the burly Russian sailor in the darkness, covered in blood from cuts and bruises, like some ghastly figure in the night. His shadow filled the doorway, lit only by Down's lantern. The man was exhausted, drenched, and freezing from exposure. He cried in broken English, "Brig ashore, sir! Right near the lighthouse tower!" Downs and his assistant tried to remove the sailor's bloody tattered rags, and then quickly give him warm garments. As they tended to his many cuts to prepare him to join them outside, the sailor told the two rescuers of the stranded wreck.

With the sailor in dry clothes, and covered in bandages, the three men grabbed a line and other equipment and headed over the icy rocks to the shoreline where they found the wreck constantly being pounded by the waves, but still intact. Downs could see that the crewmembers needed to be rescued quickly as the ship could easily break apart from its position on the rocks. He ventured out on an icy rock ledge and tried to throw a line to the rest of the crew on the vessel. After a number of attempts, the line was caught by one of the crew and secured on the wreck.

Downs looked around to find where he could secure the line on his end, and could not find anything from the rocks where they were located. He decided that the only way to anchor the line on shore was to use his own body by tying the line around his waist, and then climbing into a crevice to maintain a hold on his position. He searched in the darkness lit only by the lighthouse and was able to find a deep enough crevice nearby to climb into to gain a foothold while maintaining a firm grasp on the line. He told the Russian sailor and his friend to hold him fast as he braced himself in the freezing winds and icy spray. He them instructed his friend to shout to the crew on the vessel to come down the line one by one towards him.

Most of the fourteen men on the wreck were in fair health as each braved the bitter chill from the winds, the sting of the snow, and the icy spray of the surf. One by one they slowly climbed over the jagged rocks using the line to safety. The last two crewmembers were failing from exposure to the storm, and as they needed assistance by their crewmates, each nearly became washed off the rocks as their strength was weakening. Finally, all crewmembers had made it safely to shore, and the exhausted men started to make their way up the rocky hill through the storm, towards the lighthouse. When they reached the warmth of the little keeper's house, Downs and his friend cared for them in giving them warm blankets, any clothing they could find, food, and spirits. The house was overcrowded with so many individuals as most slept on the floor, exhausted from their ordeal.

Days passed as the storm continued, leaving all stranded at the lighthouse and keeper's dwelling without assistance from the mainland, or from the locals on the other islands who were also stranded in their homes, many unaware of the rescue. There were no other residents on White Island except for the occupants of the lighthouse. The food supply was desperately low and Downs feared that with so many mouths to feed they might starve. Finally, the storm subsided and Keeper Haley, who was stranded on the mainland from the storm and worried for the safety of his island friend, sailed back out to White Island and was able to bring provisions to the many hungry unsuspected guests at the lighthouse. When he arrived, he provided all with a hearty meal, and the fourteen grateful crewmembers were transported that afternoon to the mainland.

As he was not a government-appointed lighthouse keeper, John Bragg Downs never received a medal for risking his life that night, but did win the admiration of his fellow islanders and the locals on the mainland. For many years afterwards, Downs would venture over to White Island to the rocky shore by the lighthouse. He admired the courage and tenacity of the large Russian sailor who made such a perilous attempt in climbing over the barnacle-covered rocks, risking his life that night for his comrades where he could have easily been swept out to sea during the storm. Downs would often observe the crevice he used in making himself a human anchor, taking pride in risking his own life to save all fourteen crewmen of the Russian brig.

John Bragg Downs also had a bit of luck with him over the years. As he had grown up with other residents on Appledore Island next to White Island all his life, his property was in demand by those who bought the Oceanic Hotel and wanted the land nearby. He refused to sell to the builders, as he was comfortable in living in his home where he grew up. The hotel a few years later caught fire along with a number of uninhabited houses, and although his home was near the hotel and in the path of the fire, it was only scorched and not destroyed. He had his house repaired, and lived until just before his death at age 77 on April 23, 1888. He was one of the last of the original "shoalers" to keep his home on the island.

Isles of Shoals (White Island) Lighthouse view from nearby Appledore Island, New Hampshire.

Isles of Shoals (White Island) Lighthouse near cliffs on White Island, New Hampshire.

Vermont's Intriguing Rescue Story

At Burlington Breakwater Light

There have been over 300 shipwrecks on Lake Champlain. They vary from ships that had fought during the Revolutionary War, to modern airplanes and powerboats. With the completion of the Champlain Canal, which connected the Hudson River and Lake Champlain, Burlington became the third largest port for shipping lumber and quarried stone coming largely from Vermont, New York, and Canada. The Burlington waterfront was built because of the increasing commercial traffic on Lake Chaplain. With this increasing shipping trade came the need for a breakwater to protect mariners from the constant weather changes and storms that would plague the region. Canal boats brought in most of the stones that were used to build the breakwater. These boats helped to make the connection with the Hudson River leading into New York City, which helped Burlington develop as a world trade port.

A 1,000-foot breakwater was completed in 1854, and gradually was extended as the waterfront continued to grow. By the late 1800s, the breakwater had grown to nearly 4,200 feet long. Wooden lighthouses, known as the Burlington Breakwater Lights, were first placed on both ends of the breakwater in 1857. Over the years, the wooden structures could not survive the constant elements of strong winds, ice, and even fires. In 1870, the northern lighthouse, Burlington Breakwater North Light, burned to the ground, and in 1876 a fierce storm knocked over Burlington's southern light (Burlington Breakwater South Light).

In 1875, a keeper's dwelling was built on the breakwater, but being less than a mile from the waterfront, the keepers simply preferred to live in the city with their families, and would remain ashore. When needed, they would row out to each of the small lighthouses to tend them. It sometimes became a challenge for them to row out to the lights on those days when rough weather, which occurred quite frequently, covered the area. The keeper's house remained unoccupied for nearly ten years, before it was auctioned off and moved ashore.

Vermont's Most Famous Keeper

One of the greatest rescue stories in the region involves the wreck of the *General Butler*. In this time period, the government frowned upon and sometimes would remove those keepers who would attempt to make additional income from other occupations. James Wakefield was not only the lighthouse keeper of the Burlington Breakwater Lights, who lived on the shorefront with his family, but also had a very successful business as a ship's chandler in repairing sails and providing supplies. The successful business was apparently allowed, or ignored, by the government.

Burlington Breakwater North Lighthouse, Burlington, Vermont.

Before James Wakefield became Burlington's lighthouse keeper, he had spent many years as a sailor and as a second mate to captains on voyages involving transporting cargo all around the world. He was a large, strong man, born in 1829, and was no stranger to incidents of rescuing fellow crewmembers, aiding in saving distressed vessels during severe storms and hurricanes, and in handling drunk and unruly captains, or crewmembers.

In 1853, Wakefield was sailing as the second mate on the clipper ship *Olivia* from New Orleans to Rio de Janiero, with a load of tea. The captain of the vessel found that much of the cargo had been stolen by many crewmembers and sold on the streets for their own personal benefit. As they were heading home from port, the captain angrily told the crew he was withholding their rations of coffee and wages, which made the crew attempt a mutiny of the vessel. The captain, Wakefield, and a few others were able to drive the men below deck. They brought up the mutineers one by one and had them shackled in irons for the authorities when they arrived at the homeport. After the incident, Wakefield decided to end his career at sea, as he had been on many excursions since he was thirteen, and with his family, would leave England and spend the rest of his years in America.

As twists of fate always seemed to follow him, his lifesaving skills would be tested again. Wakefield and his family left England and sailed across the Atlantic in relatively calm weather. As they sailed off the coast of Newfoundland, they became caught in an unsuspected hurricane. The incredible force of the winds tore out the masts causing the ship to be bashed about as the wind picked up the rigging and sails. The officers and crew took refuge between the decks in hoping of either riding out the storm, or simply believing they were going to perish. Knowing that the vessel could easily be blown over into the raging sea, Wakefield secured his family as best he could, and then gallantly crept across the deck through the heavy winds and constant waves washing over the deck. He cut away the rigging to free the sails, and was able to save the ship, crew, and its passengers by keeping the vessel afloat during the storm.

After spending some time in New York near his brother, in 1857, he decided to stay in Burlington, Vermont, where he developed a prosperous business in making and repairing sails, and in dealing in ship supplies as a ship chandler. His business grew as well as his popularity for being honest and fair, and for his maritime knowledge. He had also taken the position as keeper of the Burlington Breakwater Lights, and lived in a house along the shore.

Burlington Breakwater South Lighthouse, Burlington, Vermont.

The Rescue of the *General Butler*

The vessel, the *General Butler*, was named after General Benjamin Butler, a hero of the Civil War. She was an eighty-eight-foot long canal or cargo boat built in 1862 and was designed to sail and travel through the Lake Chaplain Canal system. Captain William Montgomery was the third owner of the vessel and lived on northern Vermont's town of Isle La Motte. On December 9, 1876, the *General Butler* was heading out from Fisk Quarry on the Isle La Motte with thirty tons of marble and stone to Burlington's manufacturing shed. On board was a crewman, a quarryman with an eye injury going for medical treatment, and two teenage girls, one being the captain's teenage daughter, Cora, and her young friend.

On that December day, as the *General Butler* sailed towards Burlington, a powerful winter gale storm was approaching and came full force upon them as they came towards Burlington Harbor.

The rigging started to break apart, and all of a sudden, the steering mechanism broke on the vessel, causing it to be tossed around the thrashing waters near the Burlington breakwater. Captain Montgomery dropped anchor so he could try to jury-rig the tiller bar to the steering post, in order to gain enough momentum to steer the vessel into the harbor. The attempt to fix the steering failed and he was forced to cut the anchor line as it started dragging across the sandy bottom. Montgomery sent out a distress signal as a crowd of onlookers came out and started to watch the events unfold from the waterfront.

The *General Butler* was now being pushed helplessly by the wind and waves towards the southern end of the breakwater. The huge waves were too much for the vessel and forced the ship nearly on top of the jagged stone breakwater. Captain Montgomery knew at once the ship was about to sink in the icy waters with her heavy load and convinced all those aboard that they had to jump the ship onto the ice-covered rocks until help arrived. One by one he helped them off the ship onto the breakwater and was the last one himself to jump off. A few minutes later the *General Butler*, with her heavy load of stone, slipped off the breakwater and sank to the bottom of the harbor. That night, when the vessel finally came to rest forty feet below on the sandy bottom of the lake, she lay about seventy-five yards west of the southern end of the breakwater.

The five survivors were now in another perilous position as they were being drenched by the chilling waves washing over the breakwater and freezing from exposure. The survivors were still about a mile out in the breakwater, which was not connected to the shore, and swimming to safety would have been impossible in the bitter conditions. They could only wait for help to hopefully arrive before they would freeze to death.

At this point, a large crowd had gathered by the waterfront and were watching the survivors on the breakwater. There were many able-bodied men and experienced sea captains, but no one wanted to venture out and risk their own lives in the bitter gale-force winds and thrashing waves.

Keeper James Wakefield, now in his late 40s in age, ran towards the waterfront with his son to investigate. Upon seeing the shadowy figures of the survivors on the stone structure, he knew they were going to freeze to death if help did not come quickly. He ran back to his house near the waterfront and secured the small fourteen-foot government lighthouse boat. He and his son launched the boat amid the onlookers and started the daunting task of trying to row the craft to reach the breakwater quite

a distance away against the ferocity of the winds and pounding waves. The keeper and his son finally reached the breakwater exhausted but determined to save all from their terrifying fate. The captain of the vessel grabbed his daughter and her teenage friend and placed them first into the strong arms of the older sailor. Then one by one, as the waves would raise the boat close to the rocks, each of the three remaining crew jumped into Wakefield's little boat, risking being tossed overboard, but held on tightly to the craft.

With all their strength, Wakefield and his son pulled the boat through the violent waters and winds and safely managed to bring all ashore to a welcoming crowd. Captain Montgomery's daughter and the others received medical treatment once they were given dry clothes and were provided shelter at Wakefield's house.

What is also interesting about this rescue is that although Keeper James Wakefield successfully rescued the crew, the Burlington Breakwater South Lighthouse, near where the wreck occurred, was inoperable from a previous storm and was awaiting repairs. So there was little illumination from the south end of the breakwater to help the keeper in his efforts. He was able to rely on his knowledge of the area and expert skills to maneuver the boat to the survivors.

All the survivors recovered without any long lasting effects and James Wakefield and his son became the local heroes of Burlington. The storm itself was named as one of the worst of the century in the area, causing much damage along the shoreline as well. Wakefield was gracious and did not blame anyone for not going out to help the survivors, but simply felt it was his duty and relied on his experience to make that decision. Wakefield's business prospered to be managed by generations of Wakefields.

When she recovered from the ordeal, the captain's daughter, Cora, asked to make the return trip to Burlington and be present when the vessel would be raised. Her request never came about as the *General Butler* lay beneath the waves for eternity.

The vessel was a total loss, and had been uninsured from the year before the incident, so there were no funds left to raise her.

The *General Butler* can easily viewed by divers and on shipwreck excursions put on by the Lake Chaplain Museum. The wreck of the *General Butler* became the first shipwreck in the Vermont Underwater Historic Preserve program. The hull of the vessel is still intact, and none of the interior has collapsed. The cargo hatches that were carrying the marble are easily viewable.

Keeper's Wife Maintains Twin Lights for Days During Snowstorm

At Thacher Island Twin Lights in Massachusetts

In 1864, Alexander Bray, a Civil War veteran, was appointed as Keeper of two newly constructed towers on Thacher Island known as the Cape Anne Lighthouses, or Thacher Island Twin Lights, in Massachusetts. The new taller towers were built in 1861, replacing the two original towers constructed in 1771. Each rose 124 feet high, 166 feet above sea level, and were located about 900 feet apart, serving as the local range lights for shipping traffic and fishermen in Cape Anne passing through or into Rockport and Gloucester. The island lies about a mile from the mainland of Rockport. Bray had been an assistant keeper since 1861 and was the first to light the new south tower. He was appointed the position of Keeper when Albert Hale, the previous keeper, had to leave due to illness from typhoid fever. The two towers involved much work, as they needed tending each day, which involved climbing nearly 150 steps to the lantern room of each tower. One of the many duties would involve carrying up large containers of oil to replenish the lamps to make sure they would continue burning, and to keep the lantern room panes clear of soot. Keeper Bray had at least two assistants who worked with him to keep the two lights and fog signal operating smoothly on Thacher Island. The beams were powerful enough that they could be spotted at sea nearly twenty-two miles away.

His wife, Maria, was a learned woman of extraordinary talent in writing. She wrote articles

Maria Bray. *Image Courtesy Thacher Island Association Museum – Paul St. Germain*

for local newspapers, short stories, and served as an editor of a literary magazine called *Magnolia Leaves*. A woman who was indeed ahead of her time, her literary talents were unique where many women's abilities were overshadowed in the "man's world" of that period. She was a woman who enjoyed learning and volunteered to work alongside her husband to understand his tasks and duties. She also became passionate about marine plant life in the region and became a local authority in the field. Maria Bray had assembled quite a collection of sea mosses, algae, and other marine plant life, which became a local attraction for those who visited the island, and for local educators. She was also an activist in the anti-slavery and temperance movements, she served as the first president of the Universalist Church Ladies Mission Circle, and was superintendent of the Sunday school for many years.

On December 21, 1864, one of Bray's two assistant keepers became very ill with a fever and needed medical attention on the mainland. He and his other assistant loaded the ailing man into a boat bound for the mainland a mile away to find a doctor. Maria Bray and her nephew, Sidney Haskell, remained on Thacher Island, leaving Maria to be in charge of the tower operations. The weather was cloudy and the winds were blowing, but Keeper Bray figuring the trip would be rather short, felt he would be able to return that same day.

Upon safely reaching the mainland, Alexander Bray was able to get the necessary medical help for his assistant and a few hours later intended to head back to the island. As they were preparing to leave later that afternoon, they found an unexpected fierce snowstorm had descended on the region. They could see the raging surf and gusting winds along the shore and knew it would be too risky to try to make it back to

Thacher Island Twin Lighthouses, Rockport, Massachusetts.

Thacher Island Lighthouses, both towers, Rockport, Massachusetts.

Thacher Island. Bray realized his wife would have to take over the strenuous duties of tending both towers during the storm to keep the lights burning.

That afternoon, the snowstorm blew intensely and covered Thacher Island in blinding drifting snow. Maria knew that the lights must be kept burning for the safety of any ship caught in the disaster, and for those on the mainland. She enlisted the help of her 14-year old nephew, Sidney, to help her with the daunting task. She realized there was not only the task of climbing each tower up the nearly 150 stairs carrying oil, then performing maintenance on the lamps, but the towers were 900 feet apart in waist high snow drifts from the biting winds, making the journey a treacherous quarter mile round trip.

The storm was relentless as Maria braved the snow and wind to carry the lantern fuel to the nearest tower up 148 stairs, then trim the wicks and clean the panes. She then would have to descend the 148 stairs, and make her way through the snowdrifts and the bitter winds 900 feet to the other tower and perform the same tasks for the safety of anyone in the

Thacher Island Lighthouse, Twin Lights, North and South Towers, Rockport, Massachusetts.

region to see the lights burning. The engine room of the whistle house, which also contained the fog signal also needed to be checked and maintained through the storm.

Maria had her nephew help with the preparations and with some of the cleaning. She had to repeat the daunting trips three times during each of three nights to keep the lamps supplied with oil and the lantern room panes free of soot. She and her helper were exhausted from exposure to the snow and winds, and from fighting their way over the snowdrifts to each tower. She would only sleep a couple of hours and had to be awakened routinely to prepare and perform the strenuous tasks at least every four hours at each lighthouse tower. Alexander Bray remained stranded with his two assistants on the mainland, but much to his gratification, at times when the snows would subside, he could see the lights of the two towers were still burning.

Daybreak on Christmas Eve brought a slight calm through the still raging storm. Keeper Bray, fearing for the safety for his wife and for his nephew on Thacher Island, decided to head for the island with his assistants as the lights were still burning to guide him. It was still snowing and visibility was not very good, but the winds and waves had subsided somewhat as Bray and his men pushed the boat through the thunderous surf. The bitter blowing snow continued to cover the men as they climbed over one wave after another using the two lights from the towers on Thacher Island to navigate. After what seemed an eternity, the half frozen men successfully made the mile long trip to the island. Maria, with help from her nephew, was able to keep the lights burning during the storm and there were no marine casualties. It was a joyful Christmas Eve as the Brays and their two assistants were reunited.

There were many variations of this story, even an account that she had children during the ordeal, which is not the case. The keeper's building was set up for two families, and it is believed that the assistants were not married at the time and lived on the other side of the building.

Keeper Bray and his wife stayed on Thacher Island until 1869, when they moved back to the mainland. Alexander died in 1885, and afterwards, Maria Bray spent her last years living in Gloucester until 1921, when as Gloucester's oldest resident, she passed away at the astonishing age of 93.

In the spring of 2000, a new Coast Guard "Keeper Class" buoy tender was launched, the *Maria Bray*. On its way to its homeport in Mayport, Florida, the vessel stopped near Thacher Island where members of the Thacher Island Association, who currently maintain the island and lights, threw a ceremonial wreath into the ocean in Maria Bray's honor.

New England's "Lighthouse Storm"

Named for Destruction of Minot's Ledge Light In Massachusetts

New England's Storm of the Century

One of the worst storms in New England's recorded history occurred on Monday, April 14, 1851, and continued through that Saturday, April 19th. This storm that entered the New England coastline on a Monday morning had all the ingredients of high winds, rain, hail, and even snow over nearly a week to cause massive devastation all along the eastern seaboard, and inland of central and southern New England. Many wharves along the New Hampshire and Massachusetts coastlines were severely damaged from high winds, flooding rain, and rising tides. Homes and other buildings were swept into the sea; many vessels that were left moored in the harbors crashed into one another, or were dislodged and swept out to sea. Some lives were also lost from this ferocious storm. Inland, the hurricane-force winds blew off roofs and even some church steeples.

A butcher from Brighton was carrying a load of calves while crossing the Cambridge Bridge with his horse drawn cart during the storm. All of a sudden he, his horse, and the calves were literally blown off the bridge into the river, and were carried down to the milldam. He barely survived with his horse, but the load of calves all drowned in the swift river.

Along the Cape, many wharves were destroyed and in Boston, the rising waters, over four feet deep in some places, flooded many stores and neighborhood streets. One girl was rescued from a cellar when the water rose up to her neck. The locals created many rafts out of planks and boxes to get around the flooded streets to observe the destruction, offering any help they could for their neighbors. Deer Island, north of

Minot's Ledge Light Rescue (illustration of rescues), Cohasett, MA. *Image courtesy Jeremy D"Entremont Collection.*

Boston, was nearly completely under water and the waves had swept away a schoolhouse. The nearby sea wall was washed away as the tides continued to rise and dismantle the structure. Boston Harbor Lighthouse on Little Brewster Island suffered some damage but continued to operate.

On the Massachusetts North Shore, streets were flooded in multiple feet of water. A store was swept away in Gloucester, and Newburyport's "Water Street" was literally under water with stores and buildings flooded, carrying off large quantities of timber, wood, and other debris. The waves and wind were so ferocious that spray was thrown as high as second story windows along the shore. The Essex mill was nearly filled with surging waters.

At Newcastle Island, New Hampshire, next to Portsmouth, the sea broke through the jetty and made an island of the peninsula known as Jaffery Point, causing the locals to grab their belongings and head to higher ground, or to Portsmouth's inland areas.

Many roads were washed away all along the coast, and many railroad cars could not be operated as the tracks were either dangerously under water, or were swept away from the fierce tides. In some places, the water was so high that the steam locomotives could not drive through, as the water would extinguish their coal fires.

On Wednesday morning, April 16, the turnpike from Newburyport out to the beach on Plum Island was covered in water so high it was rendered impossible to pass through. The waves were so large and flooding so consistent that at one point the sea broke completely over the island.

Meanwhile, during that same day, the brig *Primrose*, carrying a shipment of coal, was floundering off of Salisbury Beach and heading towards the reefs near Plum Island. The captain, blinded by the rain and surging waves, was unable to make any observations and believed he was near Boston Harbor. As the *Primrose* neared Plum Island in Newburyport, the heavy gale-force winds swept through her rigging, tearing away the mainsail, and forcing the helpless vessel to approach the reefs where she wrecked a few hundred yards off shore.

Two young men, T. G. Dodge and O. Rundlett, of Newburyport, who were checking out the debris on the beach during the storm, quickly spotted the wreck. As the *Primrose* was being battered by the swells, the crew saw the two men on the beach, and communicated with them to try and secure a line from the wreck to shore. They tried numerous times, but after a couple of hours, the exhausted rescuers, standing waist deep in the cold thunderous surf, were unable to secure the line.

Luckily, within a short time later, two other men had joined them, a man whose last name was Lufkin who lived nearby, and his hired worker. After another hour's worth of attempts, the four rescuers were able

Minot's Ledge Lighthouse (illustration 1850 construction), Cohasett, MA. *Image courtesy Jeremy D"Entremont Collection.*

to secure the line to the wreck. The captain, his crew, and one passenger, totaling nine persons in all, were rescued by the tenacious efforts of the four locals. Though exhausted and suffering from exposure, the heroes and the crew of the *Primrose* all survived the ordeal and the four men were praised as local heroes. The *Primrose* lay wrecked on the sand for months, and had to have her load of coal removed. She lay beached until the following July when she was finally dislodged and towed away.

The Destruction of Minot's Ledge Light

Minot's Ledge, located south of Boston Harbor in Cohasset, Massachusetts, was a destructive rocky ledge that destroyed many a vessel and claimed many lives before Minot's Ledge Lighthouse was built there previously in January of 1850. It took three years to build as an engineering feat consisting of an enormous thirty-ton lantern perched on a huge eighty-seven-foot skeletal iron tower to protect the structure and its keepers against the strong winds and waves. It was known as the "Iron Lighthouse" from its construction and much praise was given to its engineers. The concept was that fierce winds and waves could pass through as opposed to constantly smashing a solid enclosed structure, as was the construction of most other lighthouse towers.

Almost as soon as the tower was built problems seemed to arise, with complaints from its keepers. Constant vibrations from the pounding seas and winds caused observable cracks in the locations where holes were drilled for the pillars. The pillars were becoming loosened and on the January before the storm hit, Keeper John Bennett wrote to his superiors that he felt the lighthouse would not last through the winter, as he or his assistants would be thrown off their feet when heavy seas would pound on the structure. His superiors told him that it was believed safe and he was to stay and continue his duties at the lighthouse.

Even before the terrible April storm occurred, only a month earlier, during a fierce storm on March 16, 1851, the keepers decided that the lantern room was too dangerous and retreated down into the store room, where they stayed for four days and nights, only occasionally climbing to the lantern to repair some damage done by the storm. The violent pitching and swaying of the tower almost knocked them off the rungs of the ladder, when they would try to perform their duties.

Just before the storm hit on Monday, April 14, 1851, Keeper Bennett was ordered to come ashore to gather much-needed supplies and had left his two young assistants, Joseph Antoine and Joseph Wilson, to manage and tend the lighthouse in his absence. Joseph Wilson was a proud sailor, and was reported in March, prior to the storm, in response to inquiries from reporters as to the safety of the lighthouse, that he would stay as long as Bennett would stay, and that only when they would leave the lighthouse, it would be too dangerous for anyone else to take over. Joseph Antoine was a Portuguese sailor with relatives in Cohasset, and loved working at the lighthouse. The storm had come upon the Massachusetts coast suddenly that Monday afternoon with a vengeance, preventing the two men from leaving their post.

By Wednesday afternoon, April 16, the seas were still surging and pounding Minot's Ledge Light. The only way to reach the shore would have been to descend the eighty-seven-foot structure down a rope outside to their small boat and battle the devastating waves for miles to reach the mainland. An impossible task as the two had no choice but to ride out the storm and hopefully survive.

At five o'clock, as the seas worsened, the men lit the lantern so that others might avoid a perilous fate. By nightfall, the seas continued to swell from the high tides, ferocious wind gusts, and torrential rains. The brave men continued to perform their faithful duties uncertain as to whether they would survive the night. Anxious locals observed the lantern from the shore

Minot's Ledge Lighthouse (illustration of tower collapse), Cohasett, MA. *Image courtesy Jeremy D"Entremont Collection.*

while hurricane-force wind gusts recorded at over 100 miles per hour continued to thrash at the lighthouse. The two assistant keepers managed to keep the lighthouse lamp burning as late as 10 p.m. The fog bell continued to ring until around one o'clock that morning when it was swept away with the tower.

It could only be imagined the anguish the two men were feeling as they awaited their fate. The emotions they had as the tower started to give way under the pressure of the devastating waves and hurricane-force winds. Their cries would never be heard in their last minutes as the pillars gave way, sending the entire iron structure toppling under the waves, tossing them to their watery graves.

Around four o'clock on Thursday the following morning, there was a lull in the storm and Keeper Bennett went to the beach to see if the tower was still standing. He found no evidence of the tower in sight, only the bent iron pilings where the lighthouse once stood. Plenty of debris had washed up on the shore. As he observed the debris, he found much had belonged to the lighthouse structure and keeper's living quarters, including bedding and some of his own clothing. He found two life vests washed ashore which appeared as though they had been used, but may have been washed off their inhabitants by the angry waves.

Joseph Antoine's body was found later that day near Nantasket Beach and Joseph Wilson's body was found washed on nearby Gull Island. The men have always been regarded as true heroes of Minot's Ledge Light.

By Sunday, April 20, the storm had finally cleared away from its near week long of devastation in New England. It would take many years afterwards to access and rebuild the damage caused by this fierce and destructive storm. It was later given the nickname the "Lighthouse Storm," as it was directly responsible for the destruction of Minot's Ledge Lighthouse.

Keeper Bennett became in charge of a temporary light ship beacon anchored just off Minot's Ledge where the original lighthouse stood, to serve as a temporary replacement until a new lighthouse could be built. The construction of the new Minot's Ledge Lighthouse began in 1855 and was hailed as the greatest achievement in lighthouse engineering, from lessons learned of the ill-fated previous structure. The construction of the new lighthouse took time as many of the construction workers, who were only allowed on the project if they could prove they could swim, would be swept off the rocks by the constant breaking of the waves over the ledge.

Two years into the construction of the lighthouse, the ship, *New Empire* crashed on the dangerous ledge and destroyed most of the lighthouse. Three years later, in 1860, Minot's Ledge lighthouse was finally completed as one of the most expensive lighthouses in history. The lightship guarded the ledge and lighthouse construction between 1851 and 1860. It is still considered to be one of the top engineering feats of the Lighthouse Service. Antoine and Wilson are still remembered each April, and many believe their spirits are still guarding the lighthouse.

Minot's Ledge Lighthouse (1860 construction), Cohasett, Massachusetts.

Two Miracles and Two Local Tragedies at Cape Cod

Near Cape Cod (Highland) Lighthouse
in Massachusetts

The ocean waters in New England remain quite cold during the spring months from the cold Atlantic currents until late May when they finally begin to warm up. The keeper of any lighthouse must maintain the light to guide mariners in all types of New England weather. One of the difficult aspects of any keeper's job, especially when involved in any rescue attempt, is that they must make a decision in extremely risky situations as to the amount of risk they must put their lives through to save those that are in distress off shore. It is also equally as difficult for local mariners to observe those in distress without trying to help. It is in our human nature to help those in need, sometimes at the point of possibly risking our own lives.

A treacherous collection of sand bars on Cape Cod, called the Peaked Hill Bars, became a graveyard for many ships, and lie about a mile from Highland Light, also known as Cape Cod Light. The lighthouse was constructed where high bluffs of clay and sand rose nearly 150 feet above the beach below, providing mariners with the most powerful beacon on Cape Cod.

Enoch Hamilton became keeper at Cape Cod Light in 1850. As part of his duties, he had to account for passing ships and marine vessels in his log. There were such a vast amount of ships passing by Cape Cod Lighthouse that it was almost staggering. In 1853, from a short period between July 12 and July 23, Keeper Hamilton recorded over 1,200 vessels passing by.

As was often the case, lighthouses helped many mariners steer away from dangerous shoals, sandbars, and islands, but many shipwrecks would occur during New England's many violent storms and dense fog, especially in the Cape Cod area where fog was often prevalent with changing wind currents and constant fluctuations of coastal temperatures. In 1852, the worst maritime disaster on the Cape at that time occurred during Hamilton's tenure at the light.

The British bark, the *Josepha* (also referred to as the *Josephus*) had left Bristol, England, heading for Boston with a cargo of iron rails, skins, and white lead, on March 19, 1852. Captain Cawsey commanded the six-year-old ship with a relatively young crew of fifteen. The voyage across the Atlantic was relatively calm and they were making good time as they arrived near the eastern shores by midnight on Monday, April 19. Shortly after midnight, gale-force winds were approaching and a dense fog blanketed the area. Cawsey made the decision to first head on a southeastern path to stay far enough off shore, and then sail inward towards the shoreline with the intension of entering Cape Cod Bay for safety.

Cape Cod (Highland) Lighthouse, Truro, Massachusetts.

On Tuesday, April 20, most of the upper Cape Cod area was covered in dense fog with high seas from the impending storm. With the fog thickening, all of the crew were standing guard on deck as they barely could see anything in front of them. As they tacked the depth of the water below, much to their surprise and horror, they found themselves in extremely shallow waters. By three o'clock on that Tuesday afternoon, the *Josepha* struck a dangerous outer sandbar as part of the Peaked Hill Bars about a mile from Cape Cod lighthouse, and a half mile from the beach nearby.

Because of her heavy cargo of iron in her hold, the vessel became wedged firmly onto the sandy clay ground. As the high seas washed over her, the starboard quarter broke apart and was swept away. The crew attempted to launch the ship's little side boat, but it was quickly smashed to pieces against the wreck from one of the waves. They attempted to launch a long boat and that craft also met with the same fate. As the waves continued to wash over the vessel, the young crew watched in horror as the deck gave way from the stern to the foremast, breaking two of the masts apart and washing debris overboard. Many of the crew fell into the chilly waters upon impact and found themselves struggling in the churning seas.

At about five o'clock in the afternoon, the fog had lifted a little as three boys, who were walking along the shoreline, could barely see the wreck in the distance about a half mile away. They immediately ran along the beach and scrambled up the stairs leading up the 150-foot sandy cliffs to the lighthouse. Out of breath and exhausted, they informed Keeper Hamilton of the wreck. The keeper immediately sent a messenger to run into the nearby town of Truro about a mile away yelling through the streets, "A ship ashore and all hands perishing!"

Keeper Hamilton grabbed some lifesaving rockets from the nearby Humane Society to be able to fire a line to the wreck, and informed some of his neighbors

Cape Cod (Highland) Lighthouse over cliffs before it was moved, Cape Cod, Massachusetts.

to grab some life preservers. Many of the townsfolk rushed down to the beach below, and as the fog lifted, could see the foremast with a few of the crewmembers clinging to what remained of the vessel. They could hear the screams for help amid the fog and raging seas, but were afraid to venture out into the pounding surf. Even Keeper Hamilton realized it would have been a futile effort to risk his life in such a dangerous situation.

At about seven o'clock that evening, the screams for help from the ill-fated vessel were too much for local 47-year-old fisherman Jonathan Collins to bear. He persuaded Keeper Hamilton into using the lighthouse dory and, against the pleas of Hamilton and his own neighbors, started to drag the dory towards the beach. David Smith decided to join Collins but found himself gently pushed aside by a young Daniel Cassity, aged 23, also a fisherman, who told him he would take his place, as he was younger and stronger. Cassity had just been married but felt compelled to help in the rescue. Smith obliged reluctantly as he and the crowd on shore watched Collins and Cassity pull the dory into the thunderous surf. One of the two shouted back to the crowd that they would try to rescue any survivors even if it would cost them their lives. Cassity and Smith made an attempt to fire a line from the dory over the wreck. The charge exploded prematurely and nearly endangered the lives of the rescuers.

Cassity and Collins were merely fifteen yards from the wreck when they got caught in a strong current, which positioned the boat to the leeward end of the wreck against the waves. All of a sudden, the two rescuers were caught up in a huge swell and breaking wave that capsized the dory, dumping them into the chilly waters. They struggled to right the boat but the chilly waves were too much and they slipped away, perishing from the exposure. The locals on shore saw the horrifying incident and a few ran to grab a lifeboat located about a mile from the wreck. When they returned, hide tide was coming in with huge waves and all decided that it would be too risky to lose any additional lives.

It was growing dark as the seas continued to swell. A number of fires were lit along the shore for any hope of any crewmembers reaching ashore, although many feared they would only find dead bodies and no survivors. Some of the locals who had witnessed the events, Keeper Hamilton, and other emergency personnel patrolled the shoreline for any possible survivors. As pieces of the wreck were starting to pile on shore north of the site, those on shore could still hear pieces of the doomed wreck being broken apart in the distance. They could no longer hear screams in the dark causing an eerie silence amid the crashing waves. Most feared that all had perished.

Keeper Hamilton left the shoreline at ten o'clock to tend to the lighthouse lamps briefly with the town

Cape Cod (Highland) Lighthouse at dusk, Cape Cod, Massachusetts.

Reverend, and then returned back to the shore around eleven o'clock. As he and the Reverend passed by the fires along the shoreline, they were shocked to find one of the crewmembers of the *Josepha*, George Chitney, kneeling before one of the fires. Exhausted, badly bruised and frozen, he told them he and a fellow crewmember John Jasper, whom he believed was dying, were clinging to pieces of timber from the wreck and felt both were being carried ashore. He pointed to where his comrade was lying at the edge of the surf. John Jasper was so exhausted that he could not speak or climb atop a three-foot sand bank to join the exhausted Chitney at the fire. He had only one sock on and no boots.

After bringing Jasper near the fire to try to warm him up, Hamilton and others took both crewmembers to the lighthouse to get them into dry clothes. As they removed John Jasper's wet clothing, they found him badly bruised and his hands and feet were badly swollen.

As the night progressed into the following day, only six bodies were recovered of the sixteen crewmembers. The body of young Daniel Cassity was found and given a proper burial in Truro.

At the lighthouse, the physician was called in early in the morning and found survivor John Jasper in a high fever, with his hands and feet still very swollen. The two men who miraculously survived the wreck, stayed at the lighthouse for a couple of days until they were well enough to be moved to the local hospital.

After a few days had passed, when the two miracle survivors felt better, they made statements to reporters describing how they watched in horror as their fellow crewmates were washed overboard when the ship broke apart. Both survivors were near the stern of the boat and had fastened themselves to the back of the wreck. They were both washed off a couple of times but managed to maintain their hold. They realized that they both were caught in the rigging, which had probably saved them from being washed away from the floating timbers as they were being carried towards the shoreline by the high tide.

Prior to the incident, strange coincidences had followed Daniel Cassity's family and his wife's family. Daniel Cassidy was the last of three brothers, all of whom also had met a similar type of death. One brother, Andrew Cassity was drowned from a huge rogue wave created by a boat passing by in Truro's harbor. The other brother, Timothy Cassity, drowned from injuries sustained in the sinking of the schooner *E.W. Shaw*. Of additional strange coincidence, Daniel Cassity's wife's father, and her brother had drowned in the gale of 1841, and her brother-in-law had drowned in a gale in 1851. Both Daniel Cassity and fellow fishermen, Johnathan Collins were remembered for sacrificing their lives in an effort to save others that day.

Years afterward, one of the two survivors of the *Josephus*, John Jasper, later became the captain of a trans-Atlantic ocean liner. When his vessel passed Cape Cod (Highland) Light and Keeper Hamilton, he would dip the flag as a signal of respect to Keeper Hamilton for helping to save his life and sound the horn to memorialize has fellow comrades whom had perished.

Cape Cod (Highland) Lighthouse on watch, Cape Cod, Massachusetts.

The Disaster Near Monomoy Light

In Cape Cod, Massachusetts

Monomoy Island is a large narrow island a few miles from Chatham, considered to be the elbow of Cape Cod, Massachusetts. The shoals around Monomoy Island are some of the most dangerous in New England, claiming many ships. Two large shoals, the Shovelful Shoal, and the Handkerchief Shoal stretch out under the water along the eastern and southern shores of Monomoy Island. Pollock Rip, an area of unusually strong tidal currents located off the southern shore of the island, historically has also caused numerous shipwrecks. These natural dangers created a desperate need for a lighthouse station to be built to mark the area. In 1823, Monomoy Light was built, then rebuilt in 1855 as a forty-foot, cast-iron tower lined in brick, helping to guide shipping traffic and mariners around the constantly shifting sandbars and shoals caused by those strong tidal currents at the end of Monomoy peninsula.

As lighthouses were built as navigational aids along the shore, lifesaving stations were constructed in strategic locations very near the lighthouses to house additional crewmembers strictly for purposes of rescuing those in distress off shore. The Monomoy Life Saving station was one of the original nine lifesaving stations on Cape Cod. At Monomoy, these additional men were housed at Monomoy Life Saving Station, two miles north of the lighthouse. These surfmen, or lifeboat men, as they were called, were hired as assistants to the keeper, or captain as he was also referred, when shipping traffic and tourism was at its peak. Some also stayed on as assistants year round to help the lighthouse keeper.

At Monomoy, the lighthouse keeper was also the lifesaving station keeper. During fair weather, his surfmen would perform drills on lifesaving techniques and maintain their equipment while patrolling the shoreline, keeping a close eye out for ships in distress. If a ship were found wrecked on nearby ledges or sandbars, these brave men would launch their heavy lifeboat, or surfboat, into the raging sea and row through the rough surf to attempt a rescue.

All lifeboat men were known for their motto, "You have to go out, but you don't have to come back." These brave men would perform their trained duties in risking their lives for helping stranded passengers or crew from a wrecked ship, knowing beforehand that they might perish into the sea. Many times they were successful, while other times, they ended up paying the ultimate sacrifice.

Sometimes mistakes occur in communication between stations and boats, or panic ensues when those who are rescued become too frightened, ending up as tragic events. One of the worst disasters in the history of the Life Saving Service occurred on March

USLSS to the rescue.
Painting courtesy of artist Lou Diamond and his wife Valerie.

Keeper Marshall Eldridge (back row, third from left) and members of Monomoy Lifesaving Crew, Cape Cod, Massachusetts. *Courtesy, The Chatham (MA) Historical Society.*

17, 1902, off the southern end of Monomoy Island, in the dangerous shoal called the Shovelful Shoal located near the Monomoy Lighthouse. This tragic event involved the senseless drowning of twelve persons, seven of whom were members of the lifesaving crew of Monomoy Light. This is the story of the heroism of the Monomoy Lighthouse's keeper and his crew and the loss of such brave men performing their duties to aid a ship's forgotten crew in distress.

The strange series of events leading up to this tragedy began when a severe northeastern gale struck the area on March 11, 1902. Two barges the *Wadena*, with a cargo of coal, and the *John C. Fitzpatrick*, which was being towed by the tug *Sweepstakes*, were heading towards Boston from Newport News, Virginia. They ended up lodged on Shovelful Shoal a mile apart off the southern tip of Monomoy Island as they were trying to seek shelter from the storm and a place to anchor near Hyannis on Cape Cod.

Captain Marshall W. Eldridge was Keeper at Monomoy Light Station with a crew of seven surfmen housed a couple of miles from the lighthouse. One of them, Captain Seth Ellis, was Keeper Eldridge's number one surfman and his main assistant. Eldridge and members of his crew boarded both barges and tried briefly in vain to float the vessels off the shoal but the weather made their efforts futile. The decision was made to bring crewmembers of each wreck ashore to the light station and assess the damages. When it appeared there were no signs of either vessel in danger of breaking apart, the tugboat *Sweepstakes* ferried crewmembers, and employed wreckers, who were tasked with unloading some of the cargo on each barge until they were able to float off the shoal, to the wrecks. The tug stayed for a couple of days and was replaced by the *Peter Smith* as it made port at Hyannis for needed repairs, allowing the efforts of the wreckers to continue.

The wrecker crews worked tirelessly when the weather allowed them for five days until the night of March 16 when the weather became quite severe. Nether barge was still capable of lifting off from the shoal. The tug *Peter Smith* was able to remove all but five people from the barge *Wadena*, and headed towards Hyannis Harbor. Those who had remained were the concerned owner, W. S. Mack, Captain O. D. Wilson, and three employed wreckers who had volunteered to remain on ship. The fact that these five individuals were still on board the *Wadena* was not communicated to Keeper Eldridge, or to any of his surfmen at the Monomoy Light Station. The *Fitzpatrick*, a mile away, also had a few members aboard, who had elected to stay as they tried to continue their work in floating the wreck. These individuals Keeper Eldridge was informed about.

Surfman in LSS uniform.
Image courtesy of US Coast Guard.

By eight o'clock on the morning of March 17, visual assessments were made of the barges from the light station and reported as not being in any danger of breaking apart, even as the weather was worsening. A short time later, Keeper Eldridge received a phone call from the captain of the tug *Peter Smith* still remaining in Hyannis inquiring about the remaining five men on board the *Wadena*. The keeper, upon hearing that there were still five men aboard the *Wadena*, and with the winds creating dangerously high seas, started down to the point and noticed a distress flag displayed off the stranded *Wadena* a half-mile out over the surf. Although Eldridge saw no signs of any immediate danger to those left on the *Wadena*, he could not disregard the signal of distress, and believed it was his duty to pick up the crew and bring them to shore if they felt they were in a perilous situation.

He ran to the watch house nearby and phoned Surfman Seth Ellis to get his crew together to launch a surfboat from the inside location of the beach. The heavy surfboat at that time would carry five oarsmen on two seats with the keeper at the helm, and could rescue up to five survivors. The men put on their storm clothes, and began pulling the boat by cart until they reached about two miles from the station by the beach. They met up with the keeper and launched the heavy boat into the thunderous surf. They proceeded to battle the rough seas as they headed towards the *Wadena*. Keeper Eldridge still felt that the *Wadena* was not in any immediate danger and that the vessel was still sound, but felt that this was more of a precautionary measure to get the remaining crew to safety. To his crew who asked of the risks involved, he responded, "We must go there, as there is a distress flag in the rigging."

It took some time as they maneuvered the boat through the raging seas towards the *Wadena*. Fog was also setting in making for poor visibility. The keeper and his crew made it to the vessel near the stern where the waves were less heavy and threw a line to be tied down by the grateful crew on the *Wadena*. The young survivors were quite nervous with the strong seas and gusty winds approaching. As the crew came down over the edge of the barge by rope, they were helped onto the surfboat, while the seas were pitching and rolling the craft. The fifth and last member, Captain Olsen, who was a rather large heavy man, lost grip of the rope prematurely and fell into the boat, breaking apart the second rowing seat. Keeper Eldridge positioned the additional members as best he could and directed the survivors to stay positioned low on the boat.

As the Monomoy crew tried to turn the boat around to head away from the waves hitting the *Wadena*, a huge wave crashed over the boat filling it partially with water. The rescuers stayed steadfast in their positions, but the survivors, fearing for their lives, went into a panic, stood up on the boat, and threw their arms around Eldridge's crewmen preventing the lifesavers from using the oars to get away from the barge. The boat could not be turned away as the Monomoy crew struggled to calm the panic of the frightened *Wadena* crew. As Eldridge's crew tried to restore order, another huge wave came over the boat on its broadside and capsized it, spilling all into the icy waters.

The Monomoy crewmembers were twice able to right the lifeboat, but each attempt to enter the craft was made futile by the bashing of another set of waves. As the boat pitched and rolled, the five rescued crewmembers of the *Wadena* were the first to lose their grasp and perished from exposure before the Monomoy crew's eyes. Then, one by one, each member of the Monomoy lifesaving crew, exhausted and frozen from exposure, started to lose their hold on the capsized boat in the chilly waters. The first to perish was Surfman Chase, then Surfman Nickerson and Surfman Small. Waves continued to thrash around and over the boat, as the remaining crewmembers clung for their lives. Keeper Eldridge, and Surfmen Rogers and Ellis watched in agony as their friends and comrades Surfman Foye and Surfman Kendrick slipped under the thrashing waves.

Keeper Eldridge called to Surfman Ellis to help him get a better hold of the boat. Ellis managed to position his friend to hold onto the bottom portion of the craft. As soon as it seemed safe, another huge wave struck the capsized boat and threw both men into the waters again. Surfman Ellis managed to get himself back to the boat, but Keeper Eldridge, who was holding on to the spar and sail of the craft which had broken away, started drifting away from the wooden lifesaver, unable to return. The two remaining members, Ellis and Rogers, watched in desperation as their captain fought bravely to get back to their surfboat, but finally succumbed to exposure from the cold waters, then drifted away under the rough seas.

Surfman Rogers started to panic and put his arms around Ellis' neck. Fearing he would drown under Rogers' grasp and cries for help, Ellis broke away from the grip and managed to get into the submerged boat while Rogers, clutching onto the submerged rail gave up in total exhaustion. As he started to slip away, he moaned to Ellis "I've got to go," and slipped under the waves in front of his friend.

That same morning, a foggy mist had come over the swelling seas blocking the view between the *Fitzpatrick* and the *Wadena*. No one aboard the *Fitzpatrick* saw the distress flag on the *Wadena* or the fate of the Monomoy rescuers and their struggles on the boat as the *Fitzpatrick* lay some considerable distance away about a mile from the *Wadena*. Nor did anyone hear their cries for help over the distance in the thunderous surf and gusting winds.

The *Fitzpatrick* was still intact, and also had a few crewmembers aboard, including Captain Benjamin Mallows from Chatham, Captain of the barge, Andrew Welsh, and Captain Elmer Mayo, also of Chatham who was in charge of the wreckers there. The vessel was nearly ready to float, as the crew decided to stay overnight, and continue their efforts in trying to float the barge. The *Fitzpatrick* was showing no signs of breaking up, but Captain Mayo, who was a skilled boatman, had prepared an old dory on the ship in case he needed to find help on shore. He set up pins for the oars, and cut a small section of each old oar to fit for the dory. The morning of the incident at the *Wadena*, although the weather had worsened, the few members aboard the *Fitzpatrick* felt no cause for alarm as there were no leaks reported, and continued to work on the wreck try to get her afloat.

As they were working on the barge, Captain Mayo came up on deck and looked over towards the *Wadena*, nearly a mile away. The fog was clearing, but the winds were still gusting and the waves were increasing. Grabbing a scope he could see the shadows of the capsized boat with four men clinging to it drifting slowly towards the *Fitzpatrick*, still quite some distance away. As he tried to throw over a wooden fender

Seth Ellis and Elmer Mayo. *Courtesy, The Chatham (MA) Historical Society.*

towards the survivors to cling on, the piece was carried away by the waves as neither of the Monomoy crewmen saw or heard his attempt over the howling winds. He watched in anguish while three of the men slipped under the heavy seas, and believed all had died from exposure, including Ellis.

In the capsized lifeboat, as Ellis' strength was nearly spent and fearing his own life would soon end, the drifting craft found a less turbulent area of water still some distance from the *Fitzpatrick*. He couldn't believe his luck as he saw the shadows of a few of the men still aboard the vessel. He waved his hands and cried for help with everything he could muster. Captain Mayo saw Ellis frantically waving his hands and decided he would save him, no matter what the cost to his own life.

Mayo looked at the barge's old fourteen-foot dory, which was too small to complete any rescue attempt in such dangerous seas, but still shouted to his shipmates that he has going to use the dory to rescue the one survivor. The crew warned him that he would never live through the rescue in such a small boat, but unable to change his mindset, helped him to throw the dory over the side of the barge where it landed luckily into the water right side up. Mayo quickly removed his boots and oil jacket, strapped on a life preserver, grabbed

Monomoy Lifesaving Station with Keeper Seth Ellis in dark uniform and crew after the Monomoy disaster. *Image courtesy of US Coast Guard.*

the pair of old sawed off oars, and slid down the rope from the barge into the dory.

Ellis only saw the dory being thrown over the side. He did not see Mayo and his skillful maneuvering across the breakers until to his amazement the little boat appeared next to the capsized surfboat. Ellis in complete exhaustion reached out a frozen hand, which was grabbed by Mayo and pulled into the dory.

The seas were still pounding the barge and shoreline, and Mayo realized he could not go back to the barge, nor could he go near the inside of the point with the huge sea swells pounding the shore which would certainly have capsized his little dory. Instead, he anxiously waited a few extra minutes and found Surfman Francisco Bloomer running down the beach towards the water's edge. Mayo, with all his might drove the little boat through the waves towards his rescuer while Bloomer ran into the thunderous surf to drag the boat and remove both exhausted men safely on shore.

News of the rescue and the tragedy quickly spread nationwide. The local region took up a collection to help the families of the victims and raised nearly $37,000. This was quite a sum in those days, which showed the sincere outpouring of neighbors in trying to help one another. Both the US Government and the Massachusetts Humane Society awarded medals to Captain Mayo for his bravery in risking his life at all costs to save Seth Ellis. The Secretary of the Treasury presented Mayo and Ellis with the Gold Lifesaving Medal, the highest honor given for their selfless acts of courage. With the loss of Keeper Eldridge, Ellis was promoted to Keeper of Monomoy Light Station on April 23, 1902, and served until he resigned on December 31, 1907.

With such a tragic loss of life, many felt that, with the *Wadena* remaining safely afloat for many days afterwards, that the heroic attempts of Keeper Eldridge and his crew was not mandated to rescue those aboard the *Wadena*. Seth Ellis would later write that if those who were being rescued had conducted themselves calmly, his fellow crewmembers would have landed the boat safely ashore and all would have survived the ordeal. This tragic event involved the senseless drowning of twelve persons, five from the coal barge *Wadena*, and seven who were members of the lifesaving crew of Monomoy Light. The tragedy could have been avoided if proper communication was given to the station's keeper, and those who were being rescued had not fallen into a state of alarm on rough seas.

Prior to the incident, when the new lightsaving station was being built, the older lifesaving station housing Keeper Eldridge's surfmen was scheduled to be demolished. After the Monomoy disaster, the department decided to continue the old station in memorandum of Keeper Eldridge and his six men who perished.

**Monomoy Lighthouse.
Cape Cod, Massachusetts.**

Gay Head Lighthouse overlooking cliffs of Aquinnah, Martha's Vineyard, Massachusetts.

Wampanoag Lifesavers and Cutter *Dexter* Saves 29

Near Gay Head (Aquinnah) Light in Martha's Vineyard, Massachusetts

Gay Head Lighthouse is located 130 feet above the sea on multicolored clay cliffs on the western side of the island of Martha's Vineyard, in Massachusetts. It was built in a region surrounded by the quiet Wampanoag Native American tribe, where many descendants live there today as well. The lighthouse sits atop these cliffs on the edge of the nearby town of Aquinnah, and is also referred to as "Aquinnah Light" by the locals. Gay Head Light stands guard where an underwater cluster of submerged rocky ledges known as the Devil's Bridge, reaches out from the shoreline. These ledges were considered one of the most dangerous formations in the region, threatening ships that would enter into Vineyard Sound along the main shipping route to Boston Harbor from the south.

In 1844, with the constant eroding of the sandy cliffs, the lighthouse tower had to be moved back about seventy-five feet from the edge of the bluff. In 1856, the current brick and brownstone tower replaced the original wooden lighthouse built in 1799. A huge first order Fresnel lens with 1008 prisms was also installed at that time.

In spite of this powerful lighthouse, shipwrecks would still occur quite often in the region. In 1884, Keeper Horatio Pease's assistants, or surfmen, were members of the Wampanoag tribe, who were mostly volunteers to help with the duties of the lighthouse, and they assisted him in various rescue efforts. In nearby Chilmark, the Massachusetts Humane Society Lifesavers had a lifesaving station managed by Chief Simon Johnson, with a crew of local Wampanoags. These brave men were ether local fishermen or whalers who would volunteer to assist in rescue missions.

One of New England's worst maritime disasters occurred during this time when the steamer *City of Columbus* ran aground on Devil's Bridge and sank, drowning 103 persons on board in a less than a half hour. Through their heroic efforts, Wampanoag volunteers assisted in the rescue of at least twenty-one of the twenty-nine survivors from the wreck.

The *City of Columbus* was a 275-foot steamer providing exports and passenger services up and down the eastern coast. The ship would export cotton from the South to the textile mills in New England from Boston, and export manufactured goods from New England such as clothing, shoes, and furniture, as well as canned fish to the southern states. Passengers would also travel for business and pleasure as both ends of the line provided railroad service westward for those who needed to travel to the nation's interior.

On January 17, 1884, the *City of Columbus* set sail from Nickerson's Wharf in Boston, heading for Savannah, Georgia, with a load of manufactured goods and eighty-seven passengers. Her crew of forty-five officers had been on many previous voyages without incident. Captain Shuyler E. Wright was very familiar with the area, as he had experience in making numerous trips through the reefs and sound of Martha's Vineyard. Second Officer Augustus Harding however, did not have a pilot's license to be in charge of legally navigating he ship.

Most of the passengers who were aboard the ship were heading south to escape the bitter cold of the New England winter. The wind was blowing harshly from the north, creating a bitter chill in the air. The vessel was rounding the tip of Cape Cod, and was sailing through Nantucket and Vineyard sounds at the speed of twelve knots. It was clear sailing at this time with a haze overlooking the mainland, and, as the evening progressed with a cold January wind, many passengers were socializing in the main salon or the smoking room below deck, eventually turning in for the night.

As the ship passed by Tarpaulin Cove Lighthouse, near the chain of Elizabethan Islands in Buzzard's Bay, around 2 a.m., Captain White ordered Second Officer Harding to head the ship in a southwesterly direction as he turned in for the night, believing it would be a clear, safe sail. Because of the chilly winds and

temperatures falling below freezing, officer Harding stayed in the pilot's house with the window closed while Watchman Edward Leary stayed on lookout. As the steamer headed into open waters, a stiff wind from the north continued blowing, increasing as they continued southward while the seas started churning in response.

At around 3:15 a.m., as they approached the western side of Martha's Vineyard near Gay Head Lighthouse, the winds from the open waters were increasing to gale force as the seas continued to rise. All of a sudden, Watchman Edward Leary saw the Devil's Bridge buoy approach on the wrong starboard side of the ship indicating that the vessel was too near the dangerous ledge. He quickly yelled out to Harding, but the officer could not hear Leary's cries with the window closed from the harsh winds. As precious moments went by, Leary rushed to the pilothouse to get Harding's attention to warn him of the impending danger.

The steamer was heading for Devil's Bridge at an alarming speed. After finally hearing Leary's warnings, Harding yelled, "Port!" to the quartermaster to steer the vessel away from the ledge, but he was too late.

The *City of Columbus* ran aground on Devil's Bridge. The jagged rocks had ripped a massive hole in her hull as the icy waters started pouring in.

As most of the passengers and crew were below avoiding the freezing winds, or had prepared for a night's rest when the ship crashed onto the rocks, many rushed onto the deck in only their nightclothes. The crash was so sudden many women and children were still preparing to come on deck.

Captain Wright awoke upon hearing the distress, and believing the ship was only slightly damaged,

ordered to reverse the engines in an attempt to back the ship off the dangerous reef. The attempt only made the situation worse, as the entire rear stern area of the vessel started to sink, and came to rest on the ledge with only her bow, smokestacks, and masts out of the water. He then attempted to gather the passengers together from below to explain the situation when the pounding waves caused the ship to list to the port side. A huge rush of water poured into the cabin and engine room down below, forcing passengers and crew to scramble to the main deck.

Tarpaulin Cove Lighthouse, Nashion Island, Massachusetts.

As most everyone started to grab life jackets, a series of monstrous rogue waves swept over the ship, washing many overboard into the freezing sea. Little time was left to send any kind of distress signal as the rushing water put out the fires in the boilers to drown the ship's whistle. It was impossible to launch any lifeboats on the opposite starboard side, as the steamer was literally resting on her port side. The whole back portion of the ship was now entirely underwater.

The breaking waves continued to wash survivors overboard, especially women and children as nearly forty others aboard scrambled to find safety in the rigging. Two of the lifeboats were launched in haste and became swamped. One lifeboat carried only five people in it while the other broke away, capsized, and started drifting away. The others in the first lifeboat saw the lighthouse some distance away and started to row towards the shore over the raging seas and bitter howling winds.

Within less than a half hour after the *City of Columbus* had run aground on Devil's Bridge, nearly 100 persons had drowned from being washed overboard in the ferocious seas. Those who had climbed the rigging, waited in the icy spray and gusting winds for rescue as a coat of ice covered the deck leaving those who were unable to hang on, to meet their fate in the freezing waters.

Some of those passengers, who would survive the ordeal and observed the panic, would later write that they found little signs of consideration of the men to one another, nor was much if any help provided to assist the women and children who had made up at least a third of the passengers aboard.

A couple of hours had passed as the sun started to rise on the morning of January 18, while the gale-force winds continued to wreak havoc with the rising tides. Most of the personnel had been washed off and drowned except for those who still clung to the masts and rigging.

At around 5 a.m., Keeper Horatio N. Pease at the Gay Head Lighthouse spotted the *City of Columbus* from shore. Pease gathered a volunteer crew of six Wampanoag Native Americans who were known as part of the Gay Head Lifesavers to assist him in the rescue.

Chief Simon Johnston also headed up the Massachusetts Humane Society Gay Head Life Saving Station in nearby Chilmark and helped to gather additional volunteers for another boat. A few of the Wampanoag men were sent on horseback to a telegraph station in Vineyard Haven to alert the mainland of the disaster. The one lifeboat was also sighted near the shore by the lighthouse, and the five exhausted survivors were brought into a neighboring house and given food and dry clothes.

The first boat of Wampanoag volunteers organized by Pease, and led by Captain John Peters was finally launched from the beach, but capsized from the thunderous surf. Luckily, everyone made it back to shore safely. A second attempt was made around 7:30 a.m. when it took over an hour to reach the stranded wreck. The rescuers were exhausted, drenched, and freezing from the January bitter cold after rowing over the raging waves.

The lifeboat crew feared approaching the wreck would cause their own boat to smash onto the rocks. As they neared the ship, they called to those on the rigging to jump into the icy waters to be rescued. Seven reluctant passengers made the terrifying jump into the sea and swam towards the lifeboat. The crew brought the craft alongside the survivors and hauled them aboard. With as much strength as they could muster, they made their way back over the thrashing waters and biting winds towards the shore, arriving near the beach around 10 a.m. The lifeboat was overcrowded with the additional seven survivors and got caught in the raging surf. It capsized just off from the beach, dumping all into the icy waters. All managed to swim to the beach and safely make it on dry land.

Early that same morning, the steamer *Glaucus* just happened to be passing by using the same shipping channel. Captain Bearse observed the wreck of the *City of Columbus*, but from his vantage point could not see any of the survivors on the rigging. Instead of investigating to account for any survivors, he presumed that the Gay Head Life Saving Station had rescued all survivors. He continued on his way towards Boston without stopping, an act he was severely criticized for in the newspapers afterwards.

A second boat, manned by the Massachusetts Humane Society Lifesavers, consisting also of Wampanoag Native Americans from nearby Chilmark, rowed out to gather more survivors. The volunteer crew had recently come back from a long voyage on a successful whaling hunt. The boat was tossed around effortlessly by the huge waves and gusting winds,

City of Columbus painting. *Courtesy of Mariner's Museum, Newport News, Virginia.*

City of Columbus **wrecked on Devil's Bridge in background (top left with arrow), Chief Simon Johnston (top right), and wrecked lifeboat (bottom).** *Collage of images courtesy of Quest Marine Services.*

making the rescue efforts exhausting. Through their tenacity in not giving up, the brave crew of Gay Head's Humane Society managed to bring several more survivors ashore. With little time for rest, they started out again in the heavy surf to gather another group of survivors determined to help at all costs, even at the risk of their own lives.

As the Wampanoag crew were heading for the wreck for another attempted rescue, the Revenue Cutter *Dexter* was returning from patrol along Vineyard Sound, heading for Woods Hole when she spotted the *City of Columbus* wreck around 12:30 that afternoon. Captain Gabrielson tried to maneuver the *Dexter* as close to the vessel as he dared among the monstrous waves. He anchored her in a dangerously exposed location about 200-300 yards from the wreck. Immediately, a boat was launched with Lieutenant John Rhodes in charge of five volunteers. The pounding waves carried the boat up and down as it took some time to reach the ill-fated steamer. As the lifeboat made for the wreck, it became apparent that it would be impossible to bring the craft directly

alongside the masts and rigging where the remaining survivors were clinging for their lives.

Upon reaching the vessel, the heavy seas were still breaking over the exposed bow, which was surrounded with debris and dead bodies, making the task even more difficult than expected. Rhodes yelled for the men clinging to the masts to jump into the water. One by one, seven more men jumped into the waves, as Rhodes and his crew managed to get close enough to haul each into the boat when they rose to the surface. The crew on the crowded lifeboat now made their way back to the *Dexter*, where one of the survivors died shortly afterwards on deck from exposure. Rhodes and his crew nearly exhausted and freezing from the biting winds and spray made another trip out to the wreck over the mountainous waves and were able to retrieve one other reluctant survivor back to the *Dexter*.

As Rhodes and his crew rested briefly on the *Dexter*, Lieutenant Charles Kennedy, with a party of four volunteers, was lowered into the thrashing waves and made his way over to the wreck. The debris was still everywhere and again the craft was unable to get too close to the ship, as it would certainly have been smashed against the vessel.

Kennedy managed to talk four more exhausted survivors into jumping into the icy waters. As they reluctantly jumped one by one, Kennedy and his crew managed to quickly maneuver the boat to grab the struggling men into the safety of their boat.

While Kennedy's crew were making their way over the waves towards the *Dexter*, the second lifeboat containing the six-man boat crew of Wampanoag rescuers managed to retrieve a few more survivors and transported them onto the *Dexter*.

Again, with little time for rest, the Gay Head lifesavers started heading back towards the wreck. They were exhausted and freezing from the stinging winds and spray that had been pounding them since the early morning hours, but were determined to help in the recovery efforts at all costs.

With Kennedy's return to the *Dexter*, he told Captain Gabrielson that there were still a few more survivors including the ship's captain of the *City of Columbus* on the foremast rigging. Rhodes now feeling somewhat rested, gathered a crew with Kennedy and lowered the lifeboat again from the *Dexter* to retrieve any remaining survivors. As they reached near the wreck in the churning seas, they saw the mast where Captain Wright and four men waited in earnest as they had been clinging to the mast and rigging for over twelve hours at this point.

Again the area was dangerously covered with debris and dead bodies and the rescuers could not get close enough to board the vessel. Rhodes yelled for the freezing survivors to attempt to jump in the water so his crew could help them into the boat. Two men, who were brothers, yelled that they could not swim, but Kennedy and Rhodes persuaded them to jump into the raging waves. As they jumped into the water, only one of them was able to make it near the boat. Rhodes and Kennedy had the boat placed close by the survivor and hauled him safely into the boat. The other brother, Eugene McGarry, was overcome by a huge wave and was never seen again.

At this point, Captain Wright and two unconscious men frozen to the rigging were the only survivors left. The feet and hands of his two crewmen were wrapped around the rigging, literally frozen to it. Lieutenant Rhodes shouted for the captain to jump, but Wright screamed back "Save those men first!" Rhodes replied, believing they had already perished, that the men

***City of Columbus* Rescue.** *Illustration courtesy of Quest Marine Services.*

had frozen to death, and that the captain was the last alive to leave. Captain Wright reluctantly jumped in the waters, but was unable to swim from exposure. As he rose to the surface, Lieutenant Kennedy jumped in and brought the captain safely into the boat.

As the lifeboat made its way back to the *Dexter*, Rhodes made the decision, without regard for his own life, that he would somehow board the wreck to retrieve the two men frozen on the rigging whether they were dead or still alive. When they arrived at the *Dexter*, he asked Captain Gabrielson to provide one experienced volunteer to row him out to the wreck, where he might attempt to make a swim to the vessel and rescue the two stranded men on the rigging. The captain reluctantly agreed and Lieutenant Roth volunteered to assist Rhodes in the effort.

As they neared the wreck, the Wampanoag lifesavers from Gay Head were still in the area to provide any assistance. Rhodes and Roth tried to bring their larger boat along the wreck, but the attempts proved unsuccessful as the waves and debris prevented their efforts. Rhodes saw the Gay Head lifeboat crew and called for their help. They maneuvered their smaller craft alongside his in the churning seas, and he jumped into their lifeboat to try to get closer to the wreck. He tied a rope around his waist and the lifesavers were able to bring their boat within thirty feet of the ship. Rhodes then jumped into the icy waters and started swimming towards the vessel. He nearly reached his destination over the rising waves when he was struck by a large piece of timber on the leg and started to sink. The Wampanoag crew quickly pulled him back into their boat and found that the timber had created quite a

Lieutenant John Rhodes.
Photo courtesy of Quest Marine Services.

bloody gash on his leg, which needed to be treated. All on the boat were exhausted and in danger of freezing to death from exposure. They mustered all their strength to row back to the *Dexter* through the heavy winds.

When both boats arrived at the *Dexter*, everyone was exhausted and in need of dry clothing and rest from their ordeal. Rhodes had his leg tended to and put on some dry clothes to make ready another attempt. The winds were finally calming making the waves less dangerous as Rhodes persuaded Captain Gabrielson to make one final attempt to reach the wreck. The captain tried to convince Rhodes to abandon his efforts, but Rhodes was determined to retrieve the two remaining men. The captain again reluctantly granted Rhodes permission to make the final attempt using the *Dexter's* dinghy. With another volunteer to row him out to the doomed vessel, Rhodes again tied a line to his waist and jumped into the icy waters when the craft reached within a short distance from the wreck. This time he swam with all his might and managed to scramble onto the ship. On the rigging, he found the two survivors unconscious and barely showing any signs of life. They were literally hanging with their feet and arms within the rigging, nearly frozen to death. He carefully removed them from the rigging's icy grip and hauled them into the boat to transport to the cutter. In spite of all his efforts, to his anguish and dismay, both men died from exposure before they could reach the safety of the *Dexter.*

By 4 p.m. that afternoon, Captain Gabrielson decided there were no more survivors left on the wreck and pulled up anchor of the *Dexter*. He transported twenty-one survivors along with four others who had died from exposure, and headed towards New Bedford's port.

Back at Gay Head Light in Martha's Vineyard, the local Wampanoag families opened their homes and provided assistance to those survivors from the one lifeboat that made it to the Aquinnah shore, and those brought ashore by the Gay Head Lifesavers, with food, clothing, and medical treatment. The bodies and possessions of those who had perished that had washed ashore were brought to the Gay Head Community Baptist Church to be claimed.

The *City of Columbus* had started out of Boston with forty-five officers and crewmen, and eighty-seven passengers. After the wreck, twenty-eight of the ships company and seventy-five passengers were lost. One man in Boston had lost his father, mother, brother, sister, and brother's child in the disaster. Only twenty-nine survived, and they were all men. All the women and children, who made up at least one third of the passenger list, perished in the incident.

One passenger, a Nova Scotia sea captain named Sherrington Vance who had been washed off the deck, swam to the empty lifeboat that had started to drift away from the wreck, where he struggled to right the craft. He climbed inside the icy water-filled boat, and waited for many hours until later that afternoon he was rescued by the navy tug *Speedwell*. He had nearly frozen to death, but survived the ordeal. The Speedwell had the grim task of hauling up many of the frozen bodies onto her deck, and then headed for port.

The Wampanoag Native Americans who made up the crews of the Gay Head Light and Massachusetts

Cutter *Dexter* at Woods Hole, Massachusetts. *Photo courtesy of Quest Marine Services.*

Gay Head Lifesaving crews involved in the rescue. *Image courtesy of Martha's Vineyard Museum, photographer John Chamberlain, 1884.*

Humane Society Lifesavers, and the crew of the Revenue Cutter *Dexter* were honored for their "brave and humane conduct." They were written about locally and nationally as heroes. Despite the frigid weather and terrible gale-force winds, both the Wampanoag men and the crews on the *Dexter* repeatedly went out to the wreck, risking their own lives to make sure all survivors were rescued.

The Native American volunteers of the Gay Head Lifesaving crews were directly involved in the rescue of twenty-one of the survivors from the wreck of the *City of Columbus*. They managed to row out multiple times through the thunderous surf from the beach out to the wreck and bring some of the survivors through the biting winds and raging waves back to the shore for help until the *Dexter* arrived. Determined to help at any cost, again they went out and helped in the transport of survivors from the ill-fated vessel to the *Dexter*. Lieutenant Rhodes was given additional praise for continuously risking his life as he swam through the icy waters and floating wreckage to rescue the two men frozen to the rigging.

After a lengthy investigation, Captain Bearse of the steamer *Glaucus*, who did not investigate the *City of Columbus*' dire situation was exonerated for his poor decision to pass by the ship without further inspection, although his acts were sharply criticized in the newspapers. When the investigation found that Captain Wright's Second Mate Harding had no pilot's license to navigate the ship, making it Wright's responsibility for the starboard watch that made the wrong side of the buoy, he had his pilot's license and certificate as a shipmaster removed, never to be in charge of a ship again. It is unclear as to whether Wright knew about Harding's lack of certification. There was also plenty of blame to go around as some survivors testified that the crew and many of the male passengers thought only of themselves and not the women and children in helping to rescue them to

secure them to the masts and rigging for safety. There were many questions after the incident as to why the first boat had contained mostly crewmembers.

Each of the Wampanoag Native American volunteers received rare silver or bronze medals for their heroic efforts by the Massachusetts Humane Society. For his courageous efforts, Lieutenant Rhodes was presented a Gold Lifesaving Medal from the Massachusetts Humane Society among other awards, and the Secretary of the Treasury ordered praise for the crew of the *Dexter* read on board all US cutters. Silver medals from the Massachusetts Humane Society were given to Captain Gabrielson and Lieutenant Kennedy, and citations for human efforts were given to the other officers of the *Dexter*.

The *City of Columbus* is remembered as one of the worst maritime disasters in New England at that time. In all, 103 lost their lives that day, but there were 29 grateful survivors who were rescued by the efforts of the local Wampanoag Native Americans and the crew of the *Dexter*.

Gay Head Lighthouse from Aquinnah shore in Martha's Vineyard, Massachusetts.

Ida Lewis Becomes Rhode Island's Most Famous Keeper

At Lime Rock Light, in Newport, Rhode Island

Since Lime Rock was completely surrounded by water with a constant current, the only way to reach the mainland was by boat. In the mid-nineteenth century it was highly unusual for a woman to handle a boat, but Ida Lewis rowed her siblings to school every weekday and fetched needed supplies from the town. By the age of 14, Ida had become known as the best swimmer and young rower in Newport. Her rowing skills, strength, and courage were to come into play many times during her life at Lime Rock and its lighthouse. She is credited officially with saving twenty-three lives during her thirty-nine years at Lime Rock Lighthouse, but many believe the number may be closer to thirty-five, although Ida Lewis never kept records of her lifesaving experiences.

Idawalley Zoradia Lewis, named after her mother, was the oldest of four children. Ida's father, Captain Hosea Lewis, was the Keeper of Lime Rock Lighthouse from 1857 until 1872. Her father found there wasn't a keeper's dwelling for his family, and within months, started on construction of a new building. By June of 1858, the Lewis family moved into their new home at Lime Rock. Only four months later in October, Ida's father suffered a stroke, which left him disabled. Ida's mother was having trouble helping with tending the lighthouse as her youngest child had become seriously ill and was taking all her attention. As a result, the responsibilities of keeping the light fell upon the shoulders of then 16-year-old Ida Lewis. She faithfully performed all the duties of running the lighthouse and found that she really enjoyed the work, hard as it was.

Ida's first rescue was in the fall of 1858, as she was only a teenager. She was watching from a window, as one of four youths on a sailboat climbed the mast and began deliberately rocking the boat back and forth as a prank on his friends. The sailboat capsized tossing the four youths into the water. Ida rushed to the scene in her small rowboat and hauled the four aboard one by one, where they were taken to the lighthouse and recovered. Ida's father saw the whole incident unfold from his chair and gave a sigh of relief for his daughter's efforts. The four boys returned home without mentioning the incident to their parents. The incident received no attention at the time, as the boys were probably quite embarrassed. It wasn't until eleven years later as the boys reached adulthood, and only after Ida had performed more notable rescues, that the incident became known.

In February of 1866, three drunken soldiers were walking back to Fort Adams, which was located nearby on the mainland a short distance from Lime Rock, and decided to take a small boat belonging to one of Ida's brothers as a shortcut to the fort. As they were heading towards the fort, one of the drunken men put his foot right through the floor. Two of the men slid into the icy waters into the current, and were never seen again. Ida luckily spotted the third man as she rowed out to help. He was so drunk he was barely able to move from nearly drowning, and was freezing from exposure.

Ida Lewis. *Painting courtesy of artist John Witt and US Coast Guard.*

When Ida reached the victim, and as she struggled to pull the large half-drowned man into her boat, she strained herself and was unable to get his limp body in the craft as he started to slip into unconsciousness. She had to tie a line around his body and under his armpits and tow him to shore. She saw two other men along the shore and yelled for their help. They quickly obliged and Ida was able to bring him safely to shore and revive him.

Ida's brother heard the commotion and brought warm blankets to the soldier that destroyed his boat. The man recovered and apologized to Ida's brother, but the other two soldiers were swept out to sea. It took her many months to recover from the severe strain she received when trying to bring the drunken soldier into the boat.

Ida's rescues were not only limited to people in need. One cold early morning in January, in 1877, three workers were carrying a very valuable sheep along the streets of Newport to its prominent owner. Winds were gusting and the waves were increasing as a storm was approaching the harbor. All of a sudden the frisky animal broke away and ran through the Old Mill Wharf and plunged into the icy waters. The three men followed after the sheep and grabbed Ida's brother's newly acquired skiff by Jones Bridge to set after the valuable prize. As they were nearing the sheep, the weather worsened quickly, and they found themselves in danger as the waves tossed around the small craft.

Ida was sewing by the window and saw the three men struggling in the waves with her brother's new boat. She then observed a huge rogue wave wash over the tiny boat and capsize it, spilling the men into the freezing waters. She was out the door in an instant, and launching her lifeboat towards the survivors. She rowed as fast as she could as she could hear the screams of the frightened three. As she neared the men struggling in the icy waters, she couldn't help but chuckle from her exhausting efforts, as the attention of the men were still on the valuable sheep, which was still struggling in the rough waves nearby.

She hauled each man into the boat and rowed them to shore. They were very grateful to Ida for rescuing them from what could have been a tragic situation. To their surprise, she decided she would oblige the survivors' need to capture the animal and launched the boat out again in the bitter winds to capture the sheep. She managed to maneuver the boat next to the struggling animal and haul it into the craft to safety. The sheep didn't seem to mind being out of the frigid waters and stayed in the boat as she brought it to the grateful men on shore. Ida always loved the story and would frequently tell it years later.

Ida Lewis Portrait.
Image courtesy of Newport Historical Society.

A couple of weeks passed and daybreak arrived as Ida's mother noticed a sailor stranded on an underwater ledge called Little Lime Rock, located close to the lighthouse. The mother called out to the struggling mariner that help was coming and called to Ida to assist him. The waves had risen with the tide as the man clung to the submerged ledge, with only his head above water. Ida quickly grabbed her clothes and ran to the boathouse to launch her lifeboat. She pulled the sailor into the boat and brought him to safety at the lighthouse. They offered to give him dry clothing and food, which he graciously declined and asked to quickly be brought to the nearest wharf.

They obliged the young man's request, feeling a little suspicious of his actions. As it turned out, when Ida returned the wrecked sailboat the sailor had destroyed to its rightful owner who lived nearby, the owner had been looking for it, as it had been stolen. The angry owner told Ida he would have gladly paid her fifty dollars if she had let the scoundrel drown. The authorities never found the culprit.

On March 29, 1869, a gale was raging outside the harbor area. Ida's mother was upstairs and looked out the window to find a boat had capsized with three soldiers in it. She yelled to Ida to quickly help the victims of the overturned craft as Ida rushed out the door without even taking the time to put her shoes on. She launched the lifeboat into the rising waves and proceeded towards the capsized sailboat. Before she could reach the boat, one of the soldiers had already slipped under the freezing waters while the others were clinging on for their lives. She steadied the lifeboat next to the struggling survivors and pulled each into the craft as the waves effortlessly tossed it around. Ida rowed with all her strength back to the safety of the lighthouse and got the freezing men into the kitchen. With their clothing dried and after they had rested from their ordeal, they made their way back to the fort. Colonel Henry Hunt heard of the incident and sent Ida Lewis his letter of appreciation with a contribution from the officers at the fort amounting to $218.

Ida had saved the lives of at least eight men by May of 1869. The boys and men who had been rescued previously were probably a little too embarrassed to admit that their lives had been saved by a lone girl in a small boat. Most people had not known about these rescues until 1869, when the grateful soldier saved in February of 1866 (when Ida had sprained herself in the attempt), told his story to the local press. A reporter from the New York *Herald-Tribune* read the story in the local newspaper and decided to write a feature article on Ida. She soon became a national hero when the magazines, *Harper's Weekly, Leslie's Weekly, Life,* and *Look* engraved images of her in their publications.

Because of this publicity, Ida received many awards including medals, money, two musical pieces named after her, and some other special gifts. On July 4, 1869, the residents of Newport presented Ida Lewis with a new mahogany boat named *Rescue*, complete with velvet cushions and gold-plated oarlocks. President Ulysses S. Grant even visited the 21-year old Ida in 1869 to give his thanks. They had a long talk as she showed him around the lighthouse. Grant would later remark that his time with Ida Lewis was one of the most interesting events in his life. Over the years, many prominent notable pioneers like the Astors and the Vanderbilts visited her, as she had gained quite the celebrity status in the nation. She always remained very humble, feeling she was only doing her duty.

Ida continued to assist her father over the years as his health continued to fail until his death in 1872. Ida and her mother tended the Lime Rock Lighthouse afterwards with her mother accepting the position as Keeper to replace her father.

In November 1877, Ida saved the lives of three soldiers whose catboat had run into rocks to the west of the lighthouse. This rescue was particularly stressful for Ida, and it resulted in an illness believed to be diphtheria, that lasted for months.

In 1879, with her mother's health failing, and with the help of General Sherman, from a special act of Congress, Ida Lewis was appointed Keeper of Lime Rock Lighthouse. She remained as keeper at the lighthouse until 1911.

In 1881, she performed one of her most daring rescues. Two soldiers from Fort Adams decided to walk across the half frozen Newport Harbor when they fell through the ice into the freezing waters. Ida heard their cries, and on instinct, ran across the cracking ice, and tossed her lifeline to the struggling men. One of the soldiers was able to grab hold of the line and try to position himself on the ice, but the thin ice kept breaking away and he would slide back into the frozen water. After many exhausting efforts, as the ice continued to crack and break away from the frightened survivors, Ida finally managed to pull one of the soldiers to a safe thicker area of ice, then quickly tried to get the second soldier to grab hold of the lifeline. By this time, Rudolph, her brother, had also reached the scene and together they pulled the panicking man out of the frigid waters onto the safe area of ice. Frozen from the experience, both soldiers and their two rescuers

Ida Lewis in later years.
Image courtesy of Jeremy D'Entremont.

Ida Lewis Lighthouse as part of Ida Lewis Yacht Club in Newport, Rhode Island.

recovered from the incident. The Lighthouse Board presented Ida Lewis with a Gold Lifesaving Medal for her courageous efforts.

One of her last acts of bravery occurred in 1905, at the age of 64. A close friend of hers, who was not used to using a rowboat, was making her way out to the lighthouse. She inadvertently stood up to reposition herself, and lost her balance, falling overboard. Ida, who was watching her friend from the lighthouse, saw the incident and immediately sprang into action. She ran to the boathouse and quickly launched the boat with all the strength her aged body could muster. She brought the boat alongside her friend struggling in the waters, and, as she had done countless times before, was able to haul her grateful companion into the boat and row her to the safety of the lighthouse. This rescue effort would make her friend the twenty-third documented person she had saved from drowning.

She continued at her post at Lime Rock lighthouse until 1911. The years of hard work at the lighthouse, and the strain of her rescues were starting to catch up with her. Her health started to fail, as there was news about decommissioning the lighthouse, which worried her immensely. It had turned out to be a false report.

One morning, on October 24, she became ill from an apparent stroke. The commanding officer at Fort Adams, upon hearing the news, had the coast artillery practice temporarily suspended. Idawalley Zoradia Lewis died on October 25, 1911, at the age of 69. The bells of all the vessels in Newport Harbor tolled for Ida Lewis that night.

After her death, Edward Jansen transferred from Sandy Hook Light in New Jersey to become Lime Rock's new keeper. His wife had a daughter whom they named Ida Lewis Jansen. This little girl grew up to also become a lifesaver as well in rescuing two men whose boat had capsized in a storm.

In 1924, Congress decided to change the name of Lime Rock to Ida Lewis Rock, and the lighthouse be known as Ida Lewis Light. Today the lighthouse is part of the Ida Lewis Yacht Club, which manages and owns the property.

To honor Ida Lewis, the Coast Guard built a buoy tender and named it the *Ida Lewis* in 1995. She will always be known as Rhode Island's most famous lighthouse keeper.

Connecticut's Most Experienced and Colorful Keeper

At Faulkner's Island Light

Connecticut's second oldest lighthouse, Faulkner's Island Lighthouse was built in 1802, due to the many shipwrecks that occurred around the island. Even with the lighthouse established, although the light saved many, there were still many shipwrecks occurring over the years. It was located about four miles from the main shoreline, and was within one mile distance from a tiny island known as Bruce Island.

Keeper Oliver Brooks was known as a man of many interests. He played the violin, studied ornithology and taxidermy, and conducted experiments with sound and light. He often practiced his taxidermy skills on many unfortunate birds that would be attracted to the reflecting beacon, collide into the glass surrounding the lighthouse lantern, and die. The keeper's house became a kind of a natural history museum and regional attraction for visitors to enjoy. As a taxidermist he had plenty of local birds and migrating birds. His collection included eagles, cormorants, ducks, a seal, a fox, an ox, and a rare great snowy owl from the arctic. The story goes that when he shot the owl in the neck area, it was so maimed, that he found a rooster's head and used part of it to fill what was missing on the owl's head and shoulders. One of his daughters reportedly also shot a number of birds to add to the collection.

Brooks was an avid farmer on the island with plenty of barnyard farm animals including a mule, cows, and chickens. Many times the animals would try to escape and attempt to swim or fly from the island where he had to retrieve them back to the barn. Local fisherman and lobsterman would sometimes find one of the cows trying to swim and direct them back to the island for the keeper. He also made a living as a large-scale fisherman and lobsterman and sold his catch to the locals on the mainland, or for visitors coming to the island. The family ate lobster as a main stay almost daily.

The entire Brooks family enjoyed playing musical instruments and would treat visitors to concerts at the lighthouse. Brooks himself enjoyed playing the violin. Brooks also had a huge dog named Old Tide that he taught to sing after his daughter would play the flute. It was written that the dog's voice was not in long drown howls or short barks, but "a wonderful something in between." His wife and both daughters appreciated artwork and were painters themselves. His oldest daughter studied marine botany and painted using watercolors.

Brooks was also an excellent communicator using the sun reflected into a mirror-like device known as a heliograph. In broad daylight he could communicate with friends on hilltops on the mainland up to fifteen miles away. Years later, the heliograph was used from the mainland to communicate with him when Lincoln was assassinated.

Keeper Brooks also owned nearby Bruce Island, about a mile away, where he would row out to hunt with Old Tide. It was his other getaway, if he had the opportunity, from Faulkner's Island.

He was an expert at handling small boats in all kinds of weather and was known for his extraordinary skills, especially in helping with rescue efforts. The boat he used from Faulkner's Island was an eighteen-foot skiff with a sail and long oars.

Faulkner's Island Lighthouse, Connecticut.

Aerial view of early Faulkner's Island Lighthouse with keeper's quarters. *Courtesy of US Coast Guard.*

One of the most famous rescues of the region occurred during his tenure at the lighthouse and challenged his skills as an expert boatman. On November 27, 1858, the *Moses F Webb* was anchored at about 5 p.m., between Bruce Island and Faulkner's Island for shelter for the night. She was coming up from Brunswick, New Jersey, with a load of coal heading for Hartford, Connecticut. Strong breezes came up the coast and became a violent gale storm that night. Captain Brooks stayed up during the night in the poor visibility with his Assistant Keeper Al Schofield searching for any vessels in distress.

By morning, the gale-force winds continued to worsen and the *Moses F Webb* started to drag her anchor along the bottom. The raging waves pounded and thrashed the vessel and forced the anchor chains to break apart. The vessel was now floundering in the heavy seas heading towards Bruce Island.

Keeper Brooks was on the lookout all night and saw the perilous incident that morning while looking through his spyglass. He could see the panic on board the *Moses F Webb* and everyone trying to climb and attach themselves to the rigging through the mountainous waves and piercing winds. One of the survivors he saw was a woman. He watched as a toddler was given to a sailor, who tried to hold on to the little girl as best he could, but as the ship pitched and rolled from the raging seas, he watched in horror as the agonized sailor lost his grip of her when a huge wave washed over the deck of the ship. The little girl was washed into the freezing waters and did not survive.

Brooks knew he had to do something and he also knew that he probably wouldn't survive the attempted rescue with his tiny boat in such turbulent seas. He told his young assistant, Al Schofield, that he may not make it back and that if he should perish, to keep the light burning until someone could make it to the island to relieve him. He also told him to keep a close watch on the children as his wife had gone ashore the day before the storm to get supplies. He gathered woolen blankets and provisions and set out in his small eighteen-foot boat.

As soon as he launched the boat and started battling the heaving waves, the winds shifted and continued to get stronger. As he set out alone, he felt that this was going to be too much for he and his small craft in such violent weather, but felt it was his duty to try the rescue, even if he would lose his life at the attempt. As he rowed out among the rising waves and howling winds, the effort was daunting and many times he felt it would be an impossible task. It took quite some time, but he finally was able to make it to the stranded vessel where he found five people clinging to the rigging for dear life. As the wreck was located closer to Bruce Island than Faulkner's Island, he decided to bring the survivors to Bruce Island first. His plan involved hopefully getting all survivors to Bruce Island, try to make them comfortable, and then bring them back to Faulker's Island when the winds would calm.

The woman whom he had seen with his telescope, who happened to be the captain's wife, had slipped into unconsciousness from the freezing exposure. He had only enough room in the boat to take each one at a time safely to drop off to Bruce Island, where he would quickly cover them in blankets and spirits to warm them. He learned that the little girl he had watched drown was the captain's daughter and that her mother had not known of the incident.

One by one Brooks transported each survivor to Bruce Island and made them as comfortable as he could. A few hours later, when they had regained strength, and the winds had started to subside, he brought each survivor through the still unsettling seas and wind gusts to Faulkner's Island, where his children waited for him and helped the survivors into their warm dwelling.

At the keeper's house, Brooks and his family nursed the survivors back to health and he became a local and national hero, as all the newspapers carried his story. Congress helped out by boosting his annual salary from 350 dollars to 500 dollars and he received a coveted Gold Lifesaving Medal from the New York Life Saving Society. The medal has an engraving on the back of the *Moses F Webb* being rescued by Brooks in his tiny craft.

Many years later, one other famous rescue that also serves as a testament to his valor and uncompromising character involves an incident near Thanksgiving in 1875. He was much older and so sick he was bedridden with what many believe was the flu. The paddlewheel steamer *E. A. Woodward* was making her way near the island in gale-force winds, when the captain, thinking he was going around a buoy, hit an exposed rocky ledge and broke the propeller. Brooks' family saw and heard

Faulkner's Island Lighthouse tower in Connecticut.

the vessel in distress and blew horns to indicate they were nearby. The ship was getting caught in the high winds and waves and was being tossed about heading towards the rocky shoreline of Faulker's Island.

Against all the family's wishes, the exhausted Brooks grabbed some clothes, and went out into the gale storm to try to put together a line to help those stranded on the vessel. The lifeline was too short, so with quick thinking, he decided to run back to the house and stripped the beds of the cords that were used as support for bed boards under the mattresses and was able to splice enough cordage to get the line to the stranded crew.

One by one Keeper Brooks was able to bring them safely to shore in his little boat. With the efforts successful, instead of going right back to his warm bed, he helped with his family to create a Thanksgiving dinner to his grateful guests.

Oliver N. Brooks served as keeper at Faulkner's island lighthouse from 1851 to 1882. Nearly one hundred vessels were wrecked in the vicinity during his tenure, due to the extreme weather conditions surrounding the island, not from the lighthouse itself or the lighthouse keeper. He is credited with assisting in seventy-one of these events, whether the vessels were destroyed or partially wrecked.

Famous Rescue Dogs of the Keepers

The life of a lighthouse keeper and his family was very tedious and lonely in maintaining the lighthouse tower and surrounding buildings. Most keepers had at least one dog to keep them company as they performed their often grueling and tedious tasks. Some of these animals became famous in special behaviors like pulling fog bells to warn mariners of danger in bad weather, or in response to vessels saluting to the keepers as they passed by, or were directly involved in actual rescue attempts of survivors. Here are a few of the many stories told of man's best friend.

Egg Rock Lighthouse construction from 1856 in Massachusetts. *Courtesy of US Coast Guard.*

Milo at Egg Rock Light, in Massachusetts

George B. Taylor was the first Keeper at Egg Rock Lighthouse, located a mile off near Nahant, on the Massachusetts northern shore. When he brought his family to live on Egg Rock Island, in 1855, he also brought their loving dog, Milo. The canine was a breed mix between a Newfoundland and a St. Bernard making him a rather large animal. Although the lighthouse is no longer present today, the stories and famous painting of Milo have been preserved over the years.

As the masons were completing the finishing touches on the lighthouse, they were quite fond of the playful animal and left an opening in the masonry which served as Milo's private entranceway to the lighthouse.

Milo adapted rather easily to the wildlife on the island. He was a very good swimmer and very independent. One day, as Keeper Taylor took a shot at an approaching loon for dinner, Milo started a long chase after the wounded bird. The large animal was soon out of sight chasing the prize, as it would try to fly away.

Darkness approached and the keeper and his family feared that Milo had gotten into some kind of trouble in his escapade. The Taylors finally went to sleep fearing that the dog had drowned. The following afternoon Milo was sighted in the water heading towards the island from the Nahant shoreline. The dog had apparently missed sight of the tiny rock island and lighthouse in the night, and ended up on the

Painting *Saved* by Sir Edwin Landseer (1856).

shore of Nahant, where he stayed the night and then apparently swam to the island the next day.

In foggy weather, Milo would constantly bark at any vessels approaching the lighthouse, becoming an additional fog signal. Keeper Taylor claimed that Milo was involved with assisting in the rescue of several children from drowning near the island, although there hasn't been any verification of these rescue acts.

Milo was also a favorite of local fishermen, as they would come out to the lighthouse and tie large pieces of cod to pieces of driftwood and toss them in the water. The dog would swim out from the shore to retrieve the floating fish, which sometimes were sent adrift as far as a mile from the island, and then bring them to the Taylors. The Taylors would then cook the gifts for dinner that night.

Milo's fame spread across the Atlantic where he captivated the interest of a well-known English animal painter, Sir Edwin Henry Landseer. Landseer was granted permission by Keeper Taylor to create a painting of Milo with Taylor's young son, Fred, who willingly agreed to pose with the dog. The painting displayed Milo over a young child resting between the dog's large paws, as if the child had just been rescued. The painting, entitled *Saved*, became a powerful symbol of the lighthouse service and became internationally famous.

Today, Egg Rock lighthouse has been removed and the island is used as a bird sanctuary, due to the efforts of Massachusetts Senator Henry Cabot Lodge.

Sailor at Wood Island Light, in Maine

Keeper Thomas Orcutt tended Wood Island lighthouse in Maine from 1886 to 1909. Around 1894, they brought an 8-week old puppy to the lighthouse named Sailor, who was a Scotch Collie mix from a farm in nearby Westbrook, Maine. He became the lighthouse keeper's constant companion and an eager learner with the keeper's duties as he watched his master perform with precision.

In foggy weather, the bell was sounded as two strikes in succession to identify the lighthouse station to those captains entering the region and unable to see the lighthouse through the fog. Keeper Orcutt even taught the animal to wait roughly twenty-five seconds between rings as required by regulations. In fair weather, it was also customary for passing ships to salute the lighthouse keeper with three whistle blasts, to which the keeper would respond by ringing the fog bell.

Orcutt spent many days teaching Sailor all kinds of tricks, including ringing the fog bell when needed, which involved the circumstances necessary that gave the animal the chance to ring the bell. Whenever coastal fog blanketed the area, or when he heard a ship's whistle blowing, Sailor would eagerly run out of the lighthouse quarters, towards the fog bell, grab the rope in his mouth, and ring it with precision.

Wood Island Lighthouse tower in Maine.

Keeper Thomas Orcutt and his dog Sailor at Wood Island Lighthouse in Maine. *Courtesy of Jeremy D'Entremont for Roderick Jeffers.*

One of the first to observe Sailor ringing the bell was Captain Oliver of the Casco Bay Steamship Company when he took an excursion party of several hundred visitors aboard the *Forest Green* out to Wood Island. As he passed by the lighthouse, he gave it a customary three-whistle salute and witnessed the dog running to the fog bell with Keeper Orcutt close behind. Orcutt loosened up the rope to place within the dog's reach, as Sailor grabbed the rope with his teeth and pulled to ring the bell in response to the ship's whistle.

As months went by, Sailor would learn to only ring the bell during foggy weather, or in response to ship's whistles, or bells passing by. If a ship blew their whistle, Sailor would automatically run to the fog bell and ring it in response. In foggy weather, Sailor would faithfully stay at his post for hours at a time without leaving or complaining, and ring the bell precisely to identify Wood Island Lighthouse's location.

Sailor became quite famous to the local mariners over the years as the "Wood Island Dog." The ships would ring their bells or blow their whistles as they passed by the lighthouse, and then watch as the dog would run over to the bell and ring it in response. It would never be known of the number of countless vessels he helped during dangerous foggy weather from crashing on the rocks on or near the island. The animal was perfectly content to stay alongside Keeper Orcutt while he performed his duties, and was always excited when the opportunity arose to ring the bell. Sailor also was used as a messenger to carry letters and other small articles in his mouth, and was always a tourist attraction for vacationing boaters.

Sailor died of old age in Keeper Orcutt's arms in 1905. A few months later, Keeper Orcutt, deeply depressed at the loss of his companion, and getting along in years himself, resigned his post at Wood Island lighthouse and passed away shortly afterwards.

Spot at Owls Head Light, in Maine

Owls Head lighthouse sits atop a large rocky cliff guiding ships as they enter Rockland Harbor in Maine. In the 1930s, Keeper Augustus Hamor, of Owls Head Lighthouse had a special dog named Spot who was taught by his children to ring the fog bell by tugging on the rope to the bell with its teeth every time it heard a ships whistle. The dog's entire life seemed wrapped around the family at the lighthouse, the fog bell, and the ships that would pass by the lighthouse. Spot would spend the day watching for ships passing near the lighthouse, and then would ring the fog bell when they approached near the cliff to warn them of the impending danger. When the captain of the boat returned the fog signal, Spot happily would run down to the water and bark until the boat was out of earshot.

Spot's favorite vessel was the mail boat that would make daily runs to Matinicus Island, which was a long fifteen miles from the mainland. Because of its daily schedule, Spot knew the mail boat's engine sound and when it would pass by the lighthouse. Captain Stuart Ames of the mail boat was also very fond of the animal and its owners and would always bring special treats when he visited the Hamor family. Each time the mail boat passed Owls Head Lighthouse, the skipper would give a toot for Spot, and the dog would answer by ringing the fog bell.

One wintry stormy night a fierce blizzard pounded the Maine coast and covered it in a blanket of deep snow. Keeper Hamor stayed in the light tower but

Owls Head Lighthouse overlooking cliff in Maine.

visibility was poor with near white-out conditions from the storm. As the following day wore on, fewer vessels passed by the lighthouse as most had already found shelter in the nearby harbors. The fog bell was buried in deep snowdrifts and remained silent as no one could access it in the storm. As nightfall approached, Keeper Hamor felt it safe enough to leave the tower to quickly join his family for a much needed dinner.

As the Hamors were preparing to eat, the phone rang with a desperate call from Captain Ames' wife who indicated her husband was over two hours late and asked if he had passed by the lighthouse. The dog recognized the woman's voice and listened to her tone. Keeper Hamor replied he had not seen the mail boat. Knowing of Spot's keen listening abilities, she asked the keeper if he could allow Spot outside in the blizzard to see if he could hear her husband's whistle, which they gladly obliged.

Spot disappeared in the blinding snow and went down over to the fog bell to listen for the boat's whistle, he sniffed around but could not find the rope. He stayed around the bell buried in huge snowdrifts and returned back a half hour later, cold and tired. After warming by the fire, he grew restless, whining softly knowing something was wrong, as he had not heard the mail boat on schedule. A few hours passed as Spot prepared to fall asleep.

All of a sudden, Spot jumped up from his cozy warm area as he heard the distant whistle of the lost Matinicus mail boat, which was caught in the storm trying to get home. He pawed at the door to be let out, which Keeper Hamor reluctantly opened to the storm, as Spot ran out into the darkness. Lunging over the snowdrifts, Spot again was unable to find the rope to ring the fog bell, so he ran to the edge of the cliff barking constantly as loud as he could. Keeper Hamor and his daughter Pauline got dressed and followed the barking dog to the edge of the cliff in the snowdrifts. They could hear the faint whistle of the mail boat as Spot continued to bark and yelp while the boat came nearer through the storm. Spot would continue to bark as the boat neared the cliff. Captain Ames on the mail boat, hearing Spot's barking, gave three blasts of the whistle to signal back that he had heard the dog. Two hours later, Captain Ames' wife called to thank the Hamor family, and especially Spot, in helping her husband reach the harbor home, averting what could have been a disastrous situation.

Spot is credited with saving the captain and the mail boat that night and is buried near the fog bell he loved. Over the years as the fog bell was removed, and the grave lay in a place that the many visitors to the lighthouse could not find, in 2004, Spot was given a new marker by Paul Dilger, the Coast Guard commander who resided at the lighthouse. The marker read "Spot, The Lighthouse Dog" to remind those of the dog's heroic efforts.

Owls Head Lighthouse after winter storm in Maine.

Seaboy at Great Duck Island Light, in Maine

Great Duck Island Lighthouse was built in 1890, and at the time had three keeper's dwellings near the light. This proved quite helpful with one Keeper Nathan Reed, who had one of the largest families to tend a lighthouse with his wife and seventeen children. At one time, because of the large number of keeper's children on the island, a small school was established, the only such school for lighthouse children. There were no dogs or animals however, for the children to play with.

This story is told by many fishermen in Maine about the rescue of a dog and the love of that dog for the girl that took care of him.

Sometime around 1920, a fishing vessel wrecked near Great Duck Island; the crew had a rather large dog that accompanied them on their voyage. As the ship started to sink, the crew made haste onto a lifeboat and started to pull away. The dog leaped from the wreck and swam towards the lifeboat to join them. As the crew tried to bring him into the already crowded boat, his weight made the boat tip into the water, which scared one of the crew enough to push the animal away with an oar, injuring the frightened dog. The crew watched the poor animal sink into the water and presumed he had drowned.

When the lifeboat reached Great Duck Island, the lighthouse keeper and his wife gave the crew warm clothes and food to recover from their ordeal. With their strength regained, the keeper called for assistance to meet the crew on the mainland, as they headed for the shore.

The following day, the keeper's daughter was playing along the rocky shoreline when she noticed the dog washed up on the shore. The poor animal was covered in blood and barely alive. She quickly ran to get her parents to help her. The keeper and his wife ran down to the shore and wrapped the helpless animal in warm blankets and brought it back to the

Great Duck Island Lighthouse in Maine.

house. They watched over the dog for days and nursed it back to health. As the crew of survivors had already departed days before, the dog was quickly adopted by the family and named Seaboy.

As the weeks went by, the keeper's daughter became very fond of her new best friend and the two became inseparable. She held tea parties, dressed the animal in clothes, and read to Seaboy as any little girl would. The dog in turn would not leave her side, and slept by her bed each night. For over two years the dog kept the girl safe and happy at the lighthouse.

One day, a stranger came to the lighthouse and told the keeper that he was the captain of the crew that had wrecked near the lighthouse two years before. He had heard the animal had survived and was living at the lighthouse, and had come to retrieve the dog.

The little girl was beside herself when her parents reluctantly had to tell her to give up the dog to its rightful owner. As Seaboy was led onto the fisherman's dory, the girl fell into uncontrollable sobbing and could not bear to watch as the boat rowed away. All of a sudden, the dog leaped out of the boat and started the long swim back towards the shore where her adopted owners watched in disbelief. When Seaboy reached the shore he ran to the little girl's side, soaking wet and tired, but happy. The fisherman watched the animal swim back, waved good-bye to the family ashore and never returned to try to reclaim the dog again. Seaboy lived out the remainder of years on the island with the keeper's daughter. News of the story spread and later became the basis for a popular children's book called *Captain's Castaway*.

Smut at Two Bush Island Light, in Maine

The first Keeper of Two Bush Island Light, Altiverd Norton, had a famous dog named Smut, who became a hero when, during a March storm in 1902, a fishing schooner, the *Clara Bella*, started taking in water.

Keeper Norton and his family were asleep and could not hear anything, as any sounds were deafened by the fierce winds from the storm. The dog heard the wreck crash on the rocks and the men's cries for help. Sensing the danger, he started barking to awaken Keeper Norton, and started frantically scratching the door to be let out. Keeper Norton believed something had happened to create this unusual behavior in the dog. He let Smut outside and followed the animal down to the rocks where he could see from a distance a small dory with two men aboard. The men were desperately trying to find a way to land on the island when they heard Smut's frantic barking guiding them to the shoreline.

The dory the men took to escape from the schooner overturned from a huge wave, but Norton was able to get a line to the men and hauled them ashore to safety. The two survivors were brought into the lighthouse, and cared for. Keeper Norton told the men how Smut heard their cries, and the grateful survivors continued to hug the animal, thanking it and patting it in gratitude. They offered to purchase the dog at any cost, but the keeper could not let go of his favorite four-legged companion. He told them that Smut was priceless and could never give him up.

Two Bush Island Lighthouse in Maine.

Lighthouse Keepers Rescued by Flying Santa(s)
The Tradition that Started in Maine

Lighthouse crews would risk their lives to rescue those stranded on merchant vessels or local mariners caught in New England's unpredictable storms. Most of their time was spent performing the arduous and mundane tasks of maintaining the light stations they were assigned to manage. It was an extremely lonely and desolate life, not only for themselves, but for their families as well. Holidays were very difficult emotionally, especially for those stationed off the mainland, on islands or dangerous reefs as most lighthouses in New England were located. Sometimes they themselves and their families needed an "emotional rescue."

In the late 1920s, the concept of a "Flying Santa" to bring gifts and supplies to lighthouse keepers and their families was the idea of Captain William Wincapaw, a local native of Friendship, Maine. He was known in the region as an excellent pilot who was directly involved in saving lives of islanders of Penobscot Bay and would help transport those sick or injured to safety or to nearby hospitals even in inclement weather. In those days, he navigated the region using the lighthouse beacons all along the coastline and was always appreciative of the lighthouse keepers' dedication to their duties in maintaining the lights, as they were appreciative of the Captain for his rescue efforts.

When time and weather allowed, Captain Wincapaw would land his plane at various light stations and spend some time with the keepers. With his admiration and respect for the keepers and their families, he decided in 1929, that on Christmas morning, he would load up his plane with a dozen packages of newspapers, magazines, coffee, candy, and other small luxuries for his isolated friends in the Rockland region of Maine.

Christmas morning he woke up, loaded the presents, and proceeded to drop them by his lighthouse friends. He completed the task and spent the remainder of the day with his own family. Word got around rather quickly of this saintly gesture and he was so surprised of the outpouring of thanks from the keepers and the locals that he decided to make the venture each year, increasing his range to additional stations all along the northern New England coast.

Each year the flights of the "Flying Santa," as the locals called him, continued and expanded to the rest of New England's coastline. Captain Wincapaw decided to play the role of Santa in dressing up in costume, as he would deliver his gifts. Four years later, by 1933, they were delivering presents to ninety-one lighthouses and coast guard stations all along the New England coast. In 1934, his 16-year-old son, Bill Jr., became one of the youngest licensed pilots in Massachusetts, where the family

Holiday season at Nubble (Cape Neddick) Lighthouse in Maine.

had recently moved. He also became an excellent pilot under the direction of his father. That Christmas he joined in helping his father continue the tradition, and in 1935, would fly solo to some of the stations.

As the popular tradition was growing, in 1936, Bill Jr., introduced his father to one of his teachers at Winthrop High School, Edward Rowe Snow, who was a lighthouse enthusiast and New England maritime historian. Captain Wincapaw immediately took a liking to Snow, who wanted to help in Wincapaw's efforts. He arranged to have Snow assist his son in delivering the gifts to stations in southern New England.

Captain William Wincapaw.
Photo courtesy Wincapaw family.

In 1938, Captain Wincapaw was on a mission in Bolivia and was unable to make the trip back in time to deliver the gifts, but his son, assisted by Snow, made the trips without any problems to many grateful stations all along New England's coastline. The duo also delivered without the captain in 1940 as his duties with his employer kept him again in South America during the Christmas season. Bill Wincapaw, Jr. was also getting involved in helping his father in South America afterwards and Snow found himself stepping into the captain's shoes to continue the famous tradition. Snow, who was not a pilot, would spend his own money to hire one, as he would drop off the gifts, hopefully near their designated targets.

As WWII broke out, Captain Wincapaw and his son were called to duty to aid in the war effort. Snow was also called to duty in 1942 and was wounded during a bombing mission in Northern Africa unable to continue the tradition that year as he lay in a foreign hospital bed. He was discharged in 1943 because of his wounds. Due to the uneasiness and tension all along the coast that year, it was becoming doubtful as to whether Snow would be able to deliver the gifts. He was finally granted permission just before Christmas and again hired a pilot and delivered bundles all along the New England coast to the grateful families.

By 1945, with the end of the war, the tradition was back in full force as Snow's wife started to accompany him all along the New England coast. Wiggins Airways, hearing of the gracious efforts, donated prop planes and helicopters, with additional pilots to help continue and expand the efforts to more lighthouse stations. Sponsors would also get involved in providing the necessary gifts for the expanding program.

One of the well-known stories that show Snow's big heartedness for the keepers occurred just after the war. During the Christmas season of 1945, Keeper Octave Ponsart's five-year old daughter, Seaborn, had heard that Santa would be flying over with a special doll for her. Her mother had written previously to Edward Snow that her daughter would love a little doll from the flying Santa. Snow made sure he had a doll for the little girl in the three packages he had planned to drop to the Cuttyhunk Lighthouse where the family was stationed. The family was ready for the drop, and kept their two dories prepared in case any of the packages ended up in the pond nearby, or in the ocean. As Snow threw out three packages, one landed in the pond where Keeper Ponsart launched the dory and retrieved the heavily wrapped package. The other two packages landed on the ground but one landed on a huge boulder. When the little girl opened the package that had hit the boulder, she found the doll that had been promised to her was smashed to pieces. The girl was devastated and finally cried herself to sleep that night. Her father fixed the doll as best he could with tape, glue, band-aids and slings and Seaborn called the doll her "play-sick doll."

A few months later, in 1946, Keeper Ponsart received news that Cuttyhunk Lighthouse was being condemned and would have to be torn down, and the family would have to move to West Chop Lighthouse on Martha's Vineyard that year. This was difficult for the Ponsart's realizing they were the last family to tend Cuttyhunk Lighthouse, and having to pack up all their belongings to stay at another lighthouse. Meanwhile, Snow had heard of the sad news from Seaborn's mother about the doll and promised that he would be bringing Seaborn a new doll in December at their new location.

On December 12, 1946, he made arrangements to dress in Santa costume and charter a helicopter from Wiggins Airways to land at Gay Head Station on Martha's Vineyard. He then took a horse-drawn cart to West Chop Lighthouse to personally deliver another doll to the little girl. A helicopter was never used for commercial purposes, as it was extremely expensive, but Snow paid for the deed and felt it was worth the effort and the expense, especially from the big hugs he received from the little girl. Seaborn kept in contact through the years with the Snow family, and continues to maintain contact with Snow's daughter.

On July 16, 1947, as Captain Wincapaw was taking off from Rockland Harbor with a passenger, Robert Muckenhirn; he suffered a heart attack in the air and the plane crashed in the ocean, killing both men. As the memorial service began on the afternoon of July 19, keepers sounded foghorns and bells that would be heard across Penobscot Bay in respect for the original lighthouse flying Santa. Many keepers, their families, and islanders attended the service in gratitude for his services. That December, Snow would drop a memorial wreath in Rockland Harbor in honor of his close friend.

Snow continued to carry on the now-famous tradition of delivering Christmas bundles to stations all along the New England coast and expanded the delivery to 176 lighthouses in 1947. Over the years, during many of the flights, he would still hire a pilot out of his own pay, and he and his wife would enjoy the satisfaction of their efforts as repayment. They had a daughter who would also accompany them on their flights as part of the family tradition. Wiggins Airways also helped in providing planes, and later helicopters, and occasionally provided pilots to help the Snows. On a few excursions, the Coast Guard would provide Snow with one of their own aircraft to help him with his expanding deliveries. Packages would continue to be provided by the many sponsors, and Snow began to write books about New England stories and lighthouses, which he would also provide for the keepers and their families.

As there were rare occasions of a risk of a package missing its target and destroying property, Snow still had to carry rather expensive insurance for his endeavors. Although the fifteen- to twenty-five- pound packages would usually land on their target, there were some instances where some property was destroyed and the insurance would cover the mishap, with most

Edward Snow with Seaborn Ponsart presenting gift. *Photo courtesy Jeremy D'Entremont for Dolly Snow Bicknell.*

of the "victims" recalling the experience to their families in a humorous manner. On many flights, as he would open the window to drop the gifts in his Santa costume, his fake whiskers would be blown off his face with the fierce winds. During one of his drops, they had quite a scare when two packages tied to a rope lodged themselves around the tail of the airplane near Boon Island Lighthouse in York, Maine. They were able to safely make an emergency landing safely at nearby Portsmouth, New Hampshire.

In 1953, Snow decided to fly a transcontinental Santa flight that would not only include New England stations, but also stations in California and Oregon. In 1954, he expanded his flights to include Bermuda, the Great Lakes, and a remote location known as Sable Island about 100 miles from Nova Scotia. He arrived near the destination by seaplane, and then took a horse-drawn wagon to the lighthouse where he presented gifts to three children and twenty-three grateful adults on the tiny remote island.

In the 1970s, Snow also chartered boats to help with his tasks. In 1974, with much inclement weather, only some of the gifts could be distributed, and many trips had to be cancelled, as many airports were snowbound. This hadn't happened since the war era of the 1940s. During the 1970s air space was very restricted with increasing FAA regulations and Snow found himself using a helicopter to deliver the bundles, as he had done once many years before in 1946 to deliver an unbroken doll to the keeper's daughter, Seaborn Ponsart, on Martha's Vineyard. The children and their families enjoyed the new spectacle as many times the helicopter would come very close or could land nearby.

By 1981, Snow was getting along in years and suffered a stroke, which was going to prevent him from dropping off any bundles that year. Judeth Van Hamm, director of the Hull Lifesaving Museum, approached Snow's wife to offer any assistance. With the blessing of Ana-Myrle Snow, and with a limited budget and

Snow flying over Boston Lighthouse (1947). *Photo courtesy Jeremy D'Entremont for Dolly Snow Bicknell.*

time to coordinate the undertaking, the museum was able to acquire the service of three helicopters from a local Boston television station, Wheelabrator-Frye of Maine, and the International Fund of Animal Welfare of Yarmouthport, Massachusetts. A new Santa, Ed McCabe, offered his services to carry on the tradition. Although the numbers of flights were limited compared to previous years,

Logo of Friends of Flying Santa. *Image courtesy Brian Tague of Friends of Flying Santa.*

and as many lighthouses were automated, it was greatly appreciated by those lucky recipients of the gifts.

On April 12, 1982, Snow passed away at the age of 79. He had written over ninety books on maritime history from shipwrecks, to pirates, to lighthouse stories, and remained as one of the Flying Santa's for nearly forty-four years. He is also remembered as the driving force in saving Fort Warren, a famous Civil War fort on George's Island in Boston Harbor, to be maintained as a public park for all to enjoy and remember the efforts of those veterans who fought in that war. In 2000, a granite marker was placed at the pavilion as a memorial to Snow for visitors on George's Island. It reads "Author, Historian, and 'Flying Santa.'" His efforts and writings about New England's history and folklore remain in the hearts of all who have been touched by the limitless generosity to his fellow friends.

The Hull Lifesaving Museum answered the call and continued the tradition of the Flying Santas. As years passed, other good Samaritans would follow Snow's path and become Flying Santas, helping to increase the number of flights. Although the stops would be brief, they would try to manage extra flights to additional lighthouses when at all possible. More local and corporate sponsors would provide gifts for the children to help with the efforts. In the late 1980s, local Boston news station, WCVB-TV 5, would help out the museum by providing a helicopter and much-needed public exposure. It is still involved with the Flying Santa events in Massachusetts today.

By 1997, the Flying Santa program was transferred from the Hull Lifesaving Museum to a non-profit group of volunteers calling themselves the Friends of Flying Santa. This non-profit organization would help to ensure a stable financial future in keeping the program alive, and developed the official red logo to help with fundraising efforts on clothing and novelty items.

Nowadays, it is an event where many of the lighthouses chosen, are many of the same lighthouses Captain Wincapaw and Edward Snow had flown over to deliver gifts from as far back as eighty years ago. Many sponsors still donate gifts to help with continuing this annual tradition. Since 1996, Chief Warrant Officer David Waldrip, USCG, and Chief Warrant Officer

Tom Guthlein, USCG, have become the current Flying Santas. Pilots who have helped with the flights for the flying Santas include Tom Clegg, Paul Ellis, Tony Liss, George Louzek, Art Godjikian, LaRay Todd, Leo Boucher, and Greg Harville.

Today, the Flying Santa comes down in a helicopter and calls out the name of children in attendance and presents them with a little gift to continue the annual tradition. It's an exciting experience enjoyed by adults and children alike. This annual event is promoted and scheduled to remind people of the many personnel that came before to tend the lights, and for the Flying Santas that made the process a part of their lives to help those lighthouse and Coast Guard families in need of Christmas cheer. The events are used today as a simple expression of gratitude for the work performed by the Coast Guard. Their website at www.flyingsanta.com keeps the public informed of events and helps in their efforts to raise funds for this wonderful program.

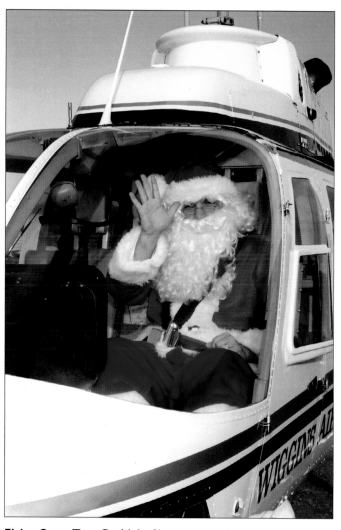

Flying Santa Tom Guthlein. *Photo courtesy of Brian Tague.*

Amusing Stories of One of the Last Surviving Lighthouse Keepers

Sometimes in life opportunities are presented, or we follow our gut feelings and things just happen to come together. I was at a family gathering and was excited about writing this book of lighthouse stories when my brother-in-law, who happens to live a couple of hours away in New Hampshire's White Mountains, approached me and told me that he had an employee whose father was one of last surviving lighthouse keepers. What was even more astounding is that this man lived with his wife about a half hour down the coast from where I lived with my family in New Hampshire. I thought to myself, "What are the odds of this particular situation?" I was very excited and asked him to have this person contact me to see if it would be possible to have an informal chat and write about his father, Paul Baptiste.

A short time later his son, John, sent me an e-mail. He was also very excited and informed me that his parents would love the opportunity to talk about their life stationed at various lighthouses and lifesaving stations. Paul Baptiste is one of the few remaining lighthouse keepers of his era. His stories encompass lighthouses and lifesaving stations where he lived with his family through most of New England's states.

Paul married his childhood sweetheart, Helen, when they were both in their late teens and began a new family during World War II. As was expected in their day, especially during the beginning of World War II, Paul enlisted in the service. His occupation was that of a Seaman patrolling the shores of Block Island located about twelve miles from Rhode Island's mainland. He was stationed at the Block Island Life Saving Station, also referred as the Block Island Surf Station, between Block Island North and Block Island Southeast lighthouses. There was much heightened security and fear of enemy boats in the area as the War progressed. He and another Seaman were each provided with revolvers, which they carried with them as they would patrol nine-mile stretches of shoreline, keeping an eye out for anything suspicious.

On one of their patrols in 1942, it was just at daybreak and a thick fog had rolled in, blocking much of their view of the ocean and surrounding shoreline. All of a sudden, they heard a strange foreign language being spoken off shore from a vessel close by. As the area was considered restricted, they feared that an enemy craft was trying to get ashore. They sounded the

Monhegan Island Lighthouse in Maine.

alarm, and soon additional forces along the beach and PT boats from the ocean side surrounded the craft still encompassed in the blanket of fog. As the fog started to lift, and as all had their guns pointed at the vessel fearing a possible attack, they found it was an Italian fishing boat of very frightened crewmembers that had ventured in the fog too near the base.

Paul remained at Block Island Life Saving station until 1944, where he was transferred to Lightship #106 located just outside busy Boston Harbor for a number of months. He was then transferred up to Greenland until the end of the war. With the end of the war, and the love for the sea, he decided he wanted to be a lighthouse keeper and raise his family at a lighthouse. He went to the Coast Guard office for a letter of recognition to be enlisted in the lighthouse service, and they told him that all he had to do was re-enlist and he could choose between two open positions: one at Boston Harbor Lighthouse, and the other at Baker's Island Light near Salem, Massachusetts. Excited, he went to the Coast Guard Base Station for more information. There, a young Coast Guardsman told Paul that when storms approached, Boston Harbor Lighthouse, being closer to sea level, and nearer the water's edge, would become awash from breaking waves at times, and there was little land for children to play. The enlisted man informed Paul that he could swim to Baker's Island from the mainland and it was much flatter and higher above sea level than Boston Harbor Light. The area surrounding the lighthouse also included more enclosed land for the children to play in, and there were frequent summer residents who would stay at nearby cottages. Paul and Helen decided not to raise their family at the historic prestigious Boston Harbor Light, but to have Paul become the Assistant Keeper of Baker's Island lighthouse, because it was the best fit for their family. As was the case with many of their decisions, Paul and Helen always put their family first.

Upon reaching Baker's Island, they realized the lighthouse was located more than three miles from Salem Harbor, which would be a long swim indeed. A short time later Paul saw the young Coast Guardsman again and asked how was he able to swim to Baker's Island Light from shore. The Coast Guardsman responded that he would stop at two other islands along the way, which he had previously neglected to tell the new keeper.

Paul and Helen were still very glad to have picked Baker's Island Light. They came to the light with two small boys, Bill and Paul, and had two more children during their five-year stay from 1946-1951. The children had plenty of room for their playground and enjoyed life on the island. Life was never dull at Baker's Island in that, during the summer months, the island would have its residents coming to stay at

Paul and Helen Baptiste before their wedding in 1943. *Image courtesy of Baptiste family.*

Sons Bill and Paul Jr. in Baker's Island wooden rescue boat with Paul in the background. *Image courtesy of Baptiste family.*

Baker's Island Lighthouse in Boston Harbor, Salem, Massachusetts.

their cottages, and then during the off season, the residents would leave the island for many months, allowing the Baptiste family and the other keeper to enjoy the island all to themselves,

During the warm weather months, their friend Edward Rowe Snow, also known as the "Flying Santa" during the holiday season, would bring tourists (known as "day trippers") to Baker's Island to meet the family and explore the lighthouse grounds. Paul and Helen were quite popular for these guests who would visit the lighthouse, as they had a flushing toilet on the island. Many of the elder tourists especially, would frequently ask to use the Baptiste's toilet to relieve themselves. At times there were long lines of grateful people to the popular commode.

During the first two years of lighthouse service on Bakers Island, Paul used a wooden rowboat for rescue as the early lighthouses keepers did. Afterwards, he was provided a twenty-foot, motorboat for rescue. The harbor was filled with sail boaters of all abilities from Marblehead and Salem, and there were many regattas during the busy summer season. During the tourist season, in addition to his regular duties of maintaining the lighthouse, he was kept rather busy helping out with rescues of the many sailboats that would get caught in the gusty New England winds and be blown over. Other rescues involved retrieving some of the older fishing boats and lobster boats to shore when their engines would give out. For his efforts, he and his family had an endless supply of lobsters whenever they wanted.

There was always plenty of work to do. As keeper, a typical day for Paul in securing the lighthouse involved cleaning the lens, polishing the brass, engine room maintenance, and charging the storage batteries. In those days, a uniform was not needed and he wore his normal clothes. About every ten days, he would need to leave before daybreak to get supplies in the mainland. He would usually try to return to the lighthouse by 10 a.m., as the seas would start to get rough. Helen would help him tie the boat and set up the towline to haul it to the boathouse. They sometimes placed seaweed on the ramp to make the move easier. Helen was mainly busy tending to their growing family, washing the daily laundry and hanging them to dry in the wind, preparing meals, and chasing the children around their home, which she loved.

One day, in 1947, Paul decided to whitewash the lighthouse. He secured himself on a seated piece of scaffolding consisting of a couple of boards tied to a rope hanging from the top of the tower, to a jeep on the ground. As he would need to be lowered to start the next area to whitewash, the jeep driver would simply put the vehicle in reverse and back it up just enough so he could start to whitewash the next area. The jeep was parked on an incline as the event drew family members and locals to the scene. A photograph was taken of Paul dangling from the tower whitewashing the lighthouse. As he was about a third of the way down the tower, the jeep slipped out of gear and started rolling down the hill, sending the very frightened keeper up the tower towards the lantern room. Luckily one of his helpers jumped into the jeep to stop it just in time. Paul was not hurt and it remains was one of his favorite stories.

Paul Baptiste whitewashing Baker's Island Lighthouse.
Image courtesy of Baptiste family.

A family member once gave the Baptiste family twelve chickens and a rooster thinking they would get plenty of fresh eggs. As the days passed, the chickens hardly ever laid any eggs and the indignant rooster became the source of the blame. Maybe it was the dog food they fed them. All was not lost as the family decided to add some local meat in their diets, so they had the rooster and his entourage plucked, chopped, and stuffed for future dinners. "They tasted good though," remarked Paul.

Sometimes, it was customary for keepers to help one another out if one needed to go ashore for a few days for special supplies or for medical reasons. Keeper Powell of Conimicut Lighthouse, which is located about a mile offshore on an isolated tiny rock ledge near Warwick, Rhode Island, needed to head to shore for a couple of days and Paul obliged to help tend the light. The grateful keeper left his wife behind and Paul stayed in one of the other rooms under the lantern room.

The first night he slept soundly and spent the day maintaining the light. The second night, the keeper's wife asked if he had seen the ghost of Mrs. Smith. She proceeded to inform him that a previous keeper's wife had committed suicide in the room Paul was sleeping in and she had seen her ghost. This new revelation scared him so much that he stayed awake all that night. He never saw any ghost, but was glad to have the Conimicut Light keeper return that following day. Paul never returned to the light again. The suicidal wife mentioned might have been Nellie Smith, wife of Keeper Ellsworth Smith, who killed herself and her two children in 1922, out of loneliness and desperation from living at the isolated structure for over a year.

On Baker's Island, the Baptiste family became friends with Edward Rowe Snow, New England's flying Santa at the time who would drop presents to lighthouse families all over New England during the lonely holiday season. Each year Edward Snow would have presents dropped to Baker's Island Lighthouse kids. One time they put out a huge sign that read "Hi Santa" for Snow as he flew by the lighthouse to drop presents. Paul and his family are also in some of the movies and photos Edward Snow made while in the air to document the events. Paul and Helen remark that their favorite place they stayed at was Baker's Island Lighthouse, with their four children.

By 1951, Paul and Helen were looking for a schoolhouse or someplace where there was a school nearby for their growing family. Paul requested to be placed in Rhode Island, but ended up at Monhegan Island Lighthouse in Maine, due to a keeper who had just quit unexpectedly. Monhegan Island is located eleven miles from the Maine shore. Not knowing what to expect, the family packed up and headed up the quiet coastline, out to the end of one Maine's tranquil peninsulas, then took a ferry out to the island. When they arrived, they found, unlike Baker's Island Light, a rather large beautiful isolated island where the islanders stayed year round. There was a one-room schoolhouse on the island that still exists today.

Upon meeting the local islanders, they found the inhabitants were very resistant to any changes and were very particular in maintaining life on the island as it been for many years previously. One week, Paul was given orders to paint the lighthouse lantern room red and the rails green. A few days after he completed preparing and painting the structure, an elderly islander told him he couldn't paint the room any color but traditional black. Paul said he was only following orders as he was told by his commander to complete the task. A few days later, Paul's commander left a communication to paint the lantern and rails black. Apparently the islander had some pull with the commander.

Monhegan Island
Lighthouse in Maine.

On Monhegan Island, the year-round islanders needed to conserve water as often as possible, leaving little water for showers. The water stored was used mainly for drinking especially during the winter months. When the Baptiste family first arrived, one of the lobstermen commented to them, "Don't take showers all winter," and explained the reasoning. The family spent the winter in their warmest clothes as New England's cold and freezing weather descended on the island. They obliged their local neighbors and would wait until spring before they could take any showers. When the weather improved, Paul would perform carpentry on the side to make some extra income. Although life was quite different in that they were among the islanders year round, they became quite fond of their neighbors, and their neighbors, in turn, appreciated the new lighthouse family.

The family developed a deep appreciation and respect for the Maine lobstermen in the Monhegan region. Here, there was one of the richest lobster beds in the world, and by law, they were allowed to catch the treasured prizes from one minute after midnight on December 31, until midnight on June 30 each year. They were a very tight group of hard workers who would always watch out for another. They were unselfish in that if one lobsterman couldn't go out due to severe illness, the other lobstermen would get the word out and would not go out as well. It was a strict code of honor that still endures today.

Paul's daily duties at Monhegan Island Light involved tending to the incandescent oil and vapor light known as an IOV. Standing inside the huge second order Fresnel lens, he would polish the numerous glass prisms. He would fill up the oil tank and wind up the weights, which rotated on solid brass wheels that he had to routinely replace.

In the early 1950s, the entire island was using kerosene for illumination and there was no electricity. Paul had a generator at the lighthouse, which was only used to pump water to the building. He asked for, and was granted permission to use the generator for electricity for the first floor of the keeper's house. He was able to complete the job, which cast a very bright light from the room. The locals saw this new brighter illumination coming from the lighthouse keeper's quarters and asked him what kind of light he was using. He simply replied that he was using a special type of kerosene lamp.

In 1952, Paul, who had now been using the generator for electricity in the house, bought and installed the first TV on the island. He then installed an antenna on top of the roof, which annoyed some of his local neighbors. He pointed the antennae out towards the sea and was able to pick up stations from as far away as North Carolina. Some of the locals

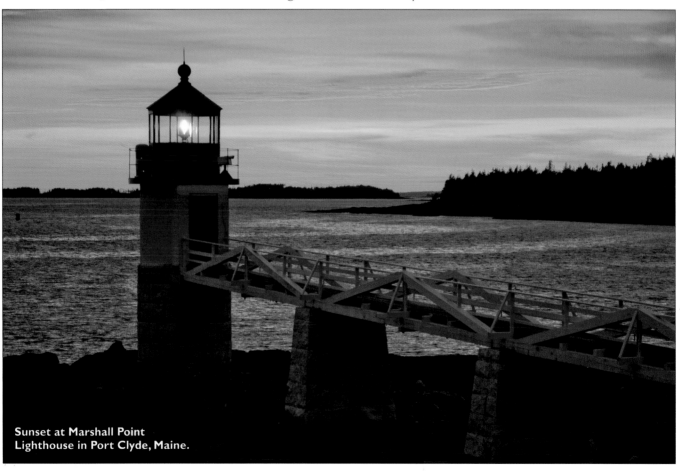

Sunset at Marshall Point Lighthouse in Port Clyde, Maine.

asked him what was on his roof, as they probably felt it was disturbing the scenery. He told them he had a TV and they responded in amazement, "You have a TV?" He became quite popular as many locals stopped in to see what shows were playing on the new black box.

The Baptistes kept their car parked by the keeper's house at Marshall Point Light on the mainland at Port Clyde and were close to the families that stayed there. They would have a willing replacement brought in to watch and tend Monhegan Light, as they would take the ferry to Port Clyde to pick up supplies or visit. Sometimes they would miss the ferry and enjoy an overnight stay at the keeper's house at Marshall Point Light, where they might enjoy some of Maine's most majestic sunsets. Their favorite replacement would sometimes even call and say, "Hey do you need to go to the mainland?" so he could go out and enjoy sightseeing at Monhegan. It was a win-win situation for all.

School life for the children in the one-room schoolhouse was quite different than for most of us when we grew up. If the teacher didn't feel like coming to class, he would just close the school for the day. One teacher had a strange name, Noellen, and sometimes would be teased by the students as the local "mammas boy." If he was angry with the children, or wanted to just stay home for the day, he simply kept the schoolhouse door locked and the kids would have the day off.

Sometimes, during recess, the children would go out back and sit on a large flat rock, watch the waves surround them, and sometimes would get drenched during high tide. One of the eldest sons remembers playing with a young boy who would come to the island for a while in the one-room schoolhouse in summer, would play with them all over the island, then would return to his home in New York. That child, James Barstol, is currently the owner of the Monhegan Boat line that makes daily trips to Monhegan Island during the fair weather months and tourist season. The one-room schoolhouse was not only used to educate the children, it was also used to host dances for everyone.

Years before the Baptiste family arrived on Monhegan Island, the tugboat *Sheridan* got caught in a storm in the 1940s, and crashed on the rocky beach at the south end of the island. The tug wreck was one of the favorite places for all the kids to play. The tug is still wrecked on the shore today and is known as one of the many attractions on this beautiful rocky island.

One time, during the summer of 1953, the three Baptiste brothers – Paul, Bill, and Tom – found this huge heavy nut about the size of a gallon of milk while playing on the hull of the wreck. The giant

Monhegan Island's one room schoolhouse today.

nut probably was a spare for the ship's propeller shaft. For some unknown reason, the boys decided that this metal object had to come home with them to the light station. This was no simple feat as the chunk was over a mile away from the lighthouse, and was very heavy. The three boys rolled it, carried it, and dragged the nut all the way from the southern end of the island where the tugboat lay, through the tiny village, past the post office, past the one-room schoolhouse, up the rugged hill to the lighthouse station. The new heavy toy remained on their sun porch for the better part of a year with all the other toys.

In early October, of 1954, the Baptistes got the news that they were transferring from Monhegan Island to Watch Hill Light in Rhode Island. The brothers decided to roll the weighty metal nut out to the edge of a cliff by the flagpole, and let it roll off into the brush some distance below. Luckily, the nut didn't make it as far as the Island Cemetery. From 1954-2009, the brothers were the only ones who knew the location of the metal chunk. In 2009, one of the brothers, Bill, visited the island with his daughter and her family and told them the nut story. They searched for the nut in the brush but it was two thick with over fifty years of growth to find the elusive object. Bill plans to return again soon for another search of the massive chunk of metal.

Monhegan Island has been a community for artists for centuries and still is. Near the top of the hill from the lighthouse, Paul saw this dead tree and decided to cut it down. He brought two of his sons to help him as he succeeded in removing the annoying site from his lighthouse. The next day, two men approached him in tears. Fearing something was wrong, he asked why they were so upset. They replied that someone

Artist painting at Monhegan Island Lighthouse, Maine.

had cut down their tree. He responded he was the guilty person as they remarked that they had been spending many hours painting the dead tree as part of the scenery.

The famous rowboat that appears next to the lighthouse that has been painted and photographed for many years was not at the lighthouse during the Baptiste's tenure. Paul remarked that it was put there by local artists and would never have been used by them, as the lighthouse was located quite a distance from the shoreline up a hill.

Their "Flying Santa" friend, Edward Rowe Snow, would still attempt to drop packages at Monhegan Island during the holiday season. Most of the time, due to the lighthouse's location, he missed his mark and the locals picked up the presents instead to bring to the Baptiste family. They had also met a famous lighthouse keeper's wife, Connie Small, who wrote a book of her experiences in her nineties. They had a special appreciation for her as she was stationed on lighthouses that were on isolated tiny "rock islands" as opposed to their stations where they had plenty of land to explore and play.

The Baptiste family stayed on Monhegan Island until 1954. Tourists would visit the island and the lighthouse from Memorial Day weekend until Columbus Day weekend; then most of the island would again belong to the natives themselves. The locals called these people "day-trippers." Many years later, one of the elder sons, now a middle-aged adult, came back to visit the lighthouse he had grown up in. He happened to visit one of the few local stores when he

**Paul and Helen Baptiste,
enjoying each other's company.**

heard one of the locals refer to him in a tired negative tone as a "day-tripper." Upon hearing the comment, the son decided to correct the elder lobsterman in commenting that he was one of keeper Paul Baptiste's sons who had grown up in the lighthouse. Upon hearing the news the atmosphere quickly changed to a hero's welcome with everyone in the building welcoming him home.

After Mohegan Island, Paul was briefly stationed at Watch Hill Light right after Hurricane Carol passed through demolishing much of the seawall structure. He then went to other assignments and ended his twenty-year career in 1962, at the Hampton Life Saving Station, on New Hampshire's seacoast. He and Helen still reside in Hampton and are now in their late 80s. They have been happily married for over sixty-eight years. They have nine children, which Helen remarks were great kids growing up, and they are proud of their family. One of their granddaughters was born on their anniversary, one of their daughters is a marine biologist who recently discovered a new species of sea worm, which is aptly named after her, and another daughter was born on Paul's birthday. One of their daughters lives near Gurnet Lighthouse in Plymouth, Massachusetts. Their nine children are spread around the country but visit their parents often, as I had the opportunity to meet three when I visited. Three of their older sons went to Monhegan's one-room schoolhouse and have great stories of their own regarding the experience. Their children loved island life, as did Paul and Helen. Both Paul and Helen remember fondly of Baker's Island Light as their favorite place to raise their family.

A few years ago, Paul and Helen went to tour Portsmouth Harbor Lighthouse in New Hampshire with the Friends of Portsmouth Harbor Light. There, Paul was quoted as saying,

Those were the good old days. You're living at home twenty-four hours a day, seven days week, raising your family, taking care of the lighthouse.

Paul's character embodies how we should view those who serve in the Coast Guard and in all branches of our military today: the love of country and the unselfish duty of helping out their fellow man. Thank you for your service.

As the population along the New England coastline dramatically increased in the early eighteenth century, this in turn created many shipping ports to accommodate the shipping trades coming into the region. With New England's numerous surprising and violent storms, many shipwrecks occurred on the plentiful ledges, reefs, shoals, and sandbars that populated the New England coastline. As these wrecks became more frequent in the eighteenth and early nineteenth centuries, many petitions were filed for some kind of warning fire or reflective device to help mariners from getting stranded, evolving into what we call today as our lighthouses. Many locals would become involved during this early period in using lanterns from someone's house, or putting a lit fire inside a tar-filled barrel, and they would leave food and survival materials that might help shipwreck victims stranded on a ledge or island.

During the nineteenth century and into the twentieth century, with the expansion of shipping and tourism, integrating the combination of cargo and passengers became a standardized and sometimes dangerous practice. The number of shipwrecks and disasters that occurred from New England's inclement weather also increased dramatically. After the Civil War, there were three branches of marine rescue service that were established to aid those in distress. They were the Lighthouse Service, the Life Saving Service, and the Revenue Cutter Service. Lightships, under the Lighthouse Service, were used as mobile floating lighthouses at dangerous locations, or in busy shipping channels where it was not possible to build a lighthouse. This profession became the most perilous due to the fact that the floating lightships were in the path of ships as they signaled, and hopefully the oncoming ship would veer away in time to avoid collision, which did not always happen. Both the Lighthouse and Life Saving branches were responsible under the US Lighthouse Service.

Although this period created a significant expansion of lighthouses, lightships, lifesaving stations, and revenue cutters to meet the demanding needs of the growing population along the eastern coast, some of New England's worst disasters still occurred from New England's many devastating storms. Many incidents occurred in most cases, as a direct result of human error, or stemming from few, if any, regulations in regards to proper safety of cargo and passengers.

New England Maritime Disasters That Pioneered Travel Safety

Beginning in the 1870s, the use of successfully coordinated rescue efforts between all three branches played key roles in saving more lives during many of New England's maritime wrecks. In 1915, Congress finally combined the services into what we now know as the Coast Guard.

This section of special stories provides a glimpse into some of those famous, and at most times tragic, events that occurred offshore from New England lighthouses. These stories, although some may be heart wrenching, also demonstrate not only accounts individually, and of coordinated efforts between the three branches of rescue service, but also efforts of local mariners, passengers and survivors, and captains of steamships who would risk their lives to help those in peril.

From many of these incidents, new tougher safety regulations, techniques, and practices would be developed to ensure the safety of future travelers that are still being used today.

Marina Sunset, New Castle near Portsmouth, New Hampshire.

The Wreck of the *Nottingham Galley*

On Boon Island, in Maine

Boon Island is a tiny rock island that lies only a few feet above water at high tide. It is roughly located about six miles from the shoreline of York, Maine. During the seventeenth and eighteenth centuries, many shipwrecks occurred there, where mariners would find themselves stranded on the rocks, only to be washed away from rogue waves breaking over the island, or perish from prolonged exposure to the elements. The wreck of the *Nottingham Galley*, though its story is horrific in nature, was one of the early incidents before lighthouses were built that spawned the need for assistance in constructing some type of warning device to help those who may find themselves wrecked on New England's coastline.

The Captain's Account

The story begins as the *Nottingham Galley* set sail for Boston from England on September 25, 1710. The first account by one of the survivors, the Captain,

Boon Island Lighthouse, York, Maine.

John Dean, was written after they were rescued and recovering at a local tavern. He wrote that the *Nottingham Galley* had been through a grueling and slow voyage hampered by storms and bad weather carrying a load of cordage and cheese.

On December 11, 1710, the *Nottingham Galley* was caught up in a winter nor'easter, being dashed about through sleet, snow, and heavy seas. The vessel crashed and sank off the rock known as Boon Island. At the time, all fourteen sailors, officers, and passengers survived and were able to make it to safety onto the icy rock island. The only items salvaged just before the wreck sank were a few small pieces of soggy cheese, pieces of torn sail, and some canvas. That night, the drenched men endured a freezing night of wind, sleet, and snow pounding the island. They made a triangle tent from the parts of the sail and canvas, and the men huddled as close together as possible to conserve heat in trying to avoid prolonged exposure to the elements.

By noon the second day, the ship's cook perished from exposure, and from an illness he had acquired while on the voyage. The crew's feet and hands were numb and starting to succumb to frostbite. They had to try to remove some of their freezing boots and clothing to expose their limbs to the cold to dry their skin. They tried to wrap their feet in parts of canvas and rope fibers to deter the discoloration.

The crew could see smoke from houses some six miles away on shore, but there were no trees or any means to create a fire on the hopeless piece of rock to signal anyone ashore of their plight, or to provide heat in the winter weather. For food, they finished off the soggy cheese within days, and then ate any kelp and rockweed sparingly, with three mussels a day rationed until the frozen supply was exhausted after a week. After the food had run out, two of the crew perished from exposure and starvation.

Captain Dean also reported that the crew, knowing that no one on shore six miles away would be able to see them in the winter weather, decided to build a crude boat to launch to shore. The ship's carpenter was extremely ill and was unable to assist in the effort. Captain Dean chose four men, including himself, to launch the craft and get help. As they started to launch it, a huge rogue wave came over it and smashed it on the rocks.

The men were now starving as their tiny rations of mussels and seaweed were not enough to survive. Their hopes were devastated from the loss of the boat, but with the help from one of their determined crewmembers, written only as the "Swede," they built a raft made of debris from whatever was left they could salvage from the wreckage. They elected two men, one being the Swede, to go on the raft and try to find help. They launched the craft amid high seas with instructions to light a fire on shore once they made it to signal their comrades on the island. As the raft came within a few miles of the mainland, it overturned and the two men perished in the icy waters.

Days went by and no sign of the raft making the shore was given. Food was unavailable, except some frozen seaweed as the end of December was approaching, nearly two weeks after the incident. The carpenter, who was too ill to help with the construction of the crude boat that was destroyed, perished from illness and exposure. The men, who were by now driven to madness by starvation, came to the captain with a plea to eat the flesh of their comrade to survive. Captain Dean, after much moral deliberation, decided to allow this horrific act to hopefully survive a few more days, with the hope that someone would find them soon before they all would perish.

He proceeded to slice the flesh for the crew, dip it in the salt water, and members placed the meat in between pieces of seaweed. The men ate so ravenously that Captain Dean became very concerned they would devour the corpse in one day. He removed the body and stored it a safe distance from the tent away from the crew. He proceeded to deal out the ghoulish delight in small portions each day. The captain would later write of the change into irrational behavior of the men, as they became fierce and reckless, and were becoming the most "pitiful objects of despair."

On January 2, over three weeks after the wreck, remains of the makeshift raft appeared on the shore. The tide carried one of the bodies to the main shore and was discovered by local fishermen, while the body of the Swede was never found. Some boats were quickly launched in the high seas to investigate and one scallop boat found the near dead survivors on Boon Island. The starved and delirious crew saw the fishing boat approaching the island. The seas were heavy as the rescue crew was only able to bring the fishing boat within a few hundred yards of the survivors. They decided to send one man in a canoe to provide materials to build a fire. The poor rescuer told his captain when he returned, how shocked he was upon setting eyes on the shipwrecked crew, that he was quite frightened. Unable to bring the crew on the vessel due to the high seas, they promised to bring help the next day. The next day came, as the seas were too rough for a rescue, but the captain would later write that they now could at least build a fire to warm themselves and boil their "meat."

The survivors were finally rescued on January 4, 1710, nearly four weeks after they were shipwrecked on Boon Island. They were brought by canoe, two or three at a time, and were given bread and spirits; they violently became sickened because of their ghastly

Winter coast of York, Maine.

diet. When the ten survivors arrived at a tavern round 8 p.m. in the evening by the shore, most were near death from starvation and exposure. Many had hands and feet blackened by frostbite, and had lost use of their limbs.

The First Mate's Contrasting Account and Controversy

Another contrasting account was made by the first mate, Christopher Langman. He claimed that Captain Dean was deliberately planning to wreck the ship previously to get insurance money for himself and his brother, who were both the owners of the ship. Other crewmembers supported Langman's claim overhearing conversations between Dean and his brother. Langman would write that Captain Dean placed the crew on short rations and beat several dissenters in attempt to break the will of any who would oppose him as the *Nottingham Galley* made its way across the Atlantic.

Langman further stated that the *Nottingham Galley* was circling in the Gulf of Maine looking for more French privateers interested in purchasing the ship without consideration for the crew, especially with a nor'easter approaching. Langman wrote that he tried to get Captain Dean to steer further out to sea, but Dean put a pistol to his head and confined him to his bunk until the *Nottingham Galley* hit the rocks of Boon Island.

Langman returned to England to publish his side of the story, but unfortunately, died shortly afterwards, which many believe from the grueling experience his body endured at Boon Island. Captain Dean survived the ordeal, and also left for England. He later enlisted to become a mercenary in the Russian Navy where he later became a spy. Dean lived to a ripe old age, republished his account several times, and died,

as many considered, as a hero. His account of what happened on Boon Island circulated worldwide for many years afterwards.

Before a lighthouse was built on the island many years later, the *Nottingham Galley* incident inspired local mariners to continuously place barrels of provisions and some survival gear on the island in case other wrecks occurred, or for mariners who found themselves stranded. This practice was performed all over the coast during the seventeenth and early eighteenth centuries. Local fishermen would also have a lantern or some device that could hold fire placed at the top floor of a designated house located outside the harbor to emit light through a window. Sometimes a lighted container of tar or oil placed on a pole on a dangerous island served as an early lighthouse to help guide mariners away from danger.

Although the *Nottingham Galley* incident occurred long before the present Boon Island Lighthouse was built on this deserted rock, the incident spawned the need for some type of light or warning device to aid mariners around this tiny rock island. Lighthouses were later funded by the government and would be built all over the coast during the latter part of the 1700s well into the nineteenth century. Boon Island Light was built on the island in 1799, as a result of so many wrecks near there. Years later, many of Boon Island's light keepers, who had duty on this barren isolated island, would speak mainly of its terrible solitude and fearful loneliness that surrounded the enclosed area.

Today Boon Island Lighthouse is the tallest lighthouse structure in New England. In 1995, nine small iron cannons and other artifacts were discovered just off Boon Island, in about twenty-five feet of water. They are believed to have been from the *Nottingham Galley* wreck.

Sheffield Island Lighthouse, Connecticut.

Fire on the Lexington With Only 4 Survivors

Between Eaton's Neck Light, New York and Sheffield Island Light, Connecticut

Although many maritime disasters in the nineteenth century occurred during stormy weather, or may have involved the collision of boats, disasters from fire were also prevalent. One of the worst steamship disasters in history occurred when the steamship *Lexington* caught fire with an estimated 150 persons aboard. The disaster caused the greatest loss of life at that time in the Long Island Sound.

The *Lexington* was a wooden paddle wheel steamer, built in 1835, over 200 feet in length. She was considered to be one of the fastest steamers on the route from New York City to Boston. The *Lexington* was one of those paddle wheel steamers that came into existence at a time when the evolution of the steam engine was also shaping the railroad systems of the future. By 1840, most investors were more interested in expanding the railroad system rather than the steamer lines, possibly causing the lack of regulations regarding safety with the dangerous route for steamers from New York Harbor, to the route around Point

Judith, heading near Providence, Rhode Island. To help with costs of operation, steamers like the *Lexington* not only were used to carry passengers, but also cargo from New York to Boston.

When she set sail on a cold day on January 13th, 1840, her Captain, Jake Vanderbilt, was ill at home, unable to make the trip, so veteran Captain George Child took command of the vessel loaded with passengers and a cargo of cotton bales. She set sail at about 4 p.m. from Manhattan, New York, bound for Stonington, Connecticut. The vessel was carrying about 150 passengers, and about 150 cotton bales, some of which were piled up near the smokestack. Each bale was about four feet long by three feet wide, and nearly a foot and a half thick.

By the time dinner was served, the temperature had plummeted to near zero and the wind was gusting. The *Lexington* was sailing under full steam, past Eaton's Neck Lighthouse outside New York, at about 7 p.m., towards Sheffield Island. All of a sudden, fire broke out near the single stack, setting the bales of cotton loaded nearby aflame. Although a fire-fighting team was quickly dispatched, they failed to put out the fire. As the fire prevented the crew from shutting down the boilers, the *Lexington* was still cruising at full speed and out of control. As a result, when full lifeboats with panicking passengers were dispatched, they capsized as soon as they hit the water, throwing everyone into

Illustration of *Lexington* Fire. *Courtesy of Library of Congress.*

the freezing waves. Those passengers who survived from being burned to death by jumping in the water instead, ended up perishing from exposure to the icy waters and drowning.

Chester Hilliard, a 24-year-old ship's captain traveling as a passenger, heard the cry of "Fire!" and ran out on deck. He waited patiently for the unattended boilers to give out so the ship would slow down. He watched in horror as passengers jumped to their deaths in the icy waters or succumbed to the raging fires. He persuaded a few of the remaining passengers and crew to throw themselves overboard attaching themselves to the cotton bales which would serve as rafts, as most of the lifeboats were swamped or destroyed by fire. By 8 p.m., an hour after the fire had started, as he and some of the survivors floated helplessly in the icy waters atop the bales of cotton, they watched the center of the main deck collapse, killing everyone there. About 3 p.m., as Hilliard looked at his watch, he observed the remaining hulk of the ship sink below the surface, carrying all those remaining aboard to their deaths.

Before that terrible freezing night of January 13, 1840 was over, all but four of the estimated 143 passengers and crew aboard the *Lexington* had perished. The many who had perished would become victims of flames or icy water in Long Island Sound's first and worst steamboat fire. Ironically, those four survivors owed their lives to the cargo of cotton bales that had fueled the fire, but also served as makeshift rafts. At the time of the disaster, only one copy of the passenger list was made. This original document sank with the *Lexington*, thus making it impossible to verify the total number lost in the disaster.

Although the *Lexington*'s fire disaster was spotted along the shore of Long Island and lower Connecticut by many mariners, most of the boats were blocked by low tide, ice, and rough seas hampering any rescue attempts to reach the burning steamboat.

Of the four survivors, three were rescued by the sloop *Merchant* and its master, Captain Meeker, by noon that following day. Those rescued included Captain Hilliard, the passenger on board the *Lexington*, Captain Stephen Manchester, pilot of the *Lexington*, and Charles Smith, fireman. All three were found frost bitten and exhausted from exposure.

The fourth survivor, second mate David Crowley, drifted for forty-three hours on a bale of cotton, coming ashore nearly fifty miles to the east, at Baiting Hollow, Long Island. Crowley was able to dig into the center of the cotton bale to stay warm. He managed to stagger nearly a mile to the nearest house before collapsing. He later fully recovered and kept the bale as a souvenir until the Civil War, when he donated it to be used for Union uniforms.

The *Lexington* burned and sank with a horrific loss of life. An unsuccessful attempt in 1842 to raise the wreck only resulted in the ship being broken apart in pieces and it sank back in 150 feet of water. Only a mass of melted silver coins was retrieved.

The inquest jury slammed the *Lexington's* crew and its owners. They felt that better judgment regarding using the buckets to put out the fire, and better discipline on the crew to launch the lifeboats would have saved some of the unnecessary loss of life. The jury charged that the use of blowers was dangerous, and that passengers and flammable cotton bales were a truly poor combination of cargo. After the facts were presented, the jury also slammed the captain and pilot in disregarding the safety of the passengers in trying only to save themselves foremost. Even though the result of their findings were published and handed down for the need for more safety regulations, there were no new safety regulations imposed regarding passengers and flammable cargo until nearly twelve years later when the steamboat *Henry Clay* burned on the Hudson River.

Survivors of *Lexington* on cotton bale. *Image courtesy of Quest Marine Services.*

Larchmont Disaster and Controversy

Near Watch Hill Lighthouse, in Rhode Island

On February 11, 1907, the paddle wheel steamer *Larchmont*, sailing out of Providence, bound for New York, and the coal-laden schooner *Harry P. Knowlton* heading to Boston, collided in the dead of night, during a fierce blizzard. The *Knowlton* tore into the *Larchmont*, causing it to keel over and fill with water. Then the boilers exploded, filling the ship with steam. The *Larchmont* sank in less than half an hour. Most of the passengers who survived the collision froze to death in their lifeboats and rafts in zero degree temperatures and howling gale-force winds. The February cold claimed 143 lives. Only 19 people survived the disaster. It would be Rhode Island's worst maritime disaster of the twentieth century.

Originally named the *Cumberland,* the *Larchmont* was over 250 feet long and touted as one of the finest side-wheel or paddle-wheel steamers of her day. She left a routine launch from Providence heading towards New York City at about 7 p.m., on February 11, 1907. Once past Point Judith Light, Rhode Island, Captain George McVey left responsibility to Pilot John L. Anson at the helm as he headed for bed. As the *Larchmont* headed west across Block Island Sound, a near gale-force wind was blowing. The full effect of the gale was not felt until the *Larchmont* rounded Point Judith near Point Judith

Lighthouse. The paddle-wheel steamer pointed her nose into the very heart of the gale and continued down through Block Island Sound as the weather worsened with snow squalls and poor visibility.

When the *Larchmont* reached about three miles from Westerly's Watch Hill Lighthouse in Rhode Island, Pilot Anson noted that two sets of lights could be seen off the bow. It was the schooner *Harry P. Knowlton* heading straight for the steamer. The coal-laden schooner, heading for Boston, was also being blown about from the bitter gale-force winds. Several blasts were sounded on the steamer's whistle as Pilot Anson and the quartermaster tried to veer the *Larchmont* away from the schooner to avoid collision.

Before another warning signal could be sounded on the steamer's whistle, the schooner crashed into the front port side of the *Larchmont* just before 11 p.m., where the passengers were awakened by the sound of the crash, and then, an explosion from the ships boilers. The impact of the schooner forced its way more than half its length over the breadth of the *Larchmont,* but the ferocity of the seas soon separated the vessels, and as the schooner slid away from the steamer, water rushed into the *Larchmont's* gaping hole.

The majority of passengers on the *Larchmont* had already retired for the night, and when the collision occurred, there were few on board prepared for the frigid weather. Literally freezing in the cold, many rushed back below to secure more clothing, while others, barefooted, and clad only in nightgowns, stood

Watch Hill Lighthouse,
Rhode Island.

on the upper decks, fearing that to go below would mean certain death. These passengers became the majority of fatalities ending up freezing to death in the icy waters. Most died of exposure on an evening when the temperature had dropped to zero degrees with gale-force winds blowing against them. Even those few who were fully dressed, and had later survived the ordeal, endured extreme hypothermia and serious frostbites.

Every boat and raft sent from the *Larchmont* immediately headed for Fishers Point, off Block Island, the nearest point of landing, which was still about five miles in the dark from where the steamer had crashed. Huge waves and spray covered the boats and survivors wore thin coatings of ice, and most were barely able to row in such ferocity. Most of the boats and rafts became separated with the heavy winds and never made it ashore with survivors, as most of the passengers and crew spilled out of the crowded boats into the freezing waters, or succumbed to exposure from the extreme cold. Some Block Island fishermen, who had heard about the disaster, braved the stormy seas to try to rescue any survivors from their frozen lifeboats and makeshift rafts.

One man in one of the full lifeboats was unable to handle the extreme cold, and after watching those around him perish from the cold, went insane and slit his own throat to end his agony. The rescuers only found one survivor left from the boat, Oliver Janvier, a 21-year-old Providence man, who managed to make it to shore to tell the tale.

Most of the details of the terrible disaster were given by Captain McVey, providing his point of view when his lifeboat came ashore. The captain later stated that it was shortly after 11 p.m. in the evening when his lifeboat was cut away from the sinking steamer, and it was not until 6:30 in the morning that it arrived at Fishers Point near Block Island to be rescued. None of the crew in the boat expected to survive the bitter cold and icy seas from the storm. The rescuers found that no one in the lifeboat was able to walk. Their feet were frozen so badly that the rescuers had to carry the survivors over their backs with their limp arms and legs to the lifesaving station.

The steamer, with a huge hole torn in her side, was so seriously damaged that no attempt was made to try to get ashore, as she sank to the bottom in less than half an hour.

The 128-foot-long schooner *Knowlton*, which was carrying a load of 400 tons of coal, began to fill with water rapidly when she started to back away from the *Larchmont's* deck, but her crew manned the pumps and kept her afloat until she reached an inlet near the mainland, where the men were able to get in their lifeboat and row ashore. There were no fatalities on the schooner, but the men suffered with hypothermia and frostbite from the extreme cold.

During the next day, forty-eight bodies and some body parts were found washed ashore, some frozen in the lifeboats and rafts. Many with their limbs encased in ice, had broken apart, and were tossed ashore in such disarray that only six of the forty-eight bodies could be identified.

Larchmont leaving Providence, Rhode, Island.
Image courtesy of Quest Marine Services.

Both captains, who survived, would blame one another for the tragedy. Captain George McVey, of the *Larchmont*, declared that the *Knowlton* had suddenly swerved off from her course, was lifted up in a huge sea swell by the gale-force winds, and crashed into the steamer. Captain Haley, of the *Knowlton*, declared that the steamer did not give his vessel sufficient sea room and that the collision occurred before he could steer the schooner away from the path of the oncoming steamer.

During the formal investigation in the days that followed, Captain McVey claimed he was the last to leave his sinking ship. Those passengers who had survived disputed his claim, stating that they observed the Captain and his crew as being in the very first lifeboat, leaving the frantic passengers on their own.

Due mostly to the freezing winter weather, over 143 people perished, and only 19 survived, 10 members of the crew including the captain, and only 9 passengers. After the investigation, the Pilot Anson, who went down with the ship, was blamed for steering the *Larchmont* in the wrong direction when approaching the schooner *Harry P. Knowlton*. An official accounting of the *Larchmont's* passengers was never made since the only original list perished with the ship.

Years later, new safety recommendations finally came about as a result of the *Larchmont* disaster in requiring multiple lists of passengers and crew to be created and distributed between the vessel and their shore destinations in case of further disasters.

The Perfect Storm
and the Sinking of the *Portland*
Near Race Point Light, in Massachusetts

One of the worst storms in New England's history occurred during the Thanksgiving week of 1898, when two storm systems, one from the Great Lakes and the other from the South, would came together over the New England coast. The collision created a "perfect storm" of blinding snow, sleet, and hurricane-force winds gusting to over 100 miles an hour, and left destruction all along the New England coastline.

Provincetown Harbor, which is well known as one of the safest on the Eastern coast, could not hold back the ferocity of the storm. The storm destroyed at least ten large vessels, twenty-seven schooners, nine wharves, and twenty-one buildings in just the harbor area alone.

Rescue Near Wood End Light, in Massachussetts

At Wood End Lighthouse, Keeper Issac G. Fisher, had climbed into the lookout tower just before daybreak and saw the morning patrolman from the lifesaving station nearby, Frank C. Wagner, running back towards the lighthouse. Wagner had seen two schooners wrecked offshore a couple of miles down, and informed Keeper Fisher to sound the alarm. The keeper had the surfmen try to bring the lifeboat on the wagon down to the shore, as the fierce winds were

Wood End Lighthouse tower, Provincetown, Massachussetts.

Launching A Surfboat. Painting by artist Sherman Groenke. *Courtesy of Jill Park and US Coast Guard.*

so strong that they were nearly blowing the craft out of the wagon. The men finally had to take the boat off the wagon and drag it to the raging surf, where they were forced to push and drag the vessel in the knee-deep freezing waters along the shore for nearly a mile and a half. This task took a couple of strenuous exhausting hours were they finally were within sight of two schooners that had wrecked during the storm.

The gale was now at its worst intensity as the surfmen tried to maneuver the boat into the surf. Each time they would try to launch the boat, the strength of the winds would force the craft towards the shore. Determined to try to save anyone in either schooner, they relentlessly pushed the boat another mile along the shore to try to gain a better angle against the gale-force winds. Hours went by as they continued their daunting task of pushing the extremely heavy craft along the surf. At 4 o'clock in the afternoon, many hours after the wrecks were initially sighted, they made another attempt to force the boat into the raging waves, and even with the help of four fishermen they had enlisted along the way, the gale force winds still kept blowing against the frustrated crew.

Again the crew tried to move the boat along the shore for a better position, and again they tried to launch the craft against the winds. This time, with all their might, they started slowly to make way towards the closest of the schooners, the *Jorden L. Mott*. There they found five members, frozen, but four still alive clinging to the rigging. The fifth member, the captain's father, had frozen to death.

The men of the *Mott* were carefully taken off the rigging and carried onto the lifeboat still heaving in the raging waves. As darkness approached, the surfmen decided that they needed to bring those still alive back to the station before wasting any additional time in carrying the corpse. With the four survivors in the boat, the lifesavers headed for shore with the wind against their backs. When they brought their boat on the beach, although the station was a short distance away from where they landed, it took nearly an hour to bring the exhausted freezing souls to the station. Two men from the *Mott*, Captain Charles Dyer, and one of his crew were too weak to walk with assistance and had to be carried to the station by the already-exhausted surfmen. The Wood End lifesavers had been enduring the storm's hurricane-force winds, sleet, and snow in trying to rescue the survivors for nearly fifteen hours, and were also exhausted and beginning to display the effects of prolonged exposure in the storm.

It was now nightfall, and any efforts to attempt a rescue of the other schooner wreck, the *Lester A Lewis*, would have been fatal for the rescuers as the storm continued in its intensity. It was believed that all aboard had already perished. The survivors and their rescuers were placed in dry clothing and provided spirits and food for the night. Captain Dyer of the *Mott* was unable to walk on his own until the following night. The rescued crew stayed at the station for three days until they had recovered enough to travel back to their homes, with their expenses paid for.

After the storm had subsided a couple of days later, the Wood End surfmen went out to the wrecks to remove the body of Captain Dyer's father on the *Jorden L. Mott*, and the five bodies of the crewmen who perished on the *Lester A. Lewis*. They brought them into Provincetown

Steamer _Portland_ on route. _Image courtesy of Jeremy D'Entremont_

largest and most luxurious steamers in New England, able to accommodate up to 800 passengers.

On November 24, 1898, Thanksgiving Day, the day started clear and cold over the New England coastline, but, as the weekend progressed, two storm systems, one from the Great Lakes and the other from the south, would came together over the New England coast producing one of the worst storms New England had ever seen. By Saturday, November 26, the seas off Boston had already begun to increase.

On Saturday, November 26, 1898, it is believed that the Captain, Hollis Blanchard, and his superiors knew a snowstorm from the South with gale-force winds was approaching that day. They did not know about the storm system coming from the Great Lakes at the same time and decided to sail figuring to outrun the approaching storm from the South. No one was prepared, however, for the intensity or duration of the storm. Captain Blanchard continued to prepare the steamer _Portland_ for its run from Boston to Portland. That evening, with snow starting to fall, over 175 passengers enjoying the Thanksgiving weekend, boarded the Portland, and left Boston Harbor at 7 p.m.

Later that evening the two storms quickly collided over the New England coast, a kind of "perfect storm system," becoming one of the worst recorded nor'easter storms in New England's history. The winds increased to hurricane force, forcing the _Portland_ further and further south until, by Sunday, on November 27th, she was floundering off the coast of Cape Cod. The ship's lights probably failed, and it would have been close to impossible to launch life rafts. With such high winds and

where they were properly taken care of. The efforts of the Wood End lifesavers were regarded as the most heroic under such extreme conditions and were highly praised by the locals and government officials alike. All of the brave rescuers recovered from their ordeal without any long-term effects.

The Portland Disaster Renames Storm as "Portland Gale"

Perhaps the most famous of New England ship disasters of the nineteenth century occurred during this storm and involved the sinking of the steamer _Portland_. It was built in 1889, and carried passengers and cargo between Boston and Portland, Maine, during the heyday of the steamship era. At over 280 feet long and 42 feet wide, the _Portland_ was one of the

Race Point Lighthouse, Provincetown, Massachusetts.

huge waves, the captain would not have been able to turn around without being capsized by the giant waves.

Several ship captains, in their own battles to stay afloat during the storm late Saturday night, reported seeing the *Portland* pitching in the seas. The ship likely got no farther than Cape Ann along the northern shoreline of Massachusetts before being driven off course, turning east to avoid the rocky coastline. Keeper Whitten of Thacher Island Twin Lights, near Rockport, Massachusetts, claimed he saw the *Portland* from the north tower about a mile off Thacher Island before she was out of site in the storm.

At 11 p.m. on Saturday, now well off-course and offshore, an account was given of the *Portland* almost colliding with the fishing schooner *Grayling*, one of the vessels that survived the storm at sea, according to the captain of the schooner.

On the morning of Sunday, Nov. 27, at 5:45 a.m., lighthouse Keeper Samuel O. Fisher, a member of the Race Point Life Saving Station near Race Point Lighthouse at the tip of Cape Cod, claimed he heard four short blasts of a steamer's whistle, which signified a distress call during a lull in the storm, but before the station could prepare a rescue boat for launching, the whistle had stopped and nothing more was heard or seen.

By Sunday evening, bodies and wreckage from the *Portland* began washing up between the Race Point and Peaked Hill Bars lifesaving stations on Cape Cod. It was believed the ship sank on Sunday, Nov. 27, around 9 a.m., because watches recovered with the bodies stopped between 9 and 10 o'clock. At the time, it was still unknown whether the *Portland* capsized, broke apart, exploded, or collided with one of the other lost ships. As the days followed, newspapers printed lists of those thought to be on board and descriptions of bodies that had washed ashore. Finally, news started to get out about the fate of the *Portland*.

With no survivors from the tragedy of the *Portland*, later accounts would print stories that the Captain had sailed against the orders of the general manager of the company because he was eager to get home to Maine to a family reunion. Other accounts suggested that the shipping line itself, not wanting to strand holiday passengers in Boston, ordered the captain to sail against his better judgment.

The storm of 1898 was one of the worst storms New England had ever seen. But with the sinking of the *Portland*, with nearly 200 lives lost, the Gale of 1898 has been known as the "Portland Gale." To this day, it is not known exactly how many passengers were aboard or who they all were, as the only passenger list was aboard the vessel. As a result of this tragedy, and others, new regulations were finally established for all passenger ships to leave a second list of passengers on shore before they depart, and a list to be sent to their destination, if possible, as well.

For years, controversy reigned as to the location of the ill-fated ship. In the summer of 2002, data from the American Underwater Search and Survey brought back images from the sea floor 400 feet deep off the tip of Cape Cod that identified the remains of the steamship *Portland*. The wreckage of the *Portland* was found near the wreckage of the schooner, *Addie E. Snow*, of Rockland, Maine, resting on the bottom less than a quarter mile away. In looking at the evidence of the bow of the schooner and the destruction on the *Portland*, it was concluded that they had both collided and sank during that fateful storm.

**Northern Cape Cod
shoreline, Massachusetts.**

The Gloucester Rides Out the Perfect Storm

During the storm there was another steamer that was also taking the same route out of Boston through Vineyard Sound as the *Portland*. The *Gloucester*, with Captain Francis Howes at the helm, was the only other steamer that ventured out on route through the storm to its destination in Norfolk, Virginia. The captain was known as one of the most experienced on the coast, and with a full load of cargo packed tightly together to keep the ship heavy enough to drill through the raging seas, he ran the vessel at its optimum speed with the intention that if it was to hit something, it would send the vessel well up shore so all the crew had a chance of survival. He relied not on buoys and markers, which were useless in such poor visibility, but on his own experience and instincts to guide the vessel through one of New England's worst storms.

The *Gloucester* left Boston around 4 o'clock that afternoon of November 26, 1898, a few hours before the *Portland* set sail, on the same route towards Norfolk, Virginia. By evening, the winds were becoming fierce, blowing at gusts of over seventy miles per hour, with blinding snow as the *Gloucester* starting heading through Vineyard Sound. There were no discernable buoys, lights, or sounds that could be heard or seen through the storm's ferocity, its blinding snow, and from the spray washing over the deck as the *Gloucester* plowed through the heavy seas. As the gale-force winds would blow the vessel off course, the captain would wait patiently for brief lulls during the storm, to set his vessel back on its charted route.

As the *Gloucester* approached Vineyard Sound, Captain Howes knew he was near the vicinity of the *Pollock Rip Shoals* Lightship and was waiting to hear the ship's whistling and to catch a glimpse of its light, when the vessel appeared a short distance right in front of him. He luckily was able to maneuver the *Gloucester* around the lightship and narrowly avoided a collision as his vessel stayed on course. He then, by experience, felt he was near the *Cross Rip* Lightship when he again nearly came directly upon the vessel, but steered clear of her as he headed around Martha's Vineyard. He could only imagine the fear and anguish the crews of both lightships must be feeling as the winds were approaching hurricane-force, bashing the waves against the stationary anchored vessels, and of the *Gloucester* nearly missing them. Again by experience, and with a lull in the storm, Captain Howes told his mate they should be seeing the light of West Chop Lighthouse shortly, which they did, giving

West Chop Lighthouse, Martha's Vineyard, Massachusetts.

the captain confidence they were still on course and remarkably still on schedule.

As the *Gloucester* made its way past Block Island heading southward, the storm was less strong the further south the vessel went. The *Gloucester*, with the trained eye of Captain Howes, made it to Norfolk Virginia, by 6 o'clock Monday morning, safely, and to the astonishment of everyone, on schedule. The amazing journey won the captain the admiration of all his peers.

The storm lasted more than 30 hours and packed coastal wind gusts of 100 mph. It buried much of New England in two feet of snow, washed away coastal buildings and destroyed neighborhoods, sank or grounded hundreds of boats and ships, and was responsible for killing more than 400 people. The blizzard had destroyed telegraph and telephone lines from Cape Cod, and it buried or washed out railroad tracks. When the storm ended, over 140 ships were lost in the storm, and it had also changed the course of the North River dividing a portion of Scituate, Massachusetts.

First Coordinated Rescue Between Lifesaving Services and Locals

Near Watch Hill Light, Rhode Island

Watch Hill Lighthouse, near Westerly, Rhode Island, is one of the oldest lighthouses in America. Its location borders the southwestern point of Rhode Island and southeastern point of Stonington, Connecticut. Initially, a watchtower and beacon were constructed in 1745 to serve as a nautical beacon to warn local residents of any naval attack. The colonial government later used it during the French and Indian Wars to track French pirates. Destroyed in a 1781 storm, President Thomas Jefferson finally approved funds to build a lighthouse in 1806. As erosion and deteriorating conditions plagued the wooden lighthouse, a taller one built of granite stones was built further away from the bluff in 1856 to marking the entrance to Fishers Island Sound and to warn mariners of a dangerous reef southwest of Watch Hill.

As with most lighthouses, although Watch Hill Light guided many vessels and their crews in fair and inclement weather, shipwrecks still occurred in the area. Unfortunately, two of the worst maritime disasters occurred near Watch Hill Lighthouse. From these incidents, however, came about special safety procedures and regulations that are used today. One of these disasters, mentioned previously, involved the sinking of the *Larchmont*. The second of these disasters occurred on August 30, 1872, when the schooner *Nettie Cushing* collided with the huge passenger steamer *Metis*. Although sixty-seven persons perished, through the coordinated efforts of various branches of the lifesaving services and personnel, including local mariners who risked their lives, eighty-five people were rescued in what could have been a more tragic incident in the loss of lives. This interaction among the three services, which initially had not been used, played a major factor in future coordination of rescue services.

In 1872, during the time of the disaster, there was not a regular lifesaving crew at Watch Hill, but a group of dedicated volunteers. Captain Daniel Larkin served as keeper at the lighthouse at Watch Hill from 1861-1868, until he developed a profitable tourist business hotel called the Larkin House. He then volunteered to head up the volunteer lifesaving crew nearby. Captain Jared Crandall took over Larkin's position as Keeper of Watch Hill light. He owned an old whaleboat, which served as the only lifesaving boat for any rescue efforts.

Watch Hill Lighthouse, Westerly, Rhode Island.

The *Metis* and *Nettie Cushing* Collision

On the afternoon of August 29, 1872, the 200-foot wooden steamer *Metis* was heading north from New York to Providence, Rhode Island, with a load of cotton cargo bound for the New England textile mills. She was also carrying a full load of 107 passengers and 45 crewmembers as a summer gale storm approached the region. The seas started churning as the storm progressed, making the journey increasingly more hazardous. During the storm, a small schooner, the *Nettie Cushing* was carrying a load of lime heading for New York. She was under sail traveling through the Sound as the wind-swept rains pounded the region. Around 8 p.m., the winds had reached to gale-force and continued through the night. By 3 o'clock in the morning, most passengers and many crewmembers were asleep as the winds and seas continued to thrash about. Around 4 o'clock, fog and mist followed the pouring rain, as both vessels were on a collision course with one another about six miles from Watch Hill Light. Neither vessel could see the another in the darkness until they were nearly on top of one another.

All of a sudden, the *Nettie Cushing* appeared in the darkness and collided into the *Metis'* front port side, creating a gaping hole. The schooner literally slipped away from the ship and disappeared in the night. Most of the passengers and crew didn't realize the incident occurred as there was little vibration felt on the ship. Those crewmembers on watch could not see if there were any survivors as the schooner fell back into the darkness. Captain Charles L. Burton, the *Metis* commander, was made aware of the incident, but believed that damage was minimal as reported by his crewmen. He ordered to briefly stop the *Metis* to try to find any possible survivors from the schooner. The wind and waves picked up and continued to batter the ship as a half hour passed with no sign of the schooner or any survivors. The chief engineer went back to check on any damages and to his surprise found water was rapidly pouring into the ship's front area. He ran up to inform the captain as they realized the ship was beginning to sink. Captain Burton ordered to prepare the passengers as the crew ran below to awaken all. He ordered to head the ship for the beach near Watch Hill Lighthouse as most passengers barely had time to dress and put on their life preservers. The ship was barely moving, as water continued to pour into the lower deck region from the gaping hole created by the schooner's bowsprit and headgear.

The steamer blew her whistle to send out a distress signal. She continued heading for the beach outside of Watch Hill Lighthouse. The vessel was still within five miles of the beach when the bow of the steamer started sinking below the waves, sucking nearly forty people under the waters. Everyone fell into panic as only three lifeboats were launched. One of these boats smashed against the steamer's side in the panic. The other two managed to break away from the doomed

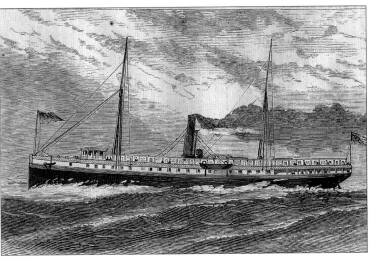

Steamer *Metis* engraving.
Image courtesy of Quest Marine Services.

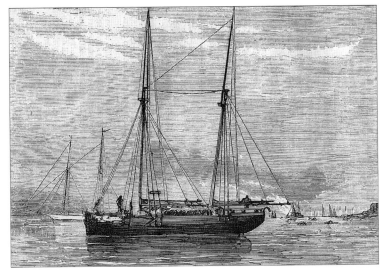

Schooner *Nettie Cushing* engraving.
Image courtesy of Quest Marine Services.

Metis **wreckage on beach engraving.** *Image courtesy of Quest Marine Services.*

vessel, carrying mostly men. A large group of about fifty passengers and crew were struggling to climb on the upper hurricane deck, when it suddenly became detached from the hull as the steamer started to sink. This made the huge deck into a giant raft for the survivors, setting it adrift over the raging waves and howling winds. Hours later, the storm began to subside, and around 8 a.m. that morning, the tide had brought the floating deck of exhausted and drenched survivors within a mile from the rocky shore near Watch Hill.

By early morning, news had spread quickly about the disaster, although no one knew the fate of the nearly 150 passengers and crew of the *Metis*. Hundreds of people lined the shoreline, unable to go out into the waters, as the surf was still dangerously breaking over the area. Anxiously, they waited and watched for any survivors to appear nearer the shore to provide any assistance.

On the same evening of the incident, around 2 a.m., the steamer *Narragansett* had reached Stonington Harbor in nearby Connecticut, on route to New York. With the storm continuing, the steamer was planning to wait until around 9 p.m. that following evening before heading out. Around 8 a.m., when the large portion of the upper deck was sighted near Watch Hill drifting with nearly fifty people clinging for dear life, Captain Allen of the *Narragansett* received a telegram from Watch Hill regarding the disaster and asked for assistance to find survivors. As he headed out towards the wreck, he quickly sent word to Captain David Richie of the Revenue Cutter *Moccasin* for help. The *Narragansett* was able to rescue seven survivors that

day, five of the *Metis* deck hand crew, one gentleman and a young woman.

The gentleman passenger was drifting nearly seven hours in the water before being picked up by the *Narragansett*. He told the story that while he was on deck of the *Metis* in all the panic; he was trying to fasten his life preserver when a woman asked to help with putting on hers. He gratefully obliged and threw a cork mattress overboard, telling her to jump with him and climb onto the floating mattress. She leaped from the vessel with him, then went under the waves, but never rose to the surface.

The young woman brought in to the *Narragansett* had reportedly lost her husband and two children in the disaster. When she was finally sighted, she was holding her youngest child, an infant who had perished, close to her chest, trying to comfort it. She had also drifted for many hours in the high seas. Her husband who had perished was picked up later, but her other child was never found. Many of the passengers on board the *Narragansett*, upon hearing the stories of the survivors tried to comfort them with money, food, and dry clothing, anything that could help them in their plight.

Luckily, the Revenue Cutter *Moccasin* was also anchored to avoid the storm in Stonington Harbor, a few miles away from the wreck when she received news of the tragedy from Watch Hill and from the Captain of the *Narragansett*. Captain David Ritchie ordered the *Moccasin* underway as soon as possible, and by 10:15 a.m., the cutter started out towards the wreck. He knew it was going to be a long and emotionally draining day for him and his men, but felt the crew were well trained and up to the task. A northeast gale had approached

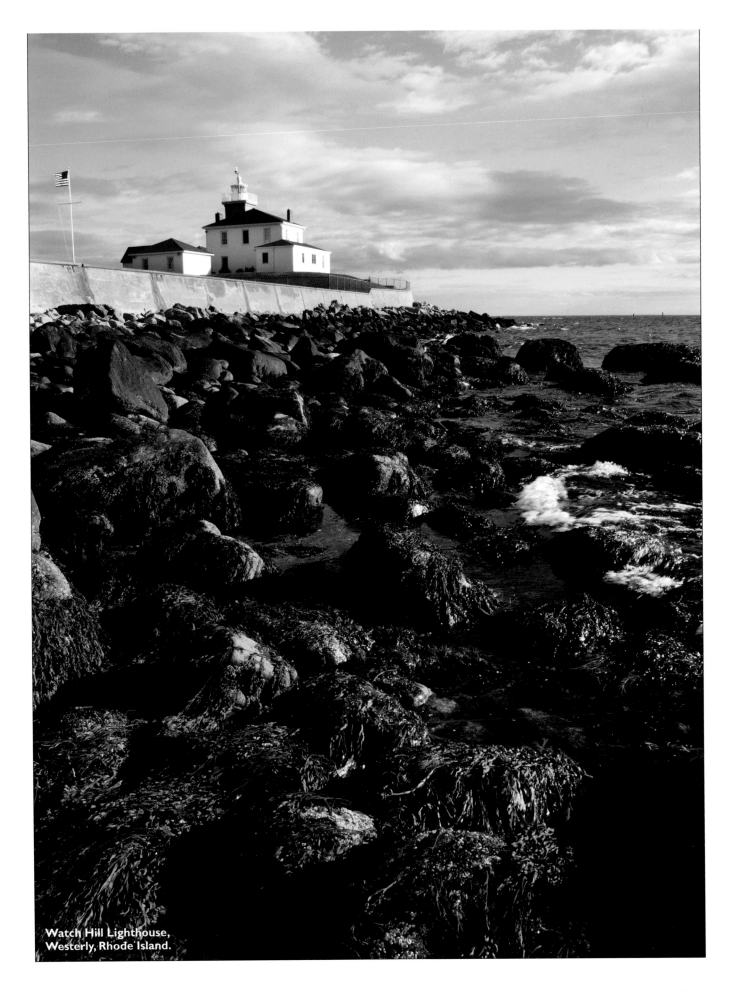

Watch Hill Lighthouse,
Westerly, Rhode Island.

to replace the rain from the other storm that had come from the southeast. The new storm created breaking waves that were crossing over the bow of the *Moccasin* as she drove towards the scene of the wreck. As the cutter came near Watch Hill Lighthouse, they found the two lifeboats being tossed around by the high seas near the edge of the rocky surf with men, women, and children aboard. Although the ship was exposed to the raging waves near the rocks, they were able to maneuver the vessel as close as possible, and then began the dangerous work of lowering the boats to bring the exhausted survivors on board the *Moccasin*. Through the skill of the rescuers, they managed to bring all aboard without incident.

The *Moccasin* also found the huge floating deck that had broken away from the doomed ship with nearly fifty survivors looking nearly lifeless, some had perished, and some were unconscious. The *Moccasin's* two boats picked up twenty-six who were alive and also recovered fourteen bodies of those who had perished. Captain's Burton and Hull of the *Metis* refused to go into the lifeboats until all personnel were taken away from the structure and decided to ride out the structure on the surf to avoid losing any more time for the *Moccasin* to pick up survivors.

Watch Hill's lighthouse Keeper, Captain Jared Crandall, had heard of the *Metis* in distress and also contacted the steamer *Narragansett* and the Revenue Cutter *Moccasin* to make way to the wreck for assistance. He assembled the volunteer lifesaving crew near the lighthouse. His crew, which included Captain Daniel Larkin, one of the volunteer lifesaving captains near the lighthouse, launched the old lifeboat and drove out through the raging waves to assist the *Moccasin* to pick up any living survivors, or bodies. Boat Captain John Harvey and his crewmen had also gotten word of the incident and launched a fishing seine boat, used to catch schools of fish with a dragging net, into the thunderous surf. Both boats retrieved survivors who were found clinging to cork mattresses, floating timbers, cotton bales, and other floating debris. Many had been battling the raging winds and violent seas for hours. The task was extremely hazardous as the crews tried to maneuver the boats to safely pick up the survivors while the winds and rising waves tried to prevent their brave efforts. Captain Harvey's fishing seine managed to retrieve eighteen people as it continued to assist the *Moccasin* in searching for survivors until late that afternoon. Keeper Crandall's boat managed to retrieve and transfer fourteen survivors and bodies to the *Moccasin*.

On what would become her last load, as Crandall's old lifeboat had just been emptied of all personnel, a huge wave caught the craft and smashed it against the cutter, splitting the boat and causing it to sink. Captain Crandall looked at the wreckage of his boat and remarked, "She was well paid for." In all, Crandall's lifeboat and the Harvey's seine boat had successfully rescued thirty-two people. The *Moccasin* also managed to retrieve another survivor who had been in the water for many hours.

A Survivor's Heart-Wrenching Story

Many of the stories of the survivors were heart wrenching to their rescuers. One survivor was in charge of a colleague's two boys, transporting them back to their father. They were all asleep, but he was awakened around 4 a.m., when he then heard the engine making a clattering noise and went out to see what was going on, leaving the two boys briefly to sleep. He found there was a commotion and one of the crew told him that the ship was starting to sink. He ran back to wake the two boys and tied life preservers around them. As the front of the boat started to sink, he ran with the children to the rear. The waves were still raging all around from the storm, and the rain was pouring in torrents, drenching all. As the hull broke apart and the waves commenced to wash over her deck, he grabbed the two boys and hugged them close.

Realizing that the ship was sinking fast he made the leap with the two children into the violent waters. As they rose to the surface he looked for a boat but none were nearby, and the current quickly carried the three to the front area of the ship. As they tried to keep afloat by pushing away from the vessel, all of a sudden the bow started to slip under the water. The area became covered with debris of timber, kegs, cotton bales, and cases as he tried to grab hold of one of them but to no avail. Both children were very quiet and obedient, but as time passed and as they were constantly being washed over from the salt waves, they grew weaker and weaker as their guardian too was exhausted trying to hold onto them for dear life.

Finally, the youngest child could not hold his head above the waves anymore and slipped away. The exhausted gentleman was determined to try to save the other child but he too, succumbed to the constant pounding of the waves and drowned. Unable to hold on anymore and fearing the he too would perish as he grew weaker and weaker; he secured the life preservers on their bodies together so they would not separate.

As he continued to be tossed about the waves, he started to give up hope and felt himself start to slip away. At that moment he saw a large gangplank coming towards him. As he tried to place himself on the large floating device, a wave washed him off the floating structure. Determined, he managed with his remaining strength to climb back on the wooden piece. The waves continued to wash over him, as he kept swallowing so much salt water making him feel very sick and exhausted as he held on. As daybreak broke he found another

Stonington Harbor
Lighthouse, Connecticut.

survivor on a cork mattress coming towards him. As they tried to comfort one another they later found to their joy a lifeboat making its way towards them. It was Captain Larkin who hauled them aboard and then transferred the grateful survivors to the *Moccasin*.

The Survivors

As the wind continued to blow hard, and the waves pounded the boats, Captain Ritchie and his crew spent the day with the dangerous task of rescuing those still alive and the grim job of picking up the bodies as well. As the seas were still high, it was equally as difficult when the survivors and bodies needed to be transferred from the lifeboat and fishing seine onto the *Moccasin*. It was nearly 4 p.m., and Captain Ritchie knew night was approaching and there were many

survivors on his vessel who were in need of immediate medical attention. His men were exhausted and there were no more visible signs of any survivors left from the wreck. They had spent many difficult and emotional hours in trying to rescue survivors and removing those bodies that were observed still floating in the waters.

The *Moccasin* then headed for port in Connecticut's Stonington Harbor, guided by Stonington Harbor Light, and reached it by 6 p.m. The Revenue Cutter, with the help of the lifesaving crews and fishing seine had rescued forty-two people and was carrying seventeen bodies to port. Many of the survivors were exhausted having been in the waters for hours. A few of the survivors were close to dying as Ritchie's trained crewmen were able to resuscitate them to keep them alive until medical attention could be given on shore. The people of Stonington who were still waiting along the shore gave the anguished survivors warm clothes and food to help.

The survivors, who were well treated by the locals and given medical attention when needed, were given free passes from the New Haven Railroad company to continue on to their destinations. Many stayed behind to identify their loved ones who had perished, or tried to stay nearby with relatives or friends. One gentleman had covered himself with a blanket and sat on the beach crying over the death of his wife. She had managed to stay with him floating on a cotton bale through the turbulent waters until they were close to shore. The surf was still high from the storm as a rogue wave came over them and washed her away. The anguished gentleman could not bring himself to leave the shore as many locals came by to provide whatever comfort they could.

The next day, the *Moccasin's* exhausted crew went back out to look for any survivors or bodies as far out as Block Island. While they were out, the winds again started to increase and seas were starting to churn indicating another storm was approaching. The *Moccasin*, unable to find any more survivors or signs of the wreck, headed towards Newport and anchored. Bodies that were found or were washed on shore were brought into Stonington for identification.

The schooner *Nettie Cushing*, which collided with the *Metis*, survived the impact. The commander of the vessel, Captain Jamison, who was from Thomaston Maine, determined that she was not sinking. The night was so dark and stormy that the crew did not see the steamer until it was too late to avoid a collision. After the collision, the vessel anchored on nearby Goshen Reef and was able to contact the revenue cutter *Campbell*. With a tow from the cutter, she made her way for Connecticut's New London Harbor. The vessel had lost her bowsprit and headgear from the impact, and damages in the bow area were sustained, but the vessel was able to make to port.

After an extensive investigation, it was decided that the crew of the *Metis* was at fault, not the schooner. The license of Captain Burke and his navigator in charge were revoked, and the First Pilot's license was suspended. The *Metis*, after being struck by the coastal schooner *Nettie Cushing* off the coast of Watch Hill, Rhode Island, sank in less than an hour of being struck, resulting with a heavy loss of life. If not for the coordinated efforts of the Lifesaving Service and lighthouse personnel,

Special medal created for lifesavers of the *Metis*.
Image courtesy of US Coast Guard.

along with the Revenue Cutter *Moccasin* and other local fishing boats helping to rescue the survivors, it would have been a worse tragic event.

Of 107 passengers and 45 crewmembers aboard when the *Metis* started her journey, accounts vary, but it is commonly viewed that a total of 85 people were rescued from the sinking vessel by those boats that rushed to the scene, although 67 souls perished in the storm-tossed sea.

On February 24, 1873, the investigation petitioned the Humane Society and Congress to provide awards to both crews of Keeper Crandall, and Captain Harvey. They each received Congressional Gold Lifesaving Medals from the Massachusetts Humane Society, in appreciation of their heroic efforts or rescuing survivors of the *Metis*. The medals were specially minted with an engraving depicting the rescue in commemoration. Both crews had managed to rescue many lives during the storm at great risk to their own lives from the steamer *Metis* as it sank five miles from Watch Hill Lighthouse on August 31, 1872. Medals for the crew of the lighthouse and volunteer lifesavers included Captain Daniel Larkin (former Watch Hill light keeper and one of the first Life-Saving Station captains), Captain Jared Crandall (Watch Hill Light Keeper), and lifeboat crewmen Albert Crandall, Frank Larkin, and Byron Green. Medals for the fishing seine boat included boat Captain John Harvey, and crewmen Courtland Gavitt, Edward Nash, Eugene Nash, and William Nash. Captain David Ritchie and his crew of the *Moccasin* received special congressional thanks by joint resolution on January 24, 1873.

The *Metis* incident signified the growing interaction between members of the newly formed Life Saving Service, the Lighthouse Service, and the Revenue Cutter Service, along with local mariners, as playing a major role in the rescue efforts. The coordination of the three branches of lifesaving service in future rescues would evolve into what is now our current Coast Guard.

In 1879, Captain Jared Crandall died while serving Watch Hill Lighthouse. His widow, Sally Ann (Gavitt) Crandall, became the first woman lighthouse keeper there.

A few years after the incident, a Life Saving Service Station was established at Watch Hill, close to the lighthouse. The station was abandoned in the 1940s and was destroyed in 1963.

Lightships Become the Most Perilous Profession

Life on a Lightship

One of the worst disasters to any lightship occurred in 1934 when the lightship *Nantucket* collided with the RMS *Olympic*, the sister ship to the ill-fated *Titanic*. Before discussing the story, it's important to understand the perilous conditions of those aboard the floating lightships.

Lighthouses were built on specific locations as navigational guides, to aid mariners in distress, or assist mariners in inclement weather. Lightships were needed as mobile floating lighthouses at places where it was not possible to build a lighthouse, usually in exposed dangerous locations, which included out to sea in deep water, shifting shoals, in busy harbors, and within busy shipping channels. Their purpose was needed as shipping traffic increased dramatically all along the coast in the 1800s, and they provided the means of needed repositioning in either serving as a landfall or a point of departure for shipping traffic.

The crews of these relatively small vessels would endure extremely cramped and lonely conditions away from the mainland, along with constant extreme weather conditions of New England. They operated through fog, violent storms, swelling seas, and hurricane-force winds, and they had to endure even natural formations like ice floes that could rip the hull of a ship. If a storm approached and vessels were trying to seek safety in nearby harbors (or even in clear weather), lightships would remain at anchor at their designated stations during the storm and provide the flashing light or sound their fog horn to help each vessel navigate to safety.

In the 1930s, radio was used where the lightship was anchored at a designated coordinate. The lightship would flash their light beacon at night and bounce the radio signal across the waves. The trans-Atlantic vessel, whether entering or leaving their destination, say a harbor, would steer towards the signals of the radio beacon or flashing light directly in the path of the guiding lightship. There was a lookout posted on the incoming vessel whose purpose was to locate the lightship from the signals received and adjust the ship's course to avoid collision with the stationary lightship. The lightship, anchored in its position was quite vulnerable in that it could easily be involved in a direct collision with a misguided vessel. Those crewmembers who were stationed aboard lightships knew they were in the most hazardous and vulnerable position, as many lightships met with tragedy in colliding with ships.

For crewmembers of lightships, it was extremely physically trying and emotionally difficult. These men were known as sailors who never went to sea and little of their existence was brought to public understanding unless tragedy or severe sickness became their fate. Many lightships were stationed just off shore where

Lightship *Nantucket* Collision Sunk By RMS *Olympic*. Painting by artist Charles J. Mazoujian. *Courtesy of Gwen Mazoujian and US Coast Guard.*

Lightship personnel in ward room.
Image Courtesy of US Coast Guard.

they could not participate in life on land but could hear society at work and at play. They would be moored over treacherous reefs, or would mark the narrow entrance to a channel or harbor. They would be stationed on board ship at least three out of four weeks each month, and with weather permitting, would be given shore leave for up to ten days. The most popular man would be the one coming back onto the lightship from the mainland with the latest newspaper for the crew to receive the most recent news. Regulations would not permit visitors, especially family members of the crew to board the ship, as these families had to endure long periods of absence from their loved ones.

During the grueling winter months, frequent nor'easters would pound the coastline and violently toss the exposed lightships, making even the most seasoned crewmembers seasick. There was also the constant ear-deafening sounds of the ship's fog signals and nauseating diesel fumes to make the experience even more uncomfortable.

Working on a lightship was known as the most hazardous profession in the marine service. New England had its share of accidents and tragedy. To make matters worse, the early lightships of the late 1800s and early 1900s were usually in deteriorating conditions from lack of funding by the government.

On February 5, 1918, the *Cross Rip* Lightship *#6* vanished off the Massachusetts coast where it was stationed with no survivors, and no distress messages sent. The aged, deteriorated wooden vessel was stationed in Vineyard Sound with no radio, masts, or sails to help her should her engine fail. She was observed from those on shore as being torn loose from her moorings by giant ice floes and drifting helplessly out to sea. No trace of her was found until fifteen years later in 1933, when a dredging vessel working in Vineyard Sound discovered her splintered hull and windlass. From observations of the debris they found, it looked like the giant ice floes had crushed her wooden hull and all the crew perished in the icy waters as she sank.

Another tragic incident occurred while hurricane-force winds swept across the New England coast on September 14, 1944. The *Vineyard Sound* Lightship *#73* was stationed near Cuttyhunk by the dangerous Sow and Pigs Reef, which marks the entrance to Buzzards Bay and Vineyard Sound. Residents of nearby Westport Harbor witnessed bright lights in the sky where the lightship was moored during the storm. The following morning the lightship was missing from its location. It was wartime and the Coast Guard established a media blackout and started a detailed investigation to determine if the vessel had been lost in the storm or had been the target of a German U-boat. The navy found the sunken ship nearly two weeks later on September 23, 1944. Many believed that the doors used to load coal in the hull had collapsed from the seas and flooded with water to sink the ship. Nearly twenty years later, in 1963, divers further investigated the wreck and the Navy determined that during the storm the crew was unable to drop the huge five-ton anchor away from the ship. It seemed that it likely became a battering ram from the pounding seas and slammed a hole in the hull, sinking the ship and drowning the crew in the frigid waters.

The Nantucket Lightship Collision
with the RMS *Olympic*

One of the worst tragedies in lightship history involved the *Nantucket* Lightship *LV-117*. The 130-foot Lightship *LV-117* was built in 1930 and went into service in 1931. It carried the most modern signaling equipment of the time. It was stationed fifty miles southeast of Nantucket Island in the deep waters placed in the middle of the trans-Atlantic shipping channel. It was considered to be the most exposed lightship on the East Coast, as it was out the furthest and subject to the unpredictable New England weather, heavy seas, and the constant fog that would encompass the region. Its position was needed as it lay near the Nantucket Shoals, an area where the depth of the ocean decreased dramatically and had claimed many ships and lives as vessels would run aground in the shallow waters. From its position, incoming ships could take bearings from its elite radio signal as far as 300 miles away.

One night, during heavy fog on January 6, 1934, the *Nantucket* transmitted radio signals to ocean liner SS *Washington*, the largest ocean-going ship ever built in the United States. The coordinates were misjudged by the SS *Washington's* lookout, and the monstrous vessel sideswiped the *Nantucket*. The *Nantucket* made it back to port for repairs and the impending tragedy was averted.

Although it nearly escaped disaster, a few months later, the ocean liner *Olympic* passed dangerously close to the *Nantucket* Lightship in April of 1934. The lightship would become involved in one of the worst tragedies in lightship history in its second encounter with the *Olympic*.

On May 15, 1934, heavy fog had engulfed the region, as the *Nantucket* Lightship *LV-117* lay anchored in 192 feet of water just of Nantucket Shoals. That night, the lightship sounded her foghorn for the incoming 47,000 ton, 900-foot ocean liner, *Olympic*, the sister of the infamous *Titanic* and *Britannic* vessels. She was traveling at a speed of 20 knots. The RMS *Olympic* had previously sailed across the Atlantic for nearly 25 years with over 250 uneventful excursions. The *Olympic* had been following the *Nantucket's* radio beacon signal with the intent of altering her course when she was close enough to the lightship. The lookout on the *Olympic* had miscalculated the location of the *Nantucket* and was unable to see the lightship in the fog until she was a mere 500 feet from colliding with the doomed vessel. The crewmen of the *Nantucket* saw the monstrous ship fast approaching and quickly sounded the alarm for the impending collision. They barely had any time to grab their life preservers as the Olympic came towards them, knowing they may not survive the impeding collision. The RMS *Olympic* was nearly seventy-five times the size of the *Nantucket* Lightship and literally ran over the helpless vessel on its broadside, cutting it in half.

The Ocean Liner *Olympic* passing closely by the *Nantucket LV-117* Lightship in April 1934 before the collision in May. *Image Courtesy of US Coast Guard.*

The current *Nantucket LV-112* Lightship as floating museum.

The Captain of the *Olympic* seeing the disaster, quickly ordered boats put over to save the crew, but the *Nantucket* sank within minutes. Seven of the eleven lightship crewmen drowned in the chilly waters and four were rescued, including Captain George Braithwaite, who died a few months later from his injuries.

A few months later, the owners of the *Olympic*, the White Star Line from Britain, began constructing a new lightship for the Coast Guard as part of an agreed -upon compensation to replace the *Nantucket*, and in remembrance to those that perished that night in 1934. It was named the *Nantucket* Lightship *LV-112* and looked like a small version of a battleship with a stronger hull and forty-three watertight compartments to keep it afloat should impending disaster strike. It was built so that whenever the foghorn would sound, the radio transmitter would broadcast a signal at the same instance so that navigators from oncoming vessels could quickly calculate the distance to the lightship. This technology was also incorporated in other lightships.

The new *Nantucket* Lightship served on the Nantucket Shoals from 1936 to 1942, then was painted gray and used as an examination vessel during World War II near the entrance to Portland Harbor in Maine. After the war, she was repainted red and returned to duty on Nantucket Shoals.

In 1960, the *Nantucket LV-112* underwent major renovations making it the largest lightship ever built. In those years, she and her crew survived two major hurricanes in 1954 and 1959 where she lost anchor, was smashed up, and had drifted many miles away from her station. The Nantucket became the longest serving lightship until she was decommissioned in 1975.

The lightship era ended in 1985, with many lightships gradually deteriorating. Many non-profit volunteer organizations stepped up to save those lightships remaining. Most have become floating museums as a testament to the courage and bravery of their crews who were stationed in the most hazardous conditions. Today, there are only seventeen lightships in existence. The *Nantucket LV-112* became the last to be removed from service, and, like other lightships, fell into disrepair. Recently, she has received funds to save her from destruction and will serve as a floating museum at the Boston Harbor Shipyard and Marina.

Greatest Coordinated Sea Rescue of the *Andrea Doria*

In dense fog on July 25, 1956, around 11 p.m. in the evening, the nearly 700-foot passenger liner *Andrea Doria*, bound for New York, was rammed broadside by the 528-foot-long Swedish steamer *Stockholm*. The collision occurred 50 miles south of Nantucket Island, Massachusetts. In one of the greatest coordinated rescue efforts between vessels and rescue services, all but 46 of the nearly 1,700 people on board were saved.

On July 17, 1956, the *Andrea Doria* left Genoa, Italy, was sailing west, and heading to New York City. On board were 1,134 passengers and 572 crewmembers. Of all Italy's ships at the time, the *Andrea Doria* was the largest, fastest, and supposedly safest vessel afloat. On the last evening of her voyage, the *Andrea Doria* encountered fog. Captain Piero Calamai, a forty-year veteran, ordered the foghorn blown repeatedly. However, he did not greatly reduce the ship's speed, which would only have enabled the ship to stop within a three-mile range. At the same time, the *Stockholm*, which had left New York that morning, was sailing east, bound for Sweden.

Johan-Ernst Carstens, the *Stockholm's* third mate who was commanding the bridge, turned his ship to the right of the *Doria* from information he received from an incorrect radar reading, believing the *Doria* to be fourteen miles away instead of its actual location only four miles away. He failed to signal the maneuver with his ship's whistle, putting the two vessels on a collision course.

When the *Andrea Doria* emerged from the fog, the crew saw the oncoming lights of the *Stockholm*. Captain Calamai of the *Andrea Doria* saw the *Stockholm's* lights and realized that it was turning directly into the *Doria*. Panicking, Calamai ordered to make a hard left turn in hopes of avoiding the approaching ship. This became

Doria, painting by Harry Ahysen. *Image courtesy of Ahysen family and US Coast Guard.*

the fatal move because it ended up exposing the *Doria's* side to the bow of the *Stockholm*. The situation was only made worse by the fact that the ships did not communicate with one another by whistle or radio, so instead of trying to sail away from one another when each spotted the other, they ended up turning towards one another and collided. The *Stockholm* crashed into the *Andrea Doria*, killing forty-five people instantly, along with five crewman of the *Stockholm*. The impact opened such a gaping hole in the *Doria's* side that, within minutes, the ship was leaning dangerously on her right side, flooding the ship's watertight compartments that helped to keep the monstrous vessel afloat. As a result, at least half of the lifeboats on the *Andrea Doria* could not be lowered because of the ship's right side listing dangerously into the water.

The Coast Guard monitoring station on Long Island quickly picked up the first SOS messages sent from both the *Andrea Doria* and the *Stockholm*. They were able to put into action probably the most effective rescue operations of the time. In addition, other ships in the area, the *Cape Ann*, the Navy Transport Pvt. *William H. Thomas* and the tidewater tanker *Robert E.*

Hopkins were all hurrying to assist in the rescue effort although they only had a few lifeboats.

The captain of the *Andrea Doria* radioed: "Danger immediate. Need boats to evacuate 1,000 persons and 500 crewmembers. We need boats." The captain of the *Ile de France*, Baron Raoul de Beaudan, was only forty-four miles away from the accident site and received the *Doria's* distress signal. The French liner *Ile de France* had just left New York with a load of passengers and was heading for France. The captain quickly decided to turn his ship around to help in the rescue effort as he had plenty of lifeboats aboard. All these ships helped to keep this accident from becoming an even greater disaster, but it was the *Ile de France* that rescued the greatest number of passengers. With repeated radio attempts of the *Andrea Doria's* captain to have the *Stockholm* aid in the rescue, the captain of the *Stockholm*, Harry Gunner Nordenson, was also concerned with the wellbeing of his own ship. After evaluating that his ship was not going to sink, he launched seven lifeboats to aid the *Andrea Doria's* passengers. The *Stockholm* left the collision scene, and with a massive amount of damage to its bow, slowly made it back safely to New York.

Andea Doria. *Image courtesy of US Coast Guard.*

On board the *Stockholm*, a sailor discovered a 14-year-old girl named Linda Morgan entangled in the wreckage near the bow. He could not find her name on the *Stockholm's* passenger list and was surprised when she told him she was a passenger on the *Andrea Doria*. She had been literally thrown from her bed on the *Andrea Doria* onto the *Stockholm* during the collision. She was known afterwards as the "miracle child," although her half-sister and stepfather died on the *Andrea Doria*.

As the night wore on, rescue ships and the Coast Guard were arriving to take the passengers to safety. Some passengers panicked and jumped overboard, to be later picked up in the lifeboats, while many slid down ropes and makeshift steps to the security of their rescuers. Many families became separated from each other in the chaos. By 6 a.m., all the survivors had been placed onto the various rescue ships that came to help and were heading to the shore.

The *Doria's* remaining crew began to abandon the ship, along with Captain Calamai by 9 a.m. The great liner began to sink at 9:45 a.m., and by 10:09 that morning, news crews witnessed the *Doria* fully disappear from sight. It sank eleven hours after the collision with the *Stockholm*, which lost five people instantly in the accident. With such a dramatic rescue effort, all but 46 (45 were killed instantly on impact) of the nearly 1,700 people on board were saved.

As the *Andrea Doria* sank beneath the waves and came to rest 235 feet below the surface southwest of Nantucket Island, accusations began to fly as to who was responsible for the collision. While Captain Calamai of the *Andrea Doria* swore that there was thick fog that evening, the *Stockholm* claimed that there was no fog, although in the month of July with such extremes of weather quite common in and around the Cape Cod region, both men may have been telling the truth. The owners of both ships settled out of court.

For many years afterwards, it was commonly held that the *Andrea Doria* and its captain were to blame for the accident. More recent investigations have cleared Captain Calamai, who died before being vindicated. As a result of this disaster, improved radar training was required, and ships were required to make contact by radio. Two years after the collision, by 1958, airlines began offering nonstop jet travel between the United States and Europe indicating an end to the passenger liner era.

New England's
Famous Haunted Lighthouses

New England is filled with tales of ghosts and other folklore. Many of these controversial stories were passed on over the years and whether believed or not, are part of the folklore that surrounds this rugged coastline. What is more important is to learn about what accurate events may have occurred beforehand that spawned these specific sightings by many respected people. Various lighthouses were built in isolated areas that sometimes were either too much for the keepers or their wives, and suicides occurred, which sometimes resulted in ghost sightings afterwards. Some keepers also became victims of foul play, were killed in tragic accidents, or from New England's ferocious storms. Other keepers were so dedicated to their lighthouse stations that sometimes their ghosts would be documented as having returned to make sure the lighthouse is well maintained.

This collection of haunted lighthouse stories, involves a journalistic approach to the documented events leading up to some of these paranormal activities, through research into the folklore of the story. Many of these sightings described were by respected townsfolk, mariners, officers, or lighthouse keepers themselves.

**Middleground (Stratford Shoal)
Lighthouse, Connecticut**

Ghosts of Suicidal Lobsterman and His Victim

At Wood Island Light in Maine

One of the best-known Maine lighthouse legends involves a murder-suicide at Wood Island Lighthouse from an altercation between a lobster fisherman, who was also a local sheriff living peacefully on the island, and a drunken resident who shot him, then shot himself. Their ghosts have reportedly been haunting the island since.

Frederick Milliken was a lobster fisherman and part-time sheriff at Biddeford Pool near Biddeford in Maine. He lived on Wood Island with his wife and three children and was a rather large peaceful man in his thirties, known as the town's "gentle giant." Two men who were drifters and part-time fisherman, Howard Hobbs and William Moses, persuaded Milliken to rent his chicken coop shack nearby for them to stay for a brief period. Both men had quite a drinking problem and over the next few months had not paid their rent to Milliken.

One summer day in June of 1896, Hobbs and Moses returned to the island from a session of heavy drinking on the mainland. Milliken found his neighbors wandering drunk on the island and told them to meet him at his house to discuss the issue about the overdue rent. Both men came to his house, with Hobbs carrying a rifle in his arms, and started arguing with Milliken, presumably about the overdue rent. Milliken tried to persuade Hobbs to hand over the weapon, but Hobbs claimed that his gun was not loaded as he waived it around. As Milliken reached to take it away, the gun fired and shot Milliken in the abdomen. Milliken's wife, who was nearby, witnessed the event in horror, along with Hobbs' friend Moses. As the two carried Milliken to his house, Hobbs followed apologizing, still holding the gun in his arms.

Still in a drunken daze, Hobbs ran off to the nearby keeper's dwelling at Wood Island Lighthouse to get help from Keeper Orcutt, still carrying the rifle. The wound proved fatal and Milliken died less than an hour later. Keeper Thomas Orcutt then advised Hobbs to give himself up to the authorities. Hobbs instead announced that he had one bullet left, which he intended to use on himself, ran off to his shack, and shot himself in the head.

Since the incident, many strange events have been reported over the years at Wood Island. Many believe both the ghosts of Hobbs and Milliken haunt Wood Island Lighthouse. Moans are still heard coming from the chicken coop shack, and locked doors have been mysteriously opened at the lighthouse. Dark shadows have been observed near the lighthouse walkway, at the top of the tower, and strange voices have also been heard. There have also been sightings of a woman, believed to be Milliken's wife.

In 1905, Keeper Charles Burke, stationed after Orcutt, was so distraught believing he was seeing and hearing ghosts, that he left his post at Wood Island Lighthouse unattended and stayed overnight

Wood Island Lighthouse and keeper's building, Maine.

Wood Island Lighthouse view from tower, Biddeford Pool, Maine.

in a boarding house on the mainland. The next day, he jumped from a window on the third floor to his death.

In the fall of 2005, the New England Ghost Project, a paranormal research team was invited to investigate the island and lighthouse area. Shadowy figures were observed and recorded near the lighthouse and walkway. A medium was brought in, and the spirit, believed to be Hobbs, was apologizing through the medium's trance. Another spirit, believed to be Milliken, made her feel as if she were severely injured and trying to get away from something.

Recently, the Wood Island Lighthouse Foundation has held special events related to the hauntings to benefit the lighthouse restoration efforts.

Wood Island Lighthouse.

The Ghost Ship *Isadore*
Near Nubble (Cape Neddick) Light in Maine

Cape Neddick Lighthouse, located in York, Maine, also known as "Nubble Light" sits atop a small rock island called a "nubble," located a few hundred feet from shore. Due to the rocky coastal area, a lighthouse was requested from many local mariners since the early 1800s. In 1837, a proposal was rejected sighting there were already enough lighthouses in the area. A lighthouse was finally erected nearly forty years later after the famous wreck of the *Isadore* in 1842. The *Isadore* sank during a fierce gale storm on a Thanksgiving night in 1842, killing all aboard. Mariners over the years still claim to see the ghost ship patrolling the area where it had perished on quiet nights.

The story of the *Isadore's* tragedy begins a couple of nights before it set sail with a load of cargo from Kennebunkport, Maine. One of the *Isadore's* crewmen, Thomas King, dreamed about the wreckage of a ship resembling the *Isadore* and its crew washed up on the shoreline. He told the dream to the Captain of the ship, Leander Foss, and begged to be left ashore, but the captain threatened that he had better be on board when the ship left or face serious consequences, especially where the crewmember was already paid a month's wages in advance for their trip to New Orleans.

The night before the *Isadore* sailed, another crewman dreamed about seven coffins, with his own body in one of them. He also came to Captain Foss about his dream, and begged not to have the ship sail the next evening fearing for the lives of all aboard, but Foss refused to listen. The frightened crewmember and King both discussed their dreams with one another fueling King's decision to stay behind.

Howling winds at Nubble (Cape Neddick) Lighthouse, Maine.

On Thanksgiving night in 1842, the call went out for all crew to make ready for sail. Thomas King, stayed away, deserting his post on the ship, and hid in town fearing the wrath of the captain, and of the fate of the ship. The *Isadore* sailed out of Kennebunkport with a load of lumber, bound for New Orleans. As it was leaving port, the wind picked up out of the northeast, and snow began to fall. By the time the crew had come around Boon Island Lighthouse, about seven miles away from Kennebunkport, the storm had intensified to gale force winds. The sea was making over twenty-foot swells in blinding snow tossing the ship closer towards Avery's Cove near the Cape Neddick island, where it crashed on the rocks and sank.

The wreckage of the ship was discovered the next morning all around Cape Neddick island, which was a few hundred feet from the main shoreline and six miles from Boon Island. The bodies of seven crewmen out of fourteen aboard were the only ones found washed ashore. One of the bodies was the other crewman who had dreamed about the seven coffins and was too frightened of the wrath of the captain to remain ashore. The body of Captain Ross was never found.

The *Isadore* still seems to appear as a phantom ship patrolling the bays. Since the day it perished in 1842, there have been sporadic sightings by mariners and visitors just offshore of Boon Island and Avery's Cove. Over the years, many fishermen have claimed to have seen it and have tried to approach the ship, but it always seems to disappear when they sail near the site. Over the years, hotel guests and tourists residing along the shoreline inns in York, near the site of the wreck, have reported seeing a faint phantom ship, even though most do not even know the story about the tragedy of the *Isadore*.

Spirits at Nubble Lighthouse in holiday season, Maine.

Storm approaching Nubble (Cape Neddick) Lighthouse, York, Maine.

The Distraught Keeper's Wife

At Boon Island Light in Maine

Boon Island Light sits atop a tiny, barren island of rock, measuring 400 square yards, and rises to only 14 feet above sea level at its highest point. It's located about 6 miles from the York shoreline and was the sight of many shipwrecks over the years. There have been sightings of a female ghost at Boon Island over the years. Some believe it is Captain Dean's wife (*Nottingham Galley* had shipwrecked on the island in 1710), although she did not accompany him in the voyage, nor were there any women aboard the ship at the time of the incident. Most believe it is the distraught wife of a former Keeper Lucas Bright, who drowned on Boon Island during a gale storm.

In the mid 1800s, First Assistant Lucas Bright arrived at Boon Island Lighthouse with his new bride, Katherine. Four months after they arrived on the tiny barren rock, gale-force winds from a severe December nor'easter storm were sending huge waves over the rocky island.

Lucus Bright was feeling ill from the past week and physically exhausted, but felt the need to check the tower and make sure the lantern was lit for any mariners stuck in the storm, so they may find safety near the shore. He tied a rope to his waist and kissed his wife as he left the warm house, into the biting winds and spray, towards the tower. The waves were breaking all around him coating the rocks in sheets of ice as he tried to secure a bolt to the door in the tower. All of a sudden, a huge rogue wave swept over the rocks and covered the keeper. He lost his grasp, slipped on the icy rocks into the freezing waters, and drowned.

His wife, Katherine, saw the accident in horror and managed to grab and hold onto the rope tied to her husband to keep him from drifting away. She went out into the storm and somehow managed to pull her husband's body ashore, then proceeded to drag it over the slippery rocks into the lighthouse tower, leaving his body at the foot of the stairs. Overcome with grief and shock, she sat with her husband and held his hand for as long as she could bear.

The storm continued and Katherine knew she had to tend the light so that others may not find the same fate as her beloved. For five days and nights, during this seemingly endless storm, Katherine, stricken with grief, took over all the lighthouse duties. She ate what little food was left and slept little. Each day, she climbed the tower's 168 stairs of Maine's tallest lighthouse, in freezing temperatures, and lit the lamp to protect any mariners during the constant storms and high waves. She would then stay near her husband's frozen corpse, sometimes holding his hand or hugging him, talking to him as if to comfort her.

Boon Island Lighthouse, Maine.

On the sixth day when the storms had finally passed over, Katherine had nearly run out of fuel, and was too exhausted and tormented to light the lighthouse, causing the light to cease. The tower was freezing cold from days of the violet storm.

Once the light had gone out, and with the seas calming, fishermen from York went out to the lighthouse to investigate. They found no one in the house and went out to the tower. The tower's temperature had fallen to a frigid ten degrees below zero. There they found Katherine Bright, freezing from exposure, and driven mad by grief and exhaustion. She was sitting on the bottom of the stairs holding the frozen corpse of her husband. The fishermen were able to bring Katherine and her husband's corpse ashore, but by that time, she'd completely lost her mind. She died a short time later after being rescued.

Over the years afterwards, many mariners and keepers have laid claim to having seen a ghostly figure of a young sad-faced woman shrouded in white on the rocks at dusk; sometimes sounds of moans and screeches were also claimed to have been heard. On some nights, keepers at the lighthouse afterwards have claimed they would hear knocking on the door, and as they'd opened the door, they would observe a faint apparition of a woman dressed in white heading to the tower. Sometimes a keeper would bring their cat or dog to the Boon Island, but most of these animals would refuse to go in the lighthouse tower. Some dogs have been witnessed to be chasing something around the rocks barking constantly as if to give warning.

One Coast Guard Keeper in the early 1970s, became a believer of the ghost stories when he and a

Boon Island Lighthouse at dusk, Maine.

fellow crewman were off the tiny rock island fishing, and drifted too far out to make it back in time to turn the light on before dark. There wasn't a person on the island, but somehow the light was glowing brightly by the time the keepers returned. He also claimed to have heard doors mysteriously opening and closing. When he would go to turn on the fog signal, he felt as if "someone was watching."

Another former Coast Guard Keeper reported that one time the station's Labrador retriever chased "something from one end of the island to the other and back again." He couldn't see what the dog was chasing, and later stated, "we figured the island must be haunted, but nothing ever bothered us." Many mariners and locals believe it is Katherine watching over the lighthouse.

Breaking waves on shore.

Lady Ghost at Dusk
Hendricks Head Light, Maine

This is the story of a woman, dressed in upper-class black garb, who perished along the shores of Southport Island, Maine, near Hendricks Head Lighthouse known today as the "Lady Ghost of the Dusk," because the last time she was ever seen alive was in the twilight of a December afternoon in 1931. Sightings of her ghost only appear in the twilight hours.

On a cold early December afternoon in 1931, a woman dressed in black, with the clothing and speech of someone in high-class society, stopped in at Charlie Pinkham's post office store and asked his wife for directions to an open sweep of ocean. Mrs. Pinkham stated, "You're near Hendricks Head Lighthouse, but it might be dark before you get back, and it's lonesome." The woman seemed to know the area Mrs. Pinkham was describing and thanked her, and was observed by Mrs. Pinkham to be walking down the road towards Hendricks Head. Mrs. Pinkham would later remark that she felt confident that the woman seemed to be familiar with Hendricks Head in the Southport area.

It was late in the afternoon as the cold winds continued to blow and the sun began to hide behind thickening clouds when Mrs. Pinkham discussed the incident with her husband. They both felt it seemed a little strange for someone to head to the shoreline with nightfall approaching on such a cold day in December. Mrs. Pinkham continued to keep her eye on the highway to watch for the woman's return.

It was dusk and Keeper Knight of Hendricks Head Lighthouse arrived at the post office store, where Mrs. Pinkham proceeded to ask him if he had met the woman on the road. He insisted he hadn't seen anyone. As he listened to the story, he became quite worried. Since the road to Hendricks Head was the only road, if she was heading that way he certainly would have seen her. They wondered why such a well-spoken woman should be walking unescorted along the shoreline in near darkness. A couple of more people arrived at the store afterwards and Mrs. Pinkham kept repeating the woman's description. Nobody seemed to know her in this small community of Southport, nor had anyone seen her.

Worried for the woman's safety, as it was now approaching twilight in the evening, Keeper Knight headed back towards Hendricks Head lighthouse keeping a close watch for her. He knew everyone in the area and would easily recognize a stranger if he saw her. He later reported seeing something flicker like a shadowy figure close to one of the cottages nearby, where he stopped, listened, and called out with no answer. Assuming it was nothing, he continued on his

Hendricks Head Lighthouse at dusk,
Boothbay Harbor, Maine.

way to the lighthouse. At the lighthouse he told his wife about the young woman. She replied that she had not seen anyone on the road.

By the next day, many of the residents in Southport had heard about the "woman in black." They decided to start looking for her. In the sandy soil a short distance from the lighthouse, they found footsteps believed to be from a woman. The location of these footsteps presumes that Keeper Knight may have walked nearby her as he was heading to the post office store. It seemed that apparently she did not want to be recognized or found, and perhaps ran into the woods upon hearing Keeper Knight heading towards or away from the post office. Many feared she might have waded into the icy water. All week there was no word as to her whereabouts. They tried to retrace her steps, but their efforts were futile all that week. In the days that followed, they found that

a woman had checked into the Fullerton Hotel in the harbor as Louise Meade, without ever returning. The entire community was now watching for her.

Suspecting something may have happened, Charlie Pinkham, who was also a volunteer firefighter in the town, gathered a search party where they found her body about a week later on Sunday, December 6, 1931. It was washed ashore on the ledge at the north end of the little beach near Hendricks Head Lighthouse. She had a leather belt fastened around her wrists and the handles around her handbag. The belt also ran though the handles of an electric flat iron, the purpose of which they had assumed was to weight her down in the water. One hand was hooked on her belt while the other hand was inside the catch of her partially opened bag. The labels on her clothes, the only identifying mark ever found, were Lord and Taylor, the fashionable New York City store. But those labels never helped at all. Nobody

ever found out a thing about her, although detectives searched and searched, and her description and her story ran in papers throughout the nation. The general theory is that she drowned herself and is still listed in the medical records as suicide.

It was learned, too, that she had asked several persons where she could get a very good view of the open ocean. In an effort to identify her, these people she had talked with came forward, willingly, during the investigation to tell all they knew. Most of those she had talked with in town had told her to go down to the wharfs of Boothbay Harbor, which apparently did not seem to interest her. As Mrs. Pinkham had remarked during many of the investigative interviews, she felt the woman knew about Hendricks Head and the surrounding territory.

The bag left at the Fullerton hotel where she signed in as Louise Meade, as well as the one fastened to her belt, did not have any evidence as to who she was or where she came from. Any identification had been carefully removed. Again, the only label ever found was that of Lord and Taylor's from New York City, on the dress and coat she had on when she washed up on shore. No evidence was found to identify this woman, who may or may not have been Louise G. Meade. Nobody ever came forward to say they'd ever even heard of this well-dressed, well-spoken woman.

Finally, on January 8, 1932, after weeks of investigation, and with no one to identify her or make claim to the body, the town of Southport buried her in their old cemetery on the road to Hendricks Head. Names on the monuments of this small cemetery included local sea captains, early settlers, and local "Southporters." The town decided to bury this woman of mystery, known as Louise Meade, to "their" cemetery under a giant tree, a little off to one side of the cemetery, and gave her a decent respectful burial. These days, the only markings are a few fieldstones put there mainly to mark the gravesite.

Over the years, many sightings of her ghost, or her shadowy figure, have been seen, mostly at twilight near Hendricks Head Lighthouse, and so she has become known as the "Lady Ghost of the Dusk." Sometimes she is seen in the very bright moonlight and there are those who swear they have seen her, when the fog comes rolling in, walking over the beach area by the rocks where she was found.

There have also been sightings over the years of a black "limousine," driving down the Hendricks Head road and parking near the spot where her body washed ashore. Some say it always comes during the first week of December that marks the anniversary of the death of this woman.

There have been many stories as to who this woman could be. Her death occurred during the Prohibition Era where much smuggling was believed to have occurred all along the Maine coastline.

This lead some folks to believe that she may have been involved in liquor smuggling, that maybe she had gone down to the coast that late afternoon in 1931 to signal a liquor boat, or that she may have been murdered because she either knew too much or because she doubled crossed someone. No one will ever know and the story still remains one of Maine's mysteries.

Hendricks Head Lighthouse at sunset, Maine.

Seguin Island Lighthouse, Maine.

Seguin Island Lighthouse's Ghosts, in Maine

Piano Playing Caused the Keeper's Insanity

Seguin Island Lighthouse, in Maine, is one of the most fogged-in lighthouses in New England. It is also famous for lots of paranormal activity witnessed by many keepers, tourists, and mariners alike. Perhaps the most tragic incident that occurred on Seguin Island is that of a former caretaker around 1850 who was driven insane, and murdered his wife, then took his own life.

According to legend, the keeper, newly married, brought his young wife out with him to tend the light. Not used to the isolation on the island, she became increasingly bored and depressed, constantly complaining about not having anything to do. Thinking it would occupy her, and keep her mind off the boredom, the keeper ordered a piano to be brought to the island before the next winter set in.

After numerous attempts trying to get the piano up the side of the rocky ledge, he proudly, and in total exhaustion, presented it to her.

The wife was delighted, but could not play without sheet music. Fortunately, only one song had come with the piano, so she set to playing it. It was a simple Scot Joplin tune. By this time, the island was icebound; no other deliveries could come in. She continually played her piano, with the same song, over and over and over again.

The isolation and constant playing of the same tune over countless hours and days eventually drove the keeper insane. Finally he had enough, took an axe and chopped the piano to bits. When she bitterly complained, he turned on her and chopped her up with the axe. Realizing the ghoulish action he just completed, he killed himself. It's said, on the Kennebec River during foggy nights, you can hear the ghost of the lighthouse keeper's wife playing the same ghostly tune on her phantom piano which can be heard floating out over the waves on those still, calm evenings.

The First Keeper Still Tending the Light

The history of Seguin Island Lighthouse is filled with strange stories. One involves the first light keeper, Count John Polereczky, who died penniless on the island. Some say his ghost has haunted the keepers who came after him. There have been sightings of a ghost who has been named the "Old Captain" climbing the staircase of the tower.

After the Lighthouse was automated in 1985, the supervisor in charge of the crew to move the furniture reported later that the "Old Captain" ghost awoke him in the middle of the night, dressed in oilskins shaking his bed. The "Old Captain" asked him not to take the furniture away and to leave his home alone. Convinced he was simply in a deep dream, the supervisor decided not to oblige the captain's ghost, and to move the furniture anyway, as he and his crew were paid to complete. The next day, all the furniture had been successfully loaded onto a boat and was being lowered into the water. All of a sudden the cable mysteriously snapped, causing the boat and all its contents to spill onto the rocks below smashing everything into pieces.

Over the years, many volunteer caretakers who sign on to help with the upkeep of the lighthouse for summer tourists to visit have reported various sightings and strange paranormal events. Items have been moved around inside the house, items have been observed being tossed from shelves onto the floor, mysterious cold spots, tools disappearing and reappearing at random, and doors have been observed opening and closing. Some have reported hearing coughing from an unseen source.

Young Girl Ghost

Many years ago a young girl is believed to have died on the island and was buried near the lighthouse. Reports have also been made of frequent sightings of a young girl running up and down the stairs and waving to those who see her. She has also been heard laughing and bouncing a ball in a room upstairs.

Stairs to Seguin Island Lighthouse, Maine.

Seguin Island Lighthouse tower, Maine.

Connecticut's Noisy Ghost Light Keepers

The Long Island Sound waterway along the New York and Connecticut boundaries contains one of the most treacherous waterways along the eastern seaboard. With its many islands and reefs, lighthouses were erected to aid mariners and the heavy shipping traffic from crashing on the rocks in stormy weather. There are three lighthouses in this area that seem to attract a lot of attention in regards to paranormal activities.

Keeper's Lost Love

At New London Ledge Lighthouse in Connecticut

The life of a lighthouse keeper was difficult and lonely. If a keeper brought his wife with him, it was usually even more difficult from lack of socializing with others and feeling stranded on an island. This was the case at the New London Ledge Lighthouse, with Keeper John Randolph's wife, who was young and enjoyed the company of others. She was known as quite the flirt to the local fisherman and sailors who would sail by the lighthouse. One day, when Randolph went ashore to fetch needed supplies, she ended up running off with the captain of the Block Island Ferry and was never seen again.

When Randolph learned that his new bride would never return, he was overcome with grief, slit his throat at the top of the lighthouse tower, and plummeted sixty-five feet to his death on the rocks below.

When his replacement soon arrived, he found he was not alone. Doors would open and close, items in locked desk drawers would be rearranged, a fishy smell was present, and chilly spots of air made him feel that someone was present.

Years later, when the Coast Guard took over running the lighthouse, the ghost whose nickname was known as "Ernie," would be blamed for tools that would mysteriously disappear and reappear, items that would be rearranged, floors that would be suddenly washed, windows that would be cleaned, and more. One Keeper stated that he found open paint cans with brushes in them, observed cups moving across tables, doors opening and closing, and a TV that would turn on and off, along with a fog horn turning on and off for no reason. Boats from local mariners and tourists that were tied ashore were mysteriously set adrift.

Legend has it that some fishermen stopped by the light for coffee and expressed their doubts about believing in the ghost. When they went to leave, they found their boat had been set adrift. Since everyone was all together having coffee, it could only be the ghost of John Randolph.

Stratford Shoal (Middleground) Lighthouse, Connecticut.

New London Ledge
Lighthouse, Connecticut.

Penfield Reef Lighthouse, Connecticut.

Drowned Keeper Playing at the Lighthouse

At Penfield Reef Light in Connecticut

The Penfield Reef Lighthouse is believed to be haunted by the ghost of an old Keeper who drowned trying to get ashore to see his family. Keeper Frederick Jordan hadn't seen his family for weeks due to a series of storms, stranding him at Penfield Reef Lighthouse until he was finally relieved by Assistant Keeper Rudolph Iten. On Christmas Eve, in 1916, the weather was still stormy with gale-force wind gusts, but Jordan chose to leave anyway to spend the holiday with his family. About 150 yards away from the lighthouse reef shoreline, Jordan's boat capsized from a large sea swell which dumped Jordan into the icy waters.

Iten watched the accident, and was too afraid to launch his boat to help rescue Jordan fearing for his own safety with the inclement weather. He could only watch Jordan's boat drift away with Jordan clinging on for dear life out of sight. Jordan's body was recovered later when the storm finally subsided, and Iten was absolved of blame for the death. He was then promoted as the next Keeper of Penfield Reef lighthouse. Weeks later, Iten claimed he felt a constant unearthly chill in the lighthouse and observed a hazy presence coming out of the dead Keeper's former room. One day, Iten found the Keeper's journal on the floor instead of on the shelf where it was placed, and it was opened to the day that Jordan had perished, describing his

death. In the months that followed, Iten claimed to have witnessed a hazy figure coming out of the lantern room at various times, and that the light would begin "behaving strangely" each time the ghost appeared.

Years later, another keeper at Penfield Reef Light reported seeing the figure of an old man dressed all in white, floating down the stairs of the tower and then disappearing after leaving the tower door. Other keepers have claimed to witness, on stormy and foggy nights, a ghost or hazy figure in the lantern room, swaying and sometimes moaning as if in pain.

One owner of a power yacht reported that in rough weather his boat was guided to safety by a mysterious figure in a rowboat, which disappeared once they were safe in calmer waters.

In 1942, a couple of youngsters were fishing near the lighthouse when they capsized their boat. An old man appeared from the nearby rocky shore and hauled the boys to safety at the base of the lighthouse, then disappeared. When they went to thank him at the lighthouse, the keeper did not know whom they were talking about. The boys then identified Jordan as their rescuer after seeing his photograph on the wall.

Decades after Jordan's death, other keepers at the Penfield Reef Lighthouse reported the light acting strangely at times, especially just before a storm. To this day mariners along the Connecticut coast claim that, in stormy weather, a human figure is seen in the lantern room gallery or floating above the reef itself. Many still believe it is the ghost of Keeper Jordan still guarding the safety of mariners who come to close to the destructive reef.

The Suicidal Assistant Keeper

At Stratford Shoals (Middleground) Lighthouse in Connecticut

Stratford Shoals Lighthouse is a sixty-foot granite tower built on a reef just off Long Island, near Connecticut. In 1905, Julius Koster, the Second Assistant Keeper and a lighthouse rookie, were left behind with First Assistant Morrell Hulse while the Head Keeper went ashore. There, Koster, who was mentally unstable, got into an argument with Hulse and lunged at Hulse with a razor. Hulse was able to avoid being cut and persuaded Koster to put away the razor. A few days later, Koster locked himself into the lantern room with an axe, he then stopped the rotation of the light and threatened to smash it and kill himself. Once again, after hours of pleading, Hulse persuaded Koster to come out and talk with him. When Koster came out of the lantern room, he then decided to jump off the tower into the water. Hulse quickly dove in and rescued him. Fearing for his safety and Koster's as well, Hulse tied Koster up and kept him at the lighthouse tower for two days until help arrived.

Koster was taken off the island and transported to an institution in New York, where he ended up killing himself a few days later. Although Koster did not perish at the lighthouse, many believe his spirit appears around the lighthouse throwing tantrums. Keepers and Coast Guardsmen have witnessed doors slamming in the middle of the night, chairs were thrown against the walls, and posters ripped down. Hot pans of water have also been observed being flung onto the floor from the stove.

Although the lighthouse was automated in 1969, local mariners going by the lighthouse still claim to hear lots of banging noises, grinding noises, and loud sounds as the ghost of Koster continues to throw tantrums.

Stratford Shoal (Middleground) Lighthouse, Connecticut.

Ghost Keepers Assisting Mariners
At Minot's Ledge Light, Massachusetts

Minot's Ledge Lighthouse lies within a dangerous group of rocky ledges called the Cohasset Rocks between the "south shore" towns of Cohasset and Scituate, located south of Boston, Massachusetts. Before the lighthouse was built in 1850, many shipwrecks were recorded from the dangerous rocks over the years with many lives lost. When the lighthouse was built on a small rocky ledge surrounded by water, it had its share of bad luck for many of those who tried to tend its lantern. The first keeper was Isaac Dunham who quit after ten months at Minot's Ledge Light because he felt the structure was inadequately built and feared for his safety.

In April of 1851, the new keeper, John Bennet, who also reported the lighthouse as unsafe, had to go ashore to gather much-needed supplies leaving two assistant keepers, Joe Wilson and Joe Antoine behind to tend the light. While he was ashore, on April 17, 1851, a fierce nor'easter storm came up by surprise in the area with winds recorded to be gusting at a hurricane force of over 100 miles per hour. The waves pounded the structure causing the lamp at Minot's Lighthouse to go out at around 10 p.m. The tower succumbed to the pounding huge waves, tidal surges, and hurricane-force wind gusts, and tumbled over, crashing over the rocks of Minot's Ledge. There was nothing left of the structure. The next morning, Antoine's body was discovered washed ashore at Nantasket Beach, while Wilson's body was later found on nearby Gull Island.

Since the tragedy, Minot's Ledge Lighthouse is believed to be haunted by the two assistant keepers. Many fishermen swear during stormy weather they've seen a man hanging from a ladder on the side of the tower, screaming, "Stay away, stay away," in Portuguese (Joe Antoine was Portuguese).

Both Joe Wilson and Joe Antoine had once worked out a method for signaling the end of the shift by making five loud taps that would echo up the very long stairway. After their deaths, other keepers stationed at Minot's Ledge Lighthouse would report hearing the five taps echoing up through the stairs at the end of a shift with no one below to make the sounds.

Other keepers, who stayed at the rebuilt granite lighthouse, have reported seeing in the middle of the night, two shadowy figures of presumably the two assistant keepers in the lantern room.

One keeper brought his cat to the tower for companionship. He would report that the cat acted very strangely when near the lantern room, running around in circles and screeching.

When birds would fly overhead many times they would dirty the windows which would take a good part of the day for the keeper to normally clean. Some other strange paranormal activities include cleaning of these lighthouse windows of bird droppings. There have been keepers who have reported that when they or their assistants would gather the materials to clean the windows, the task would be mysteriously completed ahead of time.

Some keepers could not handle the isolation of the tower in its remote location surrounded by water. One keeper went crazy and slit his throat. Another went insane and was removed from the lighthouse in a strait jacket. The ringing of a phantom bell and the taps or knocks are still frequently heard at night.

**Minot's Ledge Lighthouse
illustration of tower collapse.**
Image courtesy of Jeremy D'Entremont.

Minot's Ledge Lighthouse in Massachusetts.

Block Island Southeast Lighthouse, Rhode Island.

Block Island's Female Ghost and Ghost Ship

Female Ghost Hates Men

At Block Island Southeast Light in Rhode Island

Block Island's Southeast Light sits atop a sandy bluff 200 feet above sea level. The former (murdered) wife of a lighthouse keeper is believed to haunt the lighthouse as an angry spirit, even after the lighthouse was moved back away from the eroding cliffs in 1993.

The story goes that in the early 1900s a keeper had a violent argument with his supposedly nagging wife who was bored and depressed in the lighthouse. In a fit of anger he pushed her down the stairs of the tower causing her death. Upon investigation, although he claimed she had committed suicide, the jury convicted him of murder and of course removed him from his duties at the lighthouse.

Many islanders believe that "Mad Maggie," as she is called, continues to haunt the lighthouse harassing any male visitors or keepers of the light. They have reported to have been recipients of this ghost's wrath and have claimed to have been locked in rooms and closets, have had their beds lifted and shaken, and some have claimed that sharp objects, including knives have been thrown at them. Many have witnessed her ghost, banging pots and pans, not caring if anyone was watching her

One account involves the ghost chasing a keeper out of bed and into the cold night dressed only in his underwear, locking the door behind him. The poor embarrassed keeper had to call the Coast Guard to reopen the lighthouse so he could get back in.

Even since 1993, when the lighthouse was moved back from the eroding cliffs, men have reporting seeing the ghost of "Mad Maggie" rushing up and down the stairs in a rage, rearranging furniture, and has reportedly been observed throwing food at those men who have visited her kitchen. Women, however, have reported no such disturbances from this supposedly vengeful spirit.

The *Palatine* Ghost Ship,
Known as "The Flying Dutchman"

Block Island is surrounded by dangerous sandy shoals and rocky ledges. Dozens of ships would perish before the lighthouse authorities decided to build two lighthouses on the island named North Light in 1829, and Southeast Light in 1875. One of the most famous shipwrecks before the lighthouses were built involves the *Palatine*, which has become one of America's famous phantom ships. The area is believed to be near where Block Island Southeast Light is located a short distance from the main harbor of Block Island.

The *Palatine* was a Dutch immigrant ship that sailed for the New World in 1752. After sailing for many weeks across the Atlantic through many storms and running low on rations, tempers were high as their angry captain was continually mistreating the crew.

The Palatine continued to run into bad storms off Rhode Island. The ship was constantly being pounded with waves crashing over its deck, which eventually lead to the death of the captain as he was washed overboard from a rogue wave. When the second mate took over, the angry crew mutinied, tied him up and robbed the immigrant passengers along with anything they could find on the ship. They then took to the lifeboats leaving the passengers to fend for themselves as best they could.

With no one to guide the ship, the Palatine drifted helplessly for a few days in bad weather until it finally ran aground near Block Island. The locals, who were considered as low class in society, were not particularly interested in the immigrant passengers' plight, and although they allowed them to land, they further plundered the ship. The ship was then left unsalvageable and the locals decided to burn the remains of the ship to clear the way for other vessels. When they had taken all they could, the looters set fire to the vessel and set it out drifting to sea with the tide and gusting winds. They did not know that one scared immigrant had remained on board, too frightened to come ashore.

The ship drifted out to sea engulfed in flames. Unconfirmed reports say that local mariners could hear the screams of the poor immigrant that night as the fiery vessel disappeared in the waters.

Today the *Palatine* has become one of America's most famous phantom ghost ships, and is also known in other versions as "The Flying Dutchman," seen sailing off the coast of Block Island, often in flames.

Block Island shoreline.

First Female Keeper Visits
At Gurnet Point (Plymouth) Light
in Massachusetts

In the late 1700s, John and Hannah Thomas owned a long sandy strip of peninsula located on the northern corner of Plymouth Bay. They were asked by the Colonial government to have a lighthouse built on their land. The deal provided John Thomas to be appointed as the first Keeper, which was customary in the early days of lighthouse history. This appointment allowed John to become one of America's first light keepers in 1769. The lighthouse became known as Gurnet Point Light in Plymouth, Massachusetts. Shortly thereafter, John Thomas was called to fight in the Revolutionary War, and had to leave his wife Hannah to assume all duties at the lighthouse. In having to tend to the lighthouse all by herself, this technically made Hannah America's first woman lighthouse keeper. John Thomas never came back from the war, and in 1790, Hannah was appointed the Keeper for many years until her son took over the position until 1812.

It's believed that Hannah still haunts the house. Recently, two photographers once spent the night at Gurnet Point Light in the Keeper's house. The husband reported that during the middle of the night, he awoke and saw the ghost of a sad-faced woman hovering above his wife, who was fast asleep. The woman was wearing apparel from the colonial period, and looked to be in her thirties with long dark hair.

As he watched her, he felt no threat from her, but only her sadness. He could see the rays of light from the lighthouse come around several times, brightening the room. He looked away briefly toward the light, and then looked back to where she had appeared, and she was gone.

**Plymouth (Gurnet)
Lighthouse, Massachusetts.**

Keeper Stays on Duty With a Sense of Humor

Portsmouth Harbor Light, New Hampshire

Portsmouth Harbor lighthouse was built in 1771 on the grounds of what was once Fort William and Mary, occupied by the British during the Revolution, and involved in one of the first acts against the British where patriots stole ammunition one night. After the Revolution, the fort's name was changed to Fort Constitution. With the construction of the lighthouse, many ships and mariners were saved during the various storms that bashed against the coastline, but many others were still wrecked on the rocky coastline outside the harbor, or got caught in the dangerous tidal current of the Piscatiqua River, or were stranded a few miles out in the Isles of Shoals. The fort and lighthouse, located on New Castle Island, just outside of Portsmouth and the surrounding area, provided a safe place for bringing those who were rescued in need of attention, and also those who had perished. There were also those who had died in service there as well. There have been many ghost sightings and stories around the area ever since.

One of the most famous lighthouse keepers, in life, and afterwards, was Joshua Card. His father was a mariner, and of course Joshua would follow his father's footsteps starting out as a cabin boy on a schooner with his father as First Mate at the age of 12. He became a hardened sailor until he turned 27. When his father left to sail in the late 1840s for the gold fields of California, Joshua decided to work at the Portsmouth Naval Shipyard for good pay. He later started an express teaming business between New Castle and Portsmouth, after work was slackening at the Navy Yard. With a growing family, he later accepted a position as Keeper of Boon Island Lighthouse, which he stayed for six years. He became tired of the isolation at Boon Island, and missed the active life around New Castle and Portsmouth.

In 1874, Card was offered the position of Keeper at Fort Point Light in New Castle, next to Portsmouth, known today as Portsmouth Harbor Light, which he graciously accepted. He loved life around the fort near the lighthouse, the lighthouse itself, and his neighbors in New Castle and Portsmouth.

Card was known to have a great sense of humor. As part of his uniform, Card would wear a cap with the letter "K" surrounded by a wreath. When visitors or locals would ask him what the letter stood for, he would reply, "Why Captain of course."

Keeper Joshua Card, along with many other truly dedicated lighthouse keepers, rarely took any time off as he loved being at the lighthouse and tending

Portsmouth Harbor Lighthouse, New Hampshire.

to its needs. He would maintain the light for years without taking a single day off. He stayed at the lighthouse for over thirty-five years and became the seacoast's oldest lighthouse keeper. It is reported that in that span of thirty-five years, from 1874 to 1909, he only failed to light the lamp eleven times. This was quite a feat of dedication. He died a short time afterwards in 1911. One newspaper writer wrote that Card's manner was of high intelligence, he was punctual to the minute, had a kindly humor, and was always courteous to his neighbors and visitors to the lighthouse.

Still Staying at the Lighthouse

Nowadays, lighthouse Keeper Joshua Card seems to be involved in many of the ghost stories of the area. Although he had retired against his will at the age of 86, his ghost has been seen and heard for many years since his death in 1911. He's buried in the nearby Riverside Cemetery in New Castle Island, outside of Portsmouth, but many residents believe his spirit still visits the lighthouse. Recently reported sightings of Card's ghost range from personnel stationed at the nearby Coast Guard building observing a "shadowy figure" roaming the grounds at night, to an incident that occurred when one of the co-chairs of the Friends of Portsmouth Lighthouse, while painting in the lighthouse's lantern room heard a voice say, "How are you doing?" When the co-chair yelled down, he observed no one around.

Another experience involves a group taking a nighttime tour of Fort Constitution. One of them snapped pictures of the lighthouse that displayed in a few of the finished prints a "greenish mist" coming in and circling the area with no light observed from any cars or nearby buildings.

Recently, a woman was visiting the lighthouse when she reported seeing a figure in broad daylight standing on the wooden walkway on the front of the lighthouse, wearing an old-fashioned keeper's uniform. She reported thinking, "Wow ... a guy is giving tours in costume," and then she said he just vanished. When she was shown photos of Keeper Card at the Coast Guard Station just outside the Fort Constitution gate, she identified him as the one she saw in uniform.

One of the co-chairs of the Friends of Portsmouth Harbor Lighthouse had heard many of the these stories and was able to attract the ghost-seeking team from the program *Ghost Hunters* in October 2008 to come out and film any strange occurrences, and to help explain any strange activities perceived. He also believes to have heard a voice behind him while attending to his duties at the light.

As the ghost-seekers investigated and videotaped

Keeper Joshua Card of Portsmouth Harbor Lighthouse, New Hampshire. *Image courtesy of New Castle Historical Society.*

throughout the night inside Portsmouth Harbor Lighthouse, the Fort Constitution area, and the keeper's quarters, which were all closed to the public for the investigation, they got some very interesting evidence.

Most of the experiences seemed to happen inside the lighthouse. Two of the three teams heard strange noises in the lighthouse; such as the sounds of footsteps walking on the stairway while the team members were all up in the tower. Two female members of the team were even able to communicate with whatever entity was making the noises by knocking ("cut and a shave" sequence), with the entity responding back. Evidence of the sounds of the knocking response and footsteps were easily caught on video.

In the keeper's quarters, in the basement, that team heard some voices and a slamming of a door, with no wind drafts to cause the incident, also captured on tape. Outside in the fort, there were some different noises heard, but nothing that could be identified as possibly paranormal.

With this interesting evidence, it seems there may be more investigations forthcoming. The ghost of Keeper Joshua Card seems to enjoy the attention, while he's still visiting the lighthouse on some nights, and making sure the light is tended to and helping to guide mariners home.

Portsmouth Harbor Lighthouse
at dusk, New Hampshire.

Portsmouth Harbor Lighthouse
guiding fishermen home,
New Hampshire.

Appendix
New England Lighthouses Mentioned in Stories You Can View By Boat

Here's a list of boat rides you can take to view some of the New England lighthouses mentioned in this book. The boat cruises and ferries mentioned below may offer many types of cruises. While some may offer specific lighthouse cruises, some may pass by specific lighthouses as part of charters, narrated wildlife and historic tours, ferrying passengers, whale watching, fishing tours, and other types of excursions. Weather is also a major factor in New England, especially on sailing excursions. Website information for each boat is provided to help you get started. For more detailed information about each of New England's 168 lighthouses, regarding history, boat tours, photo galleries, and nearby attractions in the area, visit my website at www.nelights.com and click in the "Exploring" section for each region.

Lighthouse Name	State	Boat Company	Website
Baker's Island	MA	Boston Harbor Cruises	www.bostonharborcruises.com
Baker's Island	MA	Friends Of Boston Harbor Islands	www.fbhi.org
Baker's Island	MA	Mahi Mahi Cruises & Charters	www.mahicruises.com
Baker's Island	MA	Rockmore Company	www.rockmore.com
Block Island Southeast	RI	Block Island Ferry	blockislandferry.com
Boston Harbor	MA	Harbor Cruises	www.bostonharborcruises.com
Boston Harbor	MA	Boston Harbor Islands	www.bostonislands.com
Boston Harbor	MA	Friends of Boston Harbor Islands	www.fbhi.org
Burlington Breakwater	VT	Lake Champlain Cruises	www.lakechamplaincruises.com
Burlington Breakwater	VT	Lake Champlain Ferries	www.ferries.com
Burlington Breakwater	VT	Spirit of Ethan Allan III	www.soea.com
Burlington Breakwater	VT	The Whistling Man Schooner	www.whistlingman.com
Faulkner's Island	CT	Faulkner's Light Brigade	www.guilfordpreservation.org
Faulkner's Island	CT	Sound Navigation	www.soundnavigation.com
Gay Head (Aquinnah)	MA	Hy-Line Cruises	www.hy-linecruises.com
Gay Head (Aquinnah)	MA	Island Queen	www.islandqueen.com
Gay Head (Aquinnah)	MA	Martha's Vineyard Chamber of Commerce	www.mvy.com
Gay Head (Aquinnah)	MA	New Bedford to Martha's Vineyard Ferry	www.mvexpressferry.com
Gay Head (Aquinnah)	MA	New England Fast Ferry	www.nefastferry.com
Gay Head (Aquinnah)	MA	Rhode Island to Martha's Vineyard Fast Ferry	www.vineyardfastferry.com

Lighthouse Name	State	Boat Company	Website
Gay Head (Aquinnah)	MA	Steamship Authority	www.steamshipauthority.com
Hendrick's Head	ME	Cap'n Fish's Boat Trips	www.boothbayboattrips.com/
Hendrick's Head	ME	Hay Val Charters	www.hayvalcharters.com
Hendrick's Head	ME	Long Reach Cruises	www.longreachcruises.com
Hendrick's Head	ME	Maine Maritime Museum	www.mainemaritimemuseum.org
Hendrick's Head	ME	River Run Tours	riverruntours.com
Ida Lewis (Lime Rock)	RI	Bannister's Wharf	www.bannisterswharf.net
Ida Lewis (Lime Rock)	RI	Flaherty Charters	www.flahertycharters.com
Ida Lewis (Lime Rock)	RI	Rhode Island Bay Cruises	www.rhodeislandbaycruises.com
Ida Lewis (Lime Rock)	RI	Snappa Charters	www.snappacharters.com
Isles of Shoals (White Island)	NH	Granite State Whale Watch	www.granitestatewhalewatch.com
Isles of Shoals (White Island)	NH	Island Cruises	www.ryeharborcruises.com
Isles of Shoals (White Island)	NH	Isles of Shoals Steamship Company	www.islesofshoals.com
Isles of Shoals (White Island)	NH	Newburyport Whale Watch	www.newburyportwhalewatch.com/
Isles of Shoals (White Island)	NH	Portsmouth Harbor Cruises	www.portsmouthharbor.com
Isles of Shoals (White Island)	NH	Seabourne Sailing	www.sailnh.com
Matinicus Rock	ME	Matinicus Excursions	www.matinicusexcursions.com/index.html
Matinicus Rock	ME	Penobscot Ferry and Transport	www.penferry.com
Minot's Ledge	MA	Boston Harbor Cruises	www.bostonharborcruises.com
Minot's Ledge	MA	Boston Harbor Islands	www.bostonislands.com
Minot's Ledge	MA	Friends Of Boston Harbor Islands	www.fbhi.org
Monhegan Island	ME	Balmy Days Cruises	www.balmydayscruises.com
Monhegan Island	ME	Hardy Boat Cruises	www.hardyboat.com
Monhegan Island	ME	Monhegan Boat Line	www.monheganboat.com
Monomoy	MA	Monomoy Island Excursions	www.monomoysealcruise.com
Monomoy	MA	Monomoy Island Ferry	www.monomoyislandferry.com
New London Ledge	CT	Capt. John's Sport Fishing Center	www.sunbeamfleet.com
New London Ledge	CT	DownEast Lighthouse Cruises	www.owneastlighthousecruises.com
New London Ledge	CT	Mystic Seaport	www.mysticseaport.org
New London Ledge	CT	Project Oceanology	www.oceanology.org/
New London Ledge	CT	Sea Pony Cruises	www.seapone.com
Nubble (Cape Neddick)	ME	FinestKind Cruises	www.finestkindcruises.com
Nubble (Cape Neddick)	ME	Isles of Shoals Steamship Co.	www.islesofshoals.com

Lighthouse Name	State	Boat Company	Website
Owl's Head	ME	Penobscot Ferry and Transport	www.penferry.com
Penfield Reef	CT	Captain's Cove Seaport Harbor Cruises	www.captainscoveseaport.com
Penfield Reef	CT	Sound Navigation	www.soundnavigation.com
Point Judith	RI	Block Island Ferry	blockislandferry.com/
Point Judith	RI	Southland Riverboat	www.southlandcruises.com
Portland Head	ME	Bay View Cruises	www.bayviewcruises-me.com
Portland Head	ME	Casco Bay Lines	www.cascobaylines.com
Portland Head	ME	Eagle Island Tours	www.eagleislandtours.com
Portland Head	ME	Lucky Catch Cruises	www.luckycatch.com
Portland Head	ME	Portland Discovery	www.portlanddiscovery.com
Portland Head	ME	Portland Duck Tours	www.downeastducktours.com
Portsmouth Harbor	NH	Isles of Shoals Steamship Co.	www.islesofshoals.com
Portsmouth Harbor	NH	Portsmouth Harbor Cruises	www.portsmouthharbor.com
Portsmouth Harbor	NH	Seabourne Sailing	www.sailnh.com
Portsmouth Harbor	NH	Sunrise Adventure Charters	www.sunriseadventurecharters.com
Portsmouth Harbor	NH	Tug Alley Too	www.tugboatalley.com
Prospect Harbor	ME	Sea Venture Custom Boat Tours	www.svboattours.com
Seguin Island	ME	Cap'n Fish's Boat Trips	www.boothbayboattrips.com
Seguin Island	ME	Hay Val Charters	www.hayvalcharters.com
Seguin Island	ME	Long Reach Cruises	www.longreachcruises.com
Seguin Island	ME	Maine Maritime Museum	www.mainemaritimemuseum.org
Seguin Island	ME	River Run Tours	riverruntours.com
Sheffield Island	CT	Sound Navigation	www.soundnavigation.com
Stonington Harbor	CT	DownEast Lighthouse Cruises	www.downeastlighthousecruises.com
Stratford Shoal (Middleground)	CT	Sound Navigation	www.soundnavigation.com
Thacher Island Twin Lights	MA	Boston Harbor Cruises	www.bostonharborcruises.com
Thacher Island Twin Lights	MA	Cape Ann Whale Watch	www.seethewhales.com
Thacher Island Twin Lights	MA	Friends of Boston Harbor Islands	www.fbhi.org
Thacher Island Twin Lights	MA	Harbor Tours Inc. of Cape Ann	www.capeannharbortours.com
Thacher Island Twin Lights	MA	Thacher Island Association	www.thacherisland.org

Barque (also Bark)
A vessel with at least three masts, with square sails.

Bow
The front section of a ship.

Bowsprit
A long extended pole or spar in the front of the sailing ship.

Breakwater
A rock structure that extends out in a harbor, which acts like a barrier to protect from the force of waves.

Breeches Buoy
A device used in rescues, which looked like a life preserver with canvas pants attached to catch the survivor so he or she could be towed ashore.

Brig
A two masted square-sail rigged ship.

Captain
A person in command of a ship.

Congressional Gold Medal
An award bestowed by the United States Congress and is the highest civilian award in the United States.

Day-trippers
Islander's name for tourists who visit for only a day or two.

First Mate (also referred to as First Officer)
A merchant ship's officer who's rank is just below Captain.

Jetty
A wharf, or structure, such as pier, that projects out into a body of water to protect a harbor or shoreline from rising tides or strong currents.

Keeper (who also is referred to as the Captain)
In charge of all lighthouse duties, or life saving station.

Knots
A unit of length in navigation measuring exactly 1,852 meters. It is how the speed of a boat is measured in units of distance for a certain amount of time.

Life Saving Stations
Located between lighthouses and housed specially trained crews for rescuing survivors on wrecks offshore.

Listed (also list)
When a ship is tilted to one side.

Lyle Gun
A cannon like gun used to fire a line as far as 800 yards to a wreck for rescue.

Glossary of Some Mariner Terms

Mooring
is a place where a vessel can drop anchor in the water, equipped with a floating buoy to mark location, to secure it for a period of time.

Nor'easter Storm
Travels to the northeast from the south and the winds come from the northeast producing, in many cases, high winds and much precipitation.

Pilothouse (or Pilot-house)
A glass-enclosed room located on the highest or largest deck from which a ship is controlled by the ship's pilot.

Port
The left side of a ship.

Revenue Cutter Service
Named after the Civil War, was responsible for saving many lives from wrecks within harbors, or later as part of rescue coordination efforts with personnel from lighthouses and lifesaving stations.

Schooner
A sailing ship with two or more masts.

Second Mate
The third officer in command of a ship, and is a licensed member of the deck department of a merchant ship.

Seine fishing
Fishing using a large fishing net that hangs in the water due to weights along the bottom edge and floats along the top. Boats equipped for seine fishing are called seiners.

Skiff
A small flat-bottomed boat with a square stern, and a triangular bow.

Sloop
A sailboat with a single mast.

Starboard
The right side of a ship.

Steamboat, (or steamship, sometimes called a steamer)
A ship in which the primary method of propulsion is steam power, typically driven by either propellers or paddlewheels.

Stern
The rear section of a ship.

Surfman
A trained rescuer of a lifesaving station.

Thwart
A seat where the rowers were to be placed in a lifeboat.

United States Life Saving Service
A United States government agency that grew out of private and local humanitarian efforts to save the lives of shipwrecked mariners and passengers. Life Saving stations were built between lighthouses.

Wreckers
Employed to unload enough cargo on a vessel that may be wrecked offshore to try to float it off the sandbar, ledge, or shoal that grounded it, with hopefully most of the cargo intact.

Selected Bibliography

Andrea Doria – Tragedy and Rescue at Sea. http://www.andreadoria.org/.

Bachand, Robert G. *Northeast Lights: Lighthouses and Lightships, Rhode Island to Cape May, New Jersey*. Norwalk, CT: Sea Sports Publications, 1989.

Bales, Jack, and Kenneth Roberts. *Boon Island: Including Contemporary Accounts of the Wreck of the Nottingham Galley*. Hanover University Press of New England, 1996.

"Block Island, RI *Larchmont* Disaster, Feb 1907." Genealogy Events That Touched Our Ancestors' Lives, How Our Ancestors Lived and Died. http://www.gendisasters.com/data1/ri/ships/blockisland-larchmontdisaster1907.htm.

Cahill, Robert Ellis. *Lighthouse Mysteries of the North Atlantic*. Salem, MA: Old Saltbox Pub. House, 1998.

Cann, Donald, John Galluzzo, and Gayle Kadlik. *Isles of Shoals*. Charleston, SC: Arcadia Publishing, 2007.

"Cape Ann (Thacher Island) Lighthouse, Massachusetts at Lighthousefriends.com." Lighthouse Friends. http://www.lighthousefriends.com/light.asp?ID=475.

"Cape Cod Lifesavers and the Chatham Lifesavers." Chatham, Cape Cod's Online Guide: Town of Chatham, MA. http://www.mychatham.com/capecodlifesavers.html.

"CG Continues Flying Santa Tradition." Coast Guard News. http://www.military.com/news/article/coast-guard-news/cg-continues-flying-santa-tradition.html.

"*City of Columbus* – Quest Marine Services – Underwater Exploration." Research Vessel Charter, Mass, MA - Quest Marine Services. http://www.questmarineservices.com/exploration/cityOfColumbus.html.

Claflin, James. *Lighthouses and Life Saving Along the Connecticut and Rhode Island Coast*. Charleston, SC: Arcadia Pub, 2001.

Claflin, James. *Lighthouses and Life Saving Along the Maine and New Hampshire Coast*. Charleston, SC: Arcadia, 1999.

Clark, Admont G. *Lighthouses of Cape Cod, Martha's Vineyard, Nantucket: Their History and Lore*. East Orleans, MA: Parnassus Imprints, 1992.

Clark, Sue. "Christmas Memories of the Flying Santa." Lighthouse News; News, Features, Opinions and More About Lighthouses Worldwide. December 24, 2008. http://lighthouse-news.com/2008/12/24/christmas-memories-of-the-flying-santa/.

"Coast Guard Lighthouses." U. S. Coast Guard Home Page. http://www.uscg.mil/history/weblighthouses/LHCT.asp.

Cook, David E. *The Light Keepers of Lake Champlain*. Mayfield, NY: DreamChase Features, 2009.

Costopoulos, Nina. *Lighthouse Ghosts and Legends*. Birmingham, Ala.: Crane Hill Publishers, 2003.

Cutter, William Richard. *New England Families, Genealogical and Memorial: A Record of the Achievements of Her People in the Making of Commonwealths and the Founding of a Nation*. Salem, MA. Higginson Book, 2004. Google E-Books.

Dalton, J. W. *The Life Savers of Cape Cod*. Chatham, MA: Chatham Press, 1967.

De, Wire Elinor. *The Lightkeepers' Menagerie: Stories of Animals at Lighthouses*. Sarasota, FL: Pineapple Press, 2007.

D'Entremont, Jeremy. "Cape Elizabeth Lighthouse History." New England Lighthouses: A Virtual Guide – Photos, History, Tours, Cruises, Coastal Accommodations and More. http://lighthouse.cc/capeelizabeth/history.html.

D'Entremont, Jeremy. *Great Shipwrecks of the Maine Coast*. Beverly, MA: Commonwealth Editions, 2010.

D'Entremont, Jeremy. "Lime Rock Lighthouse (Ida Lewis Yacht Club) History – Page One." New England Lighthouses: A Virtual Guide – Photos, History, Tours, Cruises, Coastal Accommodations and More. http://www.lighthouse.cc/limerock/history.html.

D'Entremont, Jeremy. "Matinicus Rock Lighthouse History." New England Lighthouses: A Virtual Guide – Photos, History, Tours, Cruises, Coastal Accommodations and More. http://www.lighthouse.cc/matinicusrock/history.html.

D'Entremont, Jeremy. *The Lighthouse Handbook*. Kennebunkport, ME: Cider Mill Press Book Publishers, 2008.

D'Entremont, Jeremy. *The Lighthouses of Connecticut*. Beverly, MA: Commonwealth Editions, 2005.

D'Entremont, Jeremy. *The Lighthouses of Massachusetts*. Beverly, MA: Commonwealth Editions, 2007.

"Disaster on Devils Bridge." Research Vessel Charter, Mass, MA - Quest Marine Services. http://www.questmarineservices.com/exploration/cityOfColumbus.html.

Doherty, John. "*Nantucket* Lightship *LV117* News Story." USCG Lightship Sailors Association International Inc (USCG LSA). http://www.uscglightshipsailors.org/nantucket_lightship_lv117_newsstory.htm.

Downs, John W. "Sprays of Salt: Reminiscences of a Native Shoaler By John W. Downs." WHAT'S NEW? SeacoastNH.com. http://www.seacoastnh.com/smuttynose/downs3.html.

Downs, John William, and Gayle Patch. Kadlik. *Sprays of Salt: Reminiscences of a Native Shoaler*. Portsmouth, NH: Peter E. Randall, 1997.

The Friends of Seguin Home Page. http://www.seguinisland.org/index.htm.

"Frozen in Ice – Maine Office of Tourism." Home – Maine Office of Tourism. http://www.visitmaine.com/attractions/sightseeing_tours/lighthouse/tales_legends/frozen_in_ice/

Goldstein, Richard. *Desperate Hours: the Epic Rescue of the* Andrea Doria. New York: Wiley, 2001.

Haunted Lighthouses – Legends and Lore. http://www.hauntedlights.com/haunted2.html.

Helander, Joel. "YouTube: Capt. Oliver N. Brooks." YouTube - Broadcast Yourself. http://www.youtube.com/watch?v=Sy4IgPUcv5s.

Hickey, Walter V. "The Final Voyage of the Portland." *Final Voyage of the Portland* 38, no. 4 (Winter 2006). http://www.archives.gov/publications/prologue/2006/winter/portland.html.

"Historical Notes Regarding Nantucket Lightship Station." *Lighthouse Service Bulletin IV* 54 (June 1, 1934): 179.

"History of U.S. Lightships." PalletMaster's Work Shop. http://www.palletmastersworkshop.com/lightship.html.

Hoffer, William. *Saved! The Story of the Andrea Doria, the Greatest Sea Rescue in History*. New York: Summit Books, 1979.

Holland, F. Ross. *America's Lighthouses: An Illustrated History*. New York: Dover, 1988.

Horton, Linda. "New England Lighthouse Storm, April 1851 GenDisasters ... Genealogy in Tragedy, Disasters, Fires, Floods." GenDisasters ... Genealogy in Tragedy, Disasters, Fires, Floods; Events That Touched Our Ancestors' Lives. November 5, 2007. http://www3.gendisasters.com/new-hampshire/2125/new-england-lighthouse-storm,-apr-1851?page=0,1.

Johnson, Tim. "VPR News: History Under the Waves: The General Butler." Vermont Public Radio: Home of VPR News and VPR Classical, and Vermont's NPR News Source. http://www.vpr.net/news_detail/85417/.

King, Irving H. *The Coast Guard Expands, 1865-1915: New Roles, New Frontiers.* Annapolis, MD: Naval Institute Press, 1996. Google E Books.

Kobbe, Gustav. "Life in a Lighthouse." In *Century Magazine*, 365-74. Vol. 47. New York: Century Com, 1894. http://www.scribd.com/doc/32665948/Life-in-a-Lighthouse-Minots-Ledge.

Lanigan-Schmidt, Therese. *Ghostly Beacons: Haunted Lighthouses of North America.* Atglen, PA: Whitford Press, 2000.

"Legendary Lighthouses." PBS: Public Broadcasting Service. http://www.pbs.org/legendarylighthouses.

Licameli, Doris. *Rowing to the Rescue: the Story of Ida Lewis, Famous Lighthouse Heroine.* Morrisville, NC: Lulu Enterprises, 2006.

"Lighthouse Keepers in the Nineteenth Century." U.S. National Park Service – Experience Your America. http://www.nps.gov/history/maritime/keep/keephero.htm.

"Lightships of the US." U.S. National Park Service - Experience Your America. http://www.nps.gov/maritime/ltshipmain.htm.

Loubat, Joseph Florimond. *The Medallic History of the United States of America, 1776-1876.* New Milford: Connecticut, 1967.

Ludlum, David McWilliams. *The Country Journal New England Weather Book.* Boston: Houghton Mifflin, 1976.

Maines, Rachel. *Asbestos and Fire: Technological Tradeoffs and the Body at Risk.* New Brunswick, NJ: Rutgers University Press, 2005.

"Maria Bray: Heroine of Thacher Island." New England Lighthouses. http://nelights.blogspot.com/2010/02/maria-bray-heroine-of-thacher-island.html.

"Martha's Vineyard, MA Steamer City of Columbus Wreck, Jan 1884; GenDisasters ... Genealogy in Tragedy, Disasters, Fires, Floods." GenDisasters ... Genealogy in Tragedy, Disasters, Fires, Floods; Events That Touched Our Ancestors' Lives. http://www3.gendisasters.com/massachusetts/15358/martha-039s-vineyard-ma-wreck-steamer-city-columbus-jan-1884.

"THE METIS. – Continuation of the Official Investigation at Providence. Revelations of the Incapacity and Selfishness of the Company's Officials Indignation of the People The Search for the Missing Still in Progress. – View Article – NYTimes.com." *The New York Times* – Breaking News, World News & Multimedia. September 07, 1872. http://query.nytimes.com/mem/archive-free/pdf?res=F30F13FE345C1A7493C5A91782D85 F468784F9.

Morrison, John H. *History of American Steam Navigation.* New York: Argosy-Antiquarian, 1967.

Morse, Susan. "Historians to Mark the 300th Anniversary of Boon Island Shipwreck." Seacoast Online – Portsmouth NH, York ME, Hampton NH, Exeter NH, and Kennebunk ME Guide. http://www.seacoastonline.com/articles/20101201-NEWS-12010329?cid=sitesearch.

"The New England Lighthouse Storm." John Horrigan Historical Lecture. http://www.historylecture.org/lighthousestorm.html.

Noble, Dennis L. *Lighthouses & Keepers: The U.S. Lighthouse Service and Its Legacy.* Annapolis, MD: Naval Institute Press, 2004.

Noble, Dennis L. *Rescued by the U.S. Coast Guard: Great Acts of Heroism since 1878.* Annapolis, MD: Naval Institute Press, 2005. Google.

"PBS Online – Lost Liners – Andrea." PBS: Public Broadcasting Service. http://www.pbs.org/lostliners/andrea.html.

"Penfield Reef Lighthouse, Connecticut at Lighthousefriends.com." Lighthouse Friends. http://www.lighthousefriends.com/light.asp?ID=788.

Perley, Sidney. *Historic Storms of New England: Its Gales, Hurricanes, Tornadoes, Showers With Thunder and Lightning, Great Snow Storms, Rains, Freshets, Floods, Droughts, Cold Winters, Hot Summers, Avalanches, Earthquakes, Dark Days, Comets, Aurora Borealis, Phenomena in the Heavens, Wrecks Along the Coast, With Incidents and Anecdotes, Amusing and Pathetic.* Beverly, MA: Commonwealth Editions, 2001.

"Portland Head Lighthouse History." New England Lighthouses: A Virtual Guide – Photos, History, Tours, Cruises, Coastal Accommodations and More. http://lighthouse.cc/portlandhead/history.html.

"Rescue of Keeper's Daughter." Friends of Wood Island Light. http://www.woodislandlighthouse.org/xHistory/Rescue/index.html.

"The Rhode Island Century." *The Providence Journal*, February 28, 1999. http://www.projo.com/specials/century/month2/0228sink.htm.

Richardson, John. "Ship of Doom." Chebeague Island News. November 22, 1998. http://www.chebeague.org/shipofdoom.html.

Roberts, Bruce, and Ray Jones. *New England Lighthouses: Maine to Long Island Sound*. Guilford, CT: Globe Pequot Press, 2005.

Rojo, Heather W. "Flying Santa – the Historian Edward Rowe Snow." Genealogy Wise. December 9, 2009. http://www.genealogywise.com/profiles/blogs/flying-santa-the-historian.

"Sailor' the Famous Wood Island Light Fog Dog." Old News from Southern Maine. http://www.someoldnews.com/?p=485.

"Seguin Island Lighthouse, near Popham Beach, Maine." New England Lighthouses: A Virtual Guide – Photos, History, Tours, Cruises, Coastal Accommodations and More. http://www.lighthouse.cc/seguin/.

"Shipwrecks of Lake Champlain: Sailing Canal Boat General Butler." Lake Champlain Maritime Museum Home Page. http://www.lcmm.org/shipwrecks_history/uhp/general_butler.htm.

Simpson, Pierette Domenica. *Alive on the Andrea Doria!: The Greatest Sea Rescue in History*. Garden City, N. Y.: Morgan James, 2008.

Skomal, Lenore. *The Keeper of Lime Rock: the Remarkable True Story of Ida Lewis, America's Most Celebrated Lighthouse Keeper*. Philadelphia: Running Press, 2002.

Snow, Addie E. "Lost in the Snow, The Portland Gale – CapeLinks Cape Cod." Cape Cod Rentals, Maps, Lodging, Vacation Info & More ~ CapeLinks Cape Cod. http://www.capelinks.com/cape-cod/main/entry/lost-in-the-snow-the-portland-gale/.

Snow, Edward Rowe. *Adventures, Blizzards, and Coastal Calamities*. New York: Dodd, Mead, 1978.

Snow, Edward Rowe. *The Lighthouses of New England*. Beverly, MA: Commonwealth Editions, 2002.

Snow, Edward Rowe. *Women of the Sea*. New York: Dodd, Mead, 1962.

St. Germain, Paul. *Twin Lights of Thacher Island, Cape Ann*. Charleston, SC: Arcadia Pub., 2010.

Steamship Lexington." Wikipedia, the Free Encyclopedia. http://en.wikipedia.org/wiki/Steamship_Lexington.

Strout, John. "Portland Head Light: A Strout Tradition." The Lighthouse Depot. May 1997. http://www.lighthousedepot.com/lite_digest.asp?action=get_article&sk=170.

Tague, Brian. "History of the Flying Santa." Friends of Flying Santa. http://www.flyingsanta.com/.

Thacher Island Association. http://www.thacherisland.org.

Theroux, Joseph P. "Flying Santa: Edward Rowe Snow and the Romance of History." *Historic Nantucket* 57 (Winter 2008): 18.

"United States Coast Guard Awards – Marcus Hanna." U. S. Coast Guard Home Page. http://www.uscg.mil/history/awards/28JAN1885.asp.

"US Lifesaving Service History." U. S. Coast Guard Home Page. http://www.uscg.mil/tcyorktown/Ops/NMLBS/Surf/surf1.asp.

"USCG: Frequently Asked Questions." U. S. Coast Guard Home Page. http://www.uscg.mil/history/people/Maria_Bray.asp.

Vaughan, Marcia K., and Bill Farnsworth. *Abbie Against the Storm: the True Story of a Young Heroine and a Lighthouse*. Portland, Or. Beyond Words Pub., 1999.

"Wood Island Lighthouse, Maine at Lighthousefriends.com." Lighthouse Friends. http://www.lighthousefriends.com/light.asp?ID=549.

"The Wreck of the General Butler, State of Vermont's Underwater Historic Preserve." Victory Sports Dive Shop – Colchester Vermont. http://victorysports.net/charters/genbutler.htm.

Index

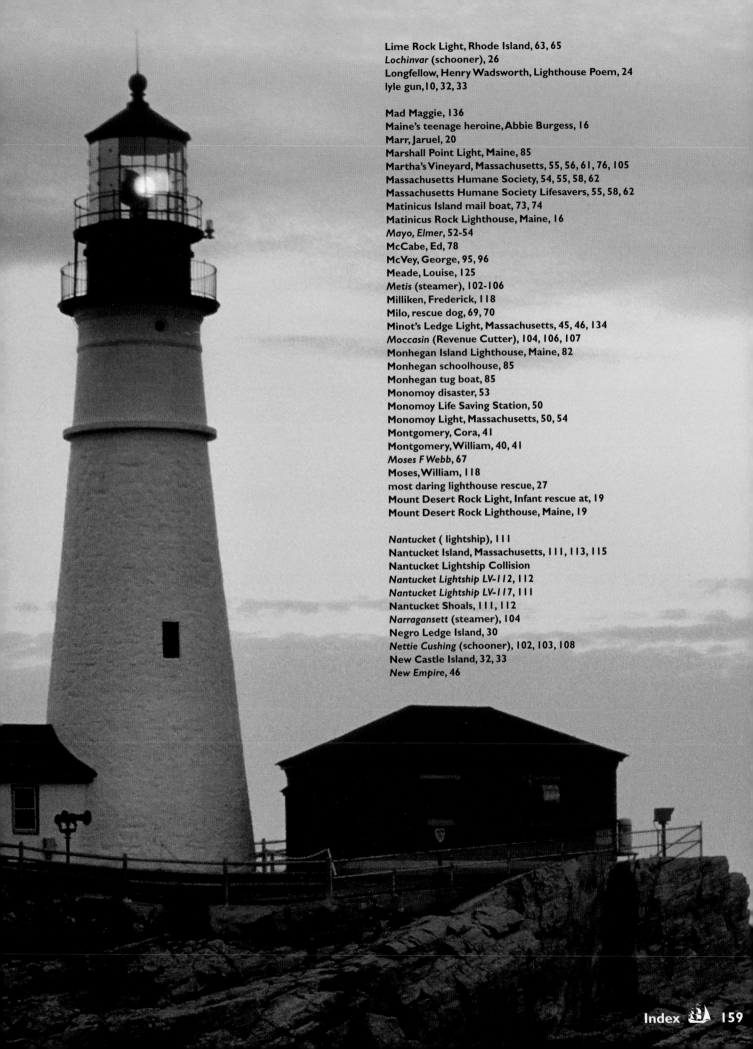